DEMOCRACY AND WAR

Democracy and War

THE END OF AN ILLUSION?

Errol A. Henderson

LYNNE
RIENNER
PUBLISHERS

BOULDER
LONDON

Published in the United States of America in 2002 by
Lynne Rienner Publishers, Inc.
1800 30th Street, Boulder, Colorado 80301
www.rienner.com

and in the United Kingdom by
Lynne Rienner Publishers, Inc.
3 Henrietta Street, Covent Garden, London WC2E 8LU

Library of Congress Cataloging-in-Publication Data
Henderson, Errol A. (Errol Anthony), 1962–
    Democracy and war : the end of an illusion? / Errol A. Henderson.
        p.   cm.
    Includes bibliographical references and index.
    ISBN 1-58826-051-8 (alk. paper) — ISBN 1-58826-076-3 (pbk. : alk. paper)
    1. Democracy.   2. War.   I. Title.

JC421.H46   2002
303.6'6—dc21
                                                                    2001048937

British Cataloging in Publication Data
A Cataloguing in Publication record for this book
is available from the British Library.

Printed and bound in the United States of America

The paper used in this publication meets the requirements
of the American National Standard for Permanence of
Paper for Printed Library Materials Z39.48-1984.

5   4   3   2   1

Contents

Tables

Preface

Unlike many studies penned by newer scholars, this one did not emerge from a grueling process begun when I was still a graduate student; its impetus is much more modest. It originated from the banter around the table at the weekly Correlates of War (COW) project seminar held dutifully every Friday afternoon in the Political Science Department at the University of Michigan in Ann Arbor. At one point, the project director, J. David Singer, admonished me: "Henderson, when are you going to do something serious and stop writing about that democratic peace stuff?" Recognizing his sarcasm, which is usually accompanied by equal parts of playfulness and insight, I responded in kind, reminding him that since he provided the seminal empirical treatment of the subject in mainstream world politics (i.e., Small and Singer, 1976), the blame for the proliferation of democratic peace research fully rested on his shoulders. But I had been concerned about Singer's agnosticism regarding the democratic peace finding ever since I'd become aware of it in my graduate courses. It struck me as strange that one of the doyen of the behavioral revolution would be such an avid critic of what some scholars hail as the closest thing to an empirical law in the field. I had published several articles both supporting and challenging the thesis (e.g., Henderson, 1998a, 1999a), so I had my own concerns about the accuracy of democratic peace arguments, as well. David didn't miss a beat and retorted that if I wanted to redeem myself I'd refute the democratic peace proposition. After reminding him that I thought that the finding was robust given the research designs commonly used to evaluate it, I pointed out that if one really wanted to refute it, then the most convincing way to go about it was to try to hoist the democratic peace on its own empirical petard by using the same basic research design used to support it. In that way, it would allow little room for maneuver for the pugilistically savvy democratic peace advocates, who had shown an almost indefatigable capacity to vigorously and quite persuasively respond to challenges leveled at their findings by quantitative-oriented scholars, and who were even more adept at parrying the intellectual jabs of their more normatively driven and less systematic critics. I added that I did not think any of the critics of the democratic peace had provided a solid empirical refutation of the thesis in the manner that I had outlined, and I did not think anyone was likely to in the near future. Undaunted, Singer responded that this would be a good research project for me. I told him something along the lines of "that's easy for you to say." Nevertheless, on that day I set out to critically examine the impact of democracy on war. This book is the result.

This project reflects the perspectives I learned in Ann Arbor from three of the most influential professors in the department at the time. First, Singer instilled in me the importance of insight and evidence in approaching world politics. His epistemological approach challenged me to look beyond anecdote and a liberal ransacking of history in order to support my claims and to, instead, appreciate that systematic evidence was the most reliable support one could provide for one's theses. Frankly, I was not surprised by his approach to world politics and his diligent pursuit of reproducible evidence on the factors leading to war and peace, which he envisioned could serve as a guide for a more informed foreign policy; but I was surprised by his humanitarianism and commitment to the education of his students, friends, and colleagues and by his willingness to challenge his own ideas. At a university like Michigan, where graduate students half-jokingly take bets on whether they will even lay eyes on certain professors during their stay at the school, much less have the opportunity to have class with them or meet and talk informally, Singer consistently made himself available to his students—and former students. He is both an institution and a bit of a maverick in the department, and because I was not a typical graduate student, his mentorship and guidance were immeasurable. Although he has made his mark in the quantitative literature, he has published in probably the most diverse array of academic, policy-oriented, and popular outlets of any professor of his generation. He consistently taught us to strive to "explain" phenomena in world politics; therefore, it's not surprising that he did not rush to accept the statistical evidence in support of the democratic peace thesis since, to his mind, there was not an adequate theoretical explanation to account for the finding. The empirical results from this study seem to vindicate Singer's skepticism.

Second, I owe an intellectual debt to A. F. K. Organski. Ken and I spent most of our time discussing the nexus between world and comparative politics. He, more than anyone else, encouraged me to reject the artificial bounds between the two and to explore the factors within states that affect their domestic and foreign policies. His work on political development (Organski, 1965) provided a point of departure for my own theorizing on the subject (Henderson, 2000). Organski's influence is evident in the discussion of the democratic peace and civil wars (Chapter 5), which reflects his comparativist interests. Those interests are sometimes, understandably, overlooked by international relations scholars because of the greater prominence of his power transition thesis in the field of world politics. But Organski's view that the comparative and world politics twain would meet is borne out by the increased interest among international relations scholars in issues of civil war, interethnic conflict, democratization, and development. Like Singer, he also encouraged systematic analysis and critical engagement of the subject matter that sometimes bordered on irreverence but was never boring.

Third, Ali Mazrui served as an intellectual mentor who would always make time in his extremely busy academic and public-speaking schedule to assume both the formal and the informal burdens of being the only progressive, black, full professor in the department prior to Hanes Walton's arrival much later in my matriculation. I had a million questions, it seemed, and he always made time for me and gave me excellent comments on my writing. His writing is among the most beautiful prose in the discipline (and his poetry is very nice, as well). Ali impressed me, first of all, with the breadth of his knowledge. He did not focus on the systematic research that was the mainstream in Ann Arbor, but his work was insightful on a diversity of levels, and it was almost always pregnant with testable propositions even though they were not stated as hypotheses in the text. Moreover, Ali's focus on African and "third world" politics was not lost on me—an African American, born and raised in Detroit's Brewster Housing Project, who commuted from the east side of Detroit to attend classes in Ann Arbor—and it provided a point of departure for much of my graduate work. My own personal experience gave me a sense of the contradictions within democracy, especially where its practice converged with issues of race and class. Ali helped me to apply insights born from such experiences to explicating world politics more generally. It remains as unfortunate as it is pervasive that within Eurocentric (mainstream) world politics, scholars who focus on racism are rarely quantitatively oriented, and those who are quantitatively oriented largely ignore issues of racism—especially white racism. Ali Mazrui challenged me to be both systematic and relevant while taking seriously the adjective "world" in world politics by addressing issues facing the majority of people in the world. Ali's influence is most evident in the discussion of the democratic peace and Western imperialism (Chapter 4) and the discussion of civil wars in postcolonial states (Chapter 5). The findings—especially regarding the former—vindicate his focus on the importance of race, culture, and class in world politics (Mazrui, 1990).

Beyond those who provided intellectual guideposts for me and in varying ways motivated this study, I'd like to thank those who have provided comments on earlier versions of chapters in the book, including James Lee Ray, Patrick Regan, Sol Polachek, Allan Stam, John Vasquez, Dan Reiter, Scott Gartner, Nils Petter Gleditsch, Patrick James, Meredith Reid-Sarkees, Will Moore, Volker Krause, Soo Yeon Kim, R. J. Rummel, John Oneal, Harwood McClerking, Asale Angel-Ajani, and participants at the Correlates of War project seminars. Also, thanks to Gancho Armianov for his technical assistance. I especially want to thank Hanes Walton for his consistent support of my research and his invaluable advice and friendship, which he has given selflessly during days when I know that he had incredible demands on his time and energy.

Also, thanks to the two anonymous reviewers, as well as to Shena Redmond, Sally Glover, and Lynne Rienner for their support of the project. Thanks to the *Journal of Peace Research* for publishing some of my earlier work on the subject: Chapter 5 draws on "Civil War in the Postcolonial World, 1946–1992," *Journal of Peace Research,* 37, 3: 275–299 (with J. David Singer), and Chapter 6 draws on "Neoidealism and the Democratic Peace," *Journal of Peace Research,* 36, 2: 203–231.

Finally, thanks to several members of my family who gave me continuous support (which means they put up with the emotional meanderings, intellectual ramblings, and general weirdness that seem to overcome me when I get really dedicated to something) as I labored to give birth to this project: Ayanna, Megan, and Karla Henderson.

Thanks also to the Kushida family and the members of AYANA. Thanks most of all to my infant son, Errol Patrick Henderson, who has been a constant joy and has given me more than enough reason to get up at 4 A.M. to put in more work on this book. And thanks to his older brother, Joseph, for helping me to endure some of those early morning sessions even as he sought to develop his own sense of the importance of academic diligence. As a small token of appreciation for his friendship, guidance, and support, I dedicate this book to Carl Taylor at Michigan State University, who has taught me so much about being a professor, a colleague, and a friend.

Errol Anthony Henderson

I

The Democratic Peace: Strong Statistics, Weak Theory

n his international bestseller *The Great Illusion*, Norman Angell (1910) forecasted the end of protracted major-power war because large-scale warfare in the industrial age, he maintained, would incur such huge costs that it would be ruinous for both victors and vanquished. Great-power war in the Clausewitzian sense was presumed to be a remnant of a bygone preindustrial era. Angell's conclusions were not unlike those of Ivan Bloch's (1899) near the turn of the previous century. Bloch posited that given the destructiveness of military technology and the economic costs of sustained large-scale combat, major-power war had become obsolete. For both Angell and Bloch, what was left was to educate the political and military elites of the major powers to understand the changed reality of warfare. Near the turn of the twenty-first century, international relations scholars forecasted the end of war among democratic states, not because warfare among these states was highly destructive, necessarily, but because their democratic systems of government acted as a brake on warfare among them. They insisted that the conflict-dampening impact of shared democracy was so great that for the community of democratic states, war in the Clausewitzian sense was a remnant of a bygone era.

Though World War I dealt a death blow to Angell's speculation and showed that the lessons Bloch drew regarding the futility of protracted international war were largely lost on the leaders of the major powers, the "democratic peace proposition" has been celebrated in the present era, which has been marked by a half-century hiatus from major-power war—a period of major-power peace longer than any since the end of the Napoleonic Wars. In this context the proposition has gained increased support among scholars while withstanding repeated attempts to refute empirically its primary claim that there is a significant negative relationship between the level of democracy between two states and their likelihood of fighting each other. Further, unlike Angell's and Bloch's pronouncements, which were largely ignored by the major powers as they fine-tuned their mobilization plans prior to World War I, the democratic peace proposition has not been lost on policymakers but has become central to the grand strategy of the world's lone superpower. Actually, since the end of World War II, U.S. presidents have consistently given at least a modicum of support to the promotion of democracy abroad as a U.S. foreign policy goal within the overall strategy of containment.[1] For example, NATO—the institutional embodiment of the containment strategy—states in its preamble that it is "founded on the principles of democracy, individual liberty and the rule of law." Advocacy of the promotion of democracy continued after the Cold War in George H. Bush's "new world order," which, inter alia, supported the promotion of democracy among adversaries as a means of encouraging peace and security. Bush stated that "democrats in the Kremlin can assure our security in a way nuclear missiles never could" (cited in Weart, 1998: 291). But it was the Clinton administration that elevated the encouragement of democracy from an ancillary desideratum of U.S. foreign policy to a central precept of U.S. grand strategy. In what one scholar has called "a textbook case of arbitrage between the ivory tower and the real world" (Gowa, 1999: 109), Clinton converted the democratic peace proposition into a "security policy manifesto" by making it the centerpiece of his post–Cold War democratic enlargement strategy.[2] Given the pronouncements during the presidential campaign and during the early part of his administration, George W. Bush appears similarly committed to the promotion of democracy abroad as a key element of his foreign policy strategy.

In this chapter, I introduce the reader to the two main variants of the democratic peace proposition, the dyadic and monadic versions, and discuss some problems with the two prominent theoretical explanations of the democratic peace. After discussing the inconsistencies in these theoretical explanations, I show how recent studies have attempted to reconcile them with emergent evidence supportive of both versions. However, these studies are beset by various research design problems. I will outline these as well, discussing how they have necessitated a reevaluation of the democratic peace proposition. This reevaluation forms the core focus of this study.

Explaining the Dyadic Democratic Peace Proposition: Structural and Cultural Arguments

Simply stated, the democratic peace proposition (hereafter, the DPP) contends that democratic states are less likely than nondemocratic states to fight wars against each other (Small and Singer, 1976; Rummel, 1979; Maoz and Abdolali, 1989; Maoz and Russett, 1992, 1993; Russett, 1993; Ray, 1995). This thesis relates to the interaction of two states, a dyad, and has come to be known as the dyadic DPP. The dyadic DPP drew its earliest empirical support from Babst's (1964, 1972) research, which was substantiated and brought to the attention of mainstream international relations scholars by Small and Singer (1976) and later Rummel (1979) before gaining much more attention—and even greater support—with the publication in the 1980s of several studies in the *Journal of Conflict Resolution* (Rummel, 1983; Chan, 1984; Weede, 1984; Maoz and Abdolali, 1989), *Philosophy and Public Affairs* (Doyle, 1983ab), and the *American Political Science Review* (Doyle, 1986). The dyadic DPP has been empirically supported in multivariate analyses that control for a variety of potentially confounding and intervening variables (Bremer, 1992, 1993; Bueno de Mesquita and Lalman, 1992; Maoz and Russett, 1992, 1993; Russett, 1993; Oneal and Russett, 1997, 1999abc, 2000; Henderson, 1998a, 2001; Russett et al., 2000; Henderson and Tucker, 2001). Though there have been challenges from detractors (Small and Singer, 1976; Cohen, 1994; Layne, 1994; Owen, 1994; Spiro, 1994; Farber and Gowa, 1995, 1997; James et al., 1999; Gowa, 1999; Henderson, 1999a; Gartzke, 1998, 2000), the robustness of the dyadic DPP has been largely confirmed in the empirical literature on world politics (Thompson and Tucker, 1997ab; Oneal and Russett, 1999ac, 2000; Russett and Oneal, 2001). This confirmation is so strong that it seems to validate the perception among some scholars that joint democracy is a "sufficient condition for peace" (Gleditsch, 1995a: 318), and the democratic peace thesis is "as close as anything we have to an empirical law in world politics" (Levy, 1989: 88).

The dyadic DPP is reputedly one of the most powerful nontautological, nontrivial empirical findings in world politics (Russett, 1993); however, the theoretical explanations for the phenomenon are neither as straightforward nor as convincing as the statistical evidence. Theoretical explanations for the democratic peace emphasize either structural/institutional factors or cultural/normative factors in preventing war between democracies (Rummel, 1983; Doyle, 1986, 1997; Morgan and Campbell, 1991; Morgan and Schwebach, 1992; Maoz and Russett, 1993; Russett, 1993; Kober, 1994; Owen, 1994; Weart, 1994, 1998; Ray, 1995).[3] The former posits that institutional constraints on the decisionmaking choices of democratic leaders make it difficult for them to use force in their foreign policies and act as a brake on conflict with other democracies.[4] The latter assumes that democracies are less disposed to fight each other due to the impact of their shared norms that proscribe the use of violence between them. Various analysts have attempted to determine which of these theoretical arguments best accounts for the democratic peace, with often-contradictory results. While some authors find that structural arguments are more compelling, others insist that cultural arguments are more convincing.

For example, Bueno de Mesquita and Lalman (1992) suggest the greater salience of institutional factors in the democratic peace (also see Morgan and Schwebach, 1992; Bueno de Mesquita et al., 1999; Schultz, 1999). They postulate that leaders in democratic states incur higher political costs for using force than their counterparts in nondemocratic states. In addition, democratic institutions ensure that dissidents in democracies incur lower costs for their actions than those in nondemocracies, and, therefore, it is easier for them to mobilize opposition to their democratic leaders' use of force abroad. The relative transparency of democratic governments ostensibly makes it easier for their leaders to observe that their democratic rivals are "restrained from using force too readily"; therefore, amicable settlements of disputes are more likely (Bueno de Mesquita and Lalman, 1992: 158). Drawing on data from 707 European dyads from 1816 to 1970, Bueno de Mesquita and Lalman find support for this institutionalist version of the DPP.

On the other hand, Maoz and Russett's (1993) study examines the relative strength of institutional and normative explanations of the democratic peace. They specify separate indicators of both concepts. Their measures of institutional factors include the degree to which power is concentrated in the hands of one individual or group, the degree of constraint on the executive, the extent of political centralization, and the scope of government actions. Their measures of normative factors include the political stability of the state in terms of the duration of the political regime and the extent of political violence in the state.

In their analysis of more than 19,000 observations of postwar dyads, they find that although institutional factors are negatively associated with dyadic war, cultural norms account for dyadic peace more generally (i.e., both dispute escalation and war involvement). They conclude that cultural norms form the hub around which the democratic peace revolves (also see Weart, 1994, 1998).

In light of the robust statistical support for the dyadic DPP, the lack of consistency with regard to the putative theoretical explanations of this "empirical law" is rather surprising. We are left, then, with a powerful empirical finding without an equally compelling theoretical justification for it. Others go further to argue that neither theoretical argument used to explain the DPP is convincing (e.g., see Layne, 1994; Polachek, 1997). For example, Gates et al. (1996: 4) quarrel with the institutional constraints argument, which, for them, appears to rely too much "on an Enlightenment faith in the pacific preferences of free citizens" while assuming that these preferences are exogenous and that decisionmakers actually follow them. Further, they allege that it is not at all clear why citizens' aversion to interstate conflict is "only evident in cases of a democratic adversary" but does not preclude conflict with nondemocracies, third party interventions, or colonial expansion. Cultural arguments, for Gates et al. (1996: 5), do not adequately fill the theoretical void left by institutionalist rationalizations; in fact, normative/cultural arguments, for them, actually teeter on tautology: "Relations between democratic states are peaceful because they are informed by a common perception that democracies are peaceful." They conclude that the democratic peace literature "lacks a firm theoretical foundation that can identify a convincing causal mechanism" (also see James et al., 1999).

Several democratic peace scholars have attempted to reconcile the two major theoretical arguments with a hybrid that shows that they are, in fact, complementary. For example, Owen (1994) asserts that liberal ideas in democracies generate liberal ideologies that proscribe war against other democracies while promoting institutions that encourage free and open debate of important issues. The combination of these forces, for Owen, constrains democratic governments from fighting wars with other democracies. Owen focuses on the role of elite perceptions of the "democratic-ness" of the adversary as an intervening factor between shared democracy and conflict; however, the manner by which the processes he outlines reduce conflict is not apparent. For example, he maintains that "liberalism is . . . more tolerant of its own kind" and that "once liberals accept a foreign state as a liberal democracy, they adamantly oppose war against that state" (p. 95). This thesis, for Owen, follows from liberal premises but in such an idiosyncratic way that democracy is pretty much in the eye of the beholder.[5] For example, among Owen's cases, he cites Franco-American relations from 1796 to 1798 wherein U.S. perceptions of France as a liberal democracy, ostensibly, quelled tensions between the two countries. Beyond the fact that it is quite a stretch to label the United States in the eighteenth century as democratic, Owen (1994: 105) himself maintains that "France [during the 1790s] does not qualify by my definition as a liberal democracy." If joint democracy is largely determined by perceptions—and in this case misperceptions—such that its alleged conflict-dampening impact is manifest even when both states are clearly not democratic, then it follows that the "liberal peace" is less a "perpetual peace" as Kant suggested and more a "perceptual peace." This begs the question of the role of perceptions—as opposed to regime type—in international conflict, while failing to provide a compelling explanation for the democratic peace.

Further, Owen's (1994: 95) assertion that "liberalism is . . . more tolerant of its own kind" exposes an unsavory as well as a potentially conflict-exacerbating tendency among democracies—especially Western democracies. For example, Oren (1995: 151) argues that "the democratic peace proposition is not about democracy *per se*; rather, it should be understood as a special case of an argument about peace among polities that are similar relative to some normative benchmarks." What is "special" about the benchmarks that indicate democracy, for Oren, is that they represent "our kind." The designation of "our kind," I submit, often transcends regime type and draws largely on the cultural characteristics of the rival society. Specifically, among culturally dissimilar disputants, the conflict-dampening impact of joint democracy may be undermined by racist or ethnocentric animus on the part of decisionmakers, which Weart (1998: 221) observes as a potential "weak point" in the democratic peace because it may promote "aggressive imperialism" on the part of a strong democracy that attempts to "enforce its hegemony over other peoples."

In a similar vein, Russett (1993: 17) argues that "Western ethnocentric attitudes at the time" prevented normative (or institutional) constraints from forestalling the United States from fighting the Philippines War of 1899 against an arguably democratic adversary. Russett (1993) seems to agree with Weart (1998: 242) that the major influence that "may undermine peace between approximately republican regimes" is the misperception of leaders, which biases them against those that are politically, economically, or culturally different.

Each of these authors agrees that the biased perceptions of democratic leaders have not resulted in interstate warfare between two clearly democratic states, although their analyses imply that democracies may pursue imperialist wars against relatively egalitarian adversaries. The latter point has rarely been investigated systematically because analysts of the DPP—and more positivist-oriented scholars in world politics, more generally—have largely ignored imperialist and anti-colonial wars when examining the DPP (I undertake such an analysis in Chapter 4). Nevertheless, it is clear that Owen's attempted synthesis of normative and institutional explanations of the DPP (as well as Russett's and Weart's assumptions) rests on the primacy of perceptions as a factor in joint democratic conflict, and his conclusions rise or fall on the merits of arguments about the role of perceptions and misperceptions in international conflict, in general.

Although hardly conclusive, the literature on these relationships suggests that in many cases democratic states suffer from problems of misperception as readily as nondemocratic states (see Holsti et al., 1968; Jervis, 1976; Levy, 1983; Stoessinger, 1998). It is not clear from Owen's analyses (or Weart's and Russett's, for that matter) the manner by which democracies overcome the problems of misperception in order to avoid war with each other. These arguments seem to rest on the implicit assumption that foreign policy among democracies is more transparent and that decisionmakers in democratic states will have more complete information regarding their potential adversaries and would, therefore, be less likely to misperceive the intentions of adversaries and, subsequently, less likely to "stumble" into war with them (see Fearon, 1994; Russett and Starr, 2000). However, Stein (1990: 86) reminds us:

> Although misunderstanding and misperception can cause otherwise avoidable conflict, full information does not guarantee cooperation and harmony. In fact, a certain amount of interpersonal ignorance may provide a lubricant of social interaction. Think what would happen if people could suddenly read each other's thoughts . . . "the first effect would be to dissolve all friendships," . . . [and] "by nightfall human society would be in chaos."

One may take the view that it is not the provision of "complete information" that provides the lubricant for peaceful international relations between democracies. Rather, all that is required is that the two states recognize each other as democratic and ipso facto more peaceful. But this position, which is consistent with the cultural/normative viewpoint, is tautological: The reason democracies are peaceful with each other is that they realize democracies are more peaceful, therefore once they perceive their rival as democratic, they do not fight them. On the other hand, one may argue that democracies in dispute recognize that they are both constrained by their institutions in the use of force abroad and in the interregnum seek third party conflict resolution (see Dixon, 1993, 1994). Similarly, one may argue that democratic leaders recognize that their democratic adversaries are more constrained by "audience costs" and these factors inhibit joint democratic warfare.

The latter rationale is evident in the case of Eyerman and Hart's (1996) attempt to reconcile the two theoretical approaches of the DPP. They tested Fearon's (1994: 587) thesis that "high audience cost states require less military escalation in disputes to signal their preferences, and are better able to commit to a cause of action in a dispute." Since democracies, Fearon alleges, have higher audience costs, it is expected that they should only become involved in disputes when they have a high level of commitment. Nondemocracies, which are presumed to have fewer audience costs, are expected to be less selective in their dispute involvement and therefore more likely to become involved in disputes—and also more likely to lose them when the adversary is a democracy because the latter is presumed to be more committed and thus more likely to prevail.

Bueno de Mesquita et al. (1992: 644) maintain that "leaders can anticipate that they will be held accountable for failed foreign policy adventures. Consequently, the choice of war-related behavior is likely to be dampened by the fear that the regime will be punished if things go awry." They assert that democratic leaders suffer the costs of failed foreign policy adventure to a much greater extent than nondemocratic leaders since the latter do not have to satisfy large segments of their society (they often have to be responsive to only a small coterie of political, economic, cultural, and military elites—who often are mere cronies). Therefore, nondemocratic leaders—as Kant suggests—can embark on foreign policy ventures more readily than democratic leaders, who will be more constrained in their foreign policy choices, and forced to pay the price of their failed policies—especially failure in international conflict. Democracies, as presumably high-audience-cost states, are selective in the disputes in which they become involved, more committed to fight and win, and, therefore, better able to signal their commitment by virtue of participation in disputes since they pay a relatively higher cost for backing down. Other democracies recognize this situation and either avoid conflict with democracies or seek peaceful outcomes to their jointly democratic disputes. The transparency of a democratic brand of government allows democratic states to effectively signal their commitment to other states and, in this way, democracies are able to "ameliorate the security dilemma among democratic states" (Fearon, 1994: 577).

Eyerman and Hart (1996: 613) find empirical support for the "audience cost" thesis and conclude that their findings suggest that a combination of normative and institutional factors account for the democratic peace. Specifically, they argue that the institutions within democracies give them the ability to communicate their nonviolent norms from the domestic sphere to the international arena. With this justification, they conclude that "the so-called competing explanations [of the democratic peace] are more complementary than contradictory." But Eyerman and Hart's analysis suffers from problems similar to those associated with constraints-based rationalizations of the DPP (e.g., Morgan and Schwebach, 1992; Bueno de Mesquita et al., 1999). Simply put, these are not explanations of the democratic peace, per se, but assertions that constrained states, or those with high audience costs—whether they are democracies or not—should be less likely to fight each other. However, unless it can be demonstrated that democracies are consistently more constrained and have higher audience costs than nondemocracies, then these arguments fail as explanations of the democratic peace. These viewpoints minimize the role of political market failures and fractures in the checks and balances system that allow leaders to circumvent "democratic constraints" on their ability to prosecute wars, while ignoring the impact of informal checks on the ability of leaders of nondemocracies to take their states to war (see Gowa, 1999: 19–27). In fact, Morgan and Schwebach (1992) have demonstrated that there are nondemocracies that are more constrained than democracies.[6] In addition, Gelpi and Grieco (2000) evaluate the extent to which leaders who lose crises have shorter postcrisis tenure, whether the costs of failure increase with the level of escalation of the dispute, and whether democratic leaders suffer higher costs for failed escalation and find no evidence in support of any of these claims. Finally, Finel and Lord (2000: 166–167) conclude from their case studies that "transparency often exacerbates crises" because (a) the media, which is a primary mechanism of transmitting information supplied by transparency, "may have an incentive to pay more attention to belligerent statements than more subtle, conciliatory signals," (b) "transparency may actually undermine behind-the-scenes efforts at negotiated settlements," (c) transparent states engaged in belligerent rhetoric are more likely to have their crises spiral out of control, and (d) "transparency may make it difficult for observers to determine which groups will control a given policy decision."[7] Therefore, using the "transparency," "audience cost," or "institutional constraints" approach as a basis to reconcile the two putative explanations of the democratic peace has not resulted in a compelling account of the phenomenon.

In actuality, most DPP authors appreciate that the distinction between the structural/institutional and cultural/normative arguments is more apparent than real. For example, Russett (1993: 92), who, with Ze'ev Maoz, went to great pains to demonstrate the greater salience of cultural/normative arguments in their 1993 *American Political Science Review* article, points out that "it would be a mistake to emphasize too strongly the subtlety or persuasiveness of the distinction between cultural/normative and structural/institutional" factors. Morgan and Schwebach (1992: 318), who favor an institutionalist explanation of the democratic peace, observe that "to a great extent, culture and structure go together. A nation imbued with a democratic culture will likely establish a correspondent political system, and a state structured to constrain will likely foster a democratic culture." Ray (1995: 36) agrees that "wherever a democratic political culture is well ensconced, in well-established democracies, there too will democratic institutions be strong, exerting their constraints." This position leads him to conclude that the dichotomy between structural/institutional and cultural/normative versions is overstated and probably not very useful (p. 37). Russett and Oneal (2001: 53) seem to agree. They argue that democratic peace scholars have mistakenly assumed that the two explanations had to be mutually exclusive, when in fact they should be viewed as complementary. For them, "Rather than ask which theory is right and which is wrong, we should ask if and how they both could be true." They add that "it is more helpful to think of peace among democracies as 'overdetermined,' explainable by several related but conceptually distinct and reinforcing, perhaps sequential, causal mechanisms" (p. 53). They point out that "just as there are multiple paths to war . . . there are multiple, 'substitutable' paths to peace" (p. 53), and they contend that the cultural/normative and structural/institutional explanations "can be reconciled to show how they affect the opportunity and willingness of decision makers to choose between conflict and cooperation under particular conditions" (p. 54).

While there is something to be said for viewing the contending theoretical explanations of the DPP as complementary, one cannot avoid the deeper problem that analysts who have tested these explanations have uncovered significant findings suggesting that they tap on competing and not complementary aspects of the democratic peace phenomenon. For example, Maoz and Russett (1993) provide a critical test of the relative explanatory capacity of both approaches and conclude that the variables associated with political culture are much more consistently significant than those measuring political institutionalization. Having accomplished this, it is difficult, if not a bit disingenuous to then suggest that both approaches are complementary, when the analysis seems to indicate that in some respects they are contrasting, if not contradictory. Similarly, although Bueno de Mesquita and Lalman (1992) do not provide a critical test of the potency of the two approaches, their analysis clearly rejects the cultural argument in favor of an institutional one, which suggests that—at least in their view—these two arguments are mutually exclusive rather than complementary.

Explaining the Monadic DPP:
Structural and Cultural Arguments

Another problem with the structural/institutional and cultural/normative explanations of the DPP is that they seem to imply that individual democracies as well as pairs of democracies should be more peaceful than nondemocracies. For example, if institutional checks and balances within democracies restrict the arbitrary use of force in domestic politics, and these institutional checks, in turn, have a restraining influence on the arbitrary use of force abroad against other democracies, then one would expect that these same institutional impediments would prevent democracies from fighting nondemocracies as well. This follows from Kant's ([1795] 1991: 100) stipulation that "if . . . the consent of the citizens is required to decide whether or not war is to be declared, it is very natural that they will have great hesitation in embarking on so dangerous an enterprise. For this would mean calling down on themselves all the miseries of war. . . . But under a constitution where the subject is not a citizen, and which is therefore not republican, it is the simplest thing in the world to go to war." Similarly, if democracies evince non-violent norms in their domestic politics and then transfer these norms to international relations, as classical liberals and many democratic peace advocates argue, one would expect individual democratic states to be generally more peaceful than nondemocratic states.[8] Therefore, the basic theoretical argument for the democratic peace seems to assume, at least in part, the peacefulness of individual democratic states; nevertheless, the empirical evidence, for the most part, indicates that democracies are just as war prone as nondemocracies (Small and Singer, 1976; Chan, 1984; Weede, 1984; Maoz and Abdolali, 1989; Bueno de Mesquita and Lalman, 1992).

In response to this apparent anomaly, DPP researchers have proffered theoretical arguments that suggest that although democracies are less likely to fight each other (accepting the dyadic DPP), they are just as war prone as nondemocracies (rejecting the monadic DPP). For example, Russett (1993) derives these arguments from both the structural/institutional and the cultural/normative explanations. In light of the structural/institutional explanation, he notes that democracies recognize each other as constrained by the institutional checks and balances in their political systems. The constraints reduce the fear of exploitation by surprise attack, and leaders use the additional time to resolve conflicts nonviolently. On the other hand, democratic leaders realize that leaders of nondemocracies are not similarly constrained and therefore can rapidly and secretly set upon a course of war. Aware that democracies are constrained, nondemocratic leaders may "press democracies to make greater concessions over issues in conflict" (p. 40). Russett observes further that "democratic leaders may initiate large-scale violence with nondemocracies rather than make the greater concessions demanded" (p. 40). In addition, democratic leaders may initiate conflicts in order to preempt their nondemocratic adversaries. In this way, Russett provides a theoretical explanation for both the absence of wars between democracies and the presence of wars between democracies and nondemocracies. He relies on a similar rationale with respect to the cultural/normative explanation. In this variant, he insists that democracies do not fight each other because of the internalization of their domestic norms of nonviolent conflict resolution, which they expect other democracies to adopt; however, they expect nondemocracies to use the same violent means of conflict resolution in the international sphere that are apparent in their domestic politics. Therefore, democracies resort to violence with nondemocracies to avoid being exploited by them.

Russett's arguments are similar to those of Doyle (1983b: 324–325), who notes, *"The very constitutional restraint, shared commercial interests, and international respect for individual rights that promote peace among liberal societies can exacerbate conflicts in relations between liberal and non-liberal societies"* (emphasis in original). Doyle, like Russett, ultimately argues in favor of the cultural/normative explanation of the DPP, which they both insist can account for the absence of war between democracies as well as the presence of war between democracies and nondemocracies. Bueno de Mesquita and Lalman (1992) make similar arguments (i.e., accepting the dyadic DPP but rejecting the monadic DPP), but they favor the structural/institutional explanation. They contend that the transparency that allows democracies to recognize each other as constrained and to seek nonviolent means of resolving their international disputes (as discussed above) also makes them vulnerable to exploitation by nondemocracies that are not as constrained. They argue that "the high domestic political constraint faced by democracies makes them vulnerable to threats of war or exploitation and liable to launch preemptive attacks against presumed aggressors" (p. 159). Since democratic leaders are more likely to suffer costs to their regime for perceived foreign policy failures—especially loss in war (see Bueno de Mesquita et al., 1992), they may opt to go to war with nondemocracies in order to avoid the domestic political costs of capitulation or to preempt an attack by their relatively unrestrained nondemocratic adversary. In this way, Bueno de Mesquita and Lalman (1992) utilize the institutional/structural explanation to account for both the finding that democracies do not fight each other and the finding that individual democracies are just as war prone as nondemocracies.

Interestingly, the extent to which these "synthetic" explanations of "dyadic democratic peace without monadic democratic peace" have been convincing may now represent a serious shortcoming in their explanatory capacity since new research suggests that democracies, in fact, are more peaceful than nondemocracies (Oneal and Russett, 1997, 1999c; Oneal and Ray, 1997; Russett and Oneal, 2001). With the evidence provided by these new studies, DPP scholars such as those discussed above could no longer rely on the "synthetic" theoretical arguments stipulating that democracies are less likely to fight each other, but are just as war prone as nondemocracies. If they desired to stick with their previous arguments that rely on structural or cultural approaches, they would be forced to concede to what they had previously rejected: Both the cultural/normative and institutional/structural explanations of the DPP imply that individual democracies should be more peaceful than nondemocracies. This would be difficult, given that these scholars had proffered their synthetic arguments to explain why there was a dyadic democratic peace and not a monadic one.[9] In light of the recent findings, they would have to show how their theoretical arguments were consistent with both the dyadic and the monadic DPP or they would have to abandon them for an explanation that fits the new evidence.[10]

Instead of providing a new or modified theoretical explanation of the new findings that democracies are more peaceful, in general, than nondemocracies, leading DPP advocates seem to have settled on a methodological resolution of the problem. Unfortunately, this solution relies on questionable research designs that severely limit our ability to test the main premise of both the dyadic and the monadic DPP. As these will be discussed in the next section and even more fully in the following chapters, I won't examine them here. It is sufficient, at this point, to note that today, as in the past, the strongest empirical findings in support of the DPP rely on theoretical explanations that are not very persuasive. Further, and even more importantly, the empirical evidence on which the DPP relies is less convincing than often noted. Since it has been the apparent empirical regularity of the democratic peace that has led scholars, at least in the past few years, to attempt to explain it, I intend to bypass the theoretical debate and go to the heart of the empirical evidence and attempt to provide support for my agnostic claims regarding the DPP. In the next section, I outline the point of departure of this study before providing an overview of the subsequent chapters of the book.

The Point of Departure

To my mind, the empirical evidence in support of both the dyadic and the monadic DPP is problematic for several reasons. The most recent studies alluded to earlier, which indicate that democracies are less likely to fight each other and are more peaceful, in general, than nondemocracies, are beset by research design problems that severely hinder their reliability (e.g., Oneal and Russett, 1997; Oneal and Ray, 1997; Russett and Oneal, 2001). For example, many of them rely on a questionable operationalization of joint democracy that conflates the level of democracy of two states with their political dissimilarity. Only by teasing out the effects of each factor are we in a position to confidently argue that shared democracy, rather than other factors, is actually the motivating force driving democratic states toward their allegedly more peaceful international relations. In addition, the findings used to support monadic DPP claims also rely on questionable research designs that exclude whole categories of international war—namely, extrastate wars, which are usually imperialist and colonial wars. The exclusion of these wars from recent tests of the DPP leaves us unable to determine the actual applicability of the DPP to the full range of international war. In addition, given that some scholars suggest that the DPP is applicable to civil wars (Krain and Myers, 1997; Rummel, 1997), it is important to determine to what extent we observe a "domestic democratic peace" for the most civil war prone states—the post-colonial, or third world, states. Previous work has not tested the DPP for this specific group of states, and it is important that our research design address this omission.

In this study, I provide a straightforward examination of the dyadic DPP, which posits that democracies rarely if ever fight each other; the monadic DPP, which alleges that democracies are more peaceful, in general, than nondemocracies; and the "domestic DPP," which suggests that democracies are less likely to experience civil wars. What is most interesting about this study—and what makes it not simply one more on a long a list of articles and monographs on the DPP—is that it hoists the DPP on its own petard by using data from the main proponents of the DPP, using similar statistical methods, replicating their findings, and then, by only slightly revising their research designs (in very straightforward and noncontroversial ways), refuting the DPP for the post–World War II era and for several different types of armed conflicts. I analyze the DPP for all states during the postwar era—the period within which the democratic peace is most evident and for which the most unambiguous claims in support of the dyadic and monadic DPP have been advanced (e.g., Oneal and Russett, 1997, 1999c; Oneal and Ray, 1997; Leeds and Davis, 1999; Russett and Oneal, 2001). The statistical rarity of both war and democracy leaves few observations through which to acquire significant findings on the relationship between democracy and war in the pre–World War II period (see Spiro,

1994; Jaggers and Gurr, 1996). A temporal focus that concentrates on the post–World War II period, which is the era in which we find—by far—most of the cases of democratic states, actually biases the analysis *in favor* of the DPP and, therefore, makes refuting the thesis more daunting and also much more compelling if accomplished. In the following section, I provide an outline of the remaining chapters of the book.

Overview of Remaining Chapters

In Chapter 2, I examine the extent to which democracies are less likely to fight each other through a replication and extension of one of the most prominent and compelling studies of the DPP. In "The Classical Liberals Were Right," Oneal and Russett (1997) put forth a purportedly definitive empirical substantiation of the democratic peace proposition. In this chapter, I replicate and extend their results using more straightforward measures of joint democracy and dyadic conflict, as well as a control for "political distance" or political dissimilarity. With these modifications and using Oneal and Russett's data and identical statistical techniques, I find no significant relationship between joint democracy and the likelihood of international conflict. Instead, I find that having fused political dissimilarity with joint democracy, Oneal and Russett incorrectly ascribe to the latter a statistical significance it does not warrant—especially once one controls for the impact of trade interdependence. The results suggest that Oneal and Russett's findings are largely the result of several questionable research design choices and seriously call into question the dyadic version of the democratic peace thesis, thereby undermining the empirical support for democratic enlargement strategies.

In Chapter 3, I examine the monadic version of the DPP, which maintains that democracies are more peaceful, in general, than nondemocracies. As noted earlier, recent studies aver that the DPP is not only a dyadic level phenomenon (i.e., a phenomenon that applies to pairs of states) but a monadic level one (i.e., a phenomenon that applies to individual states) as well. I argue that these studies often relied on faulty research designs that required one to infer monadic level relationships from dyadic level processes. By explicitly focusing on state level relationships I avoid the levels of analysis problems evident in the earlier studies. The findings using an explicitly state level research design indicate not only that democracies are not more peaceful but that they are in fact significantly *more likely* to become involved in—and to initiate—interstate wars and militarized international disputes. The results are robust whether one uses continuous or dichotomous measures of democracy. The findings clearly refute the monadic DPP and have dire implications for strategies aimed at promoting peace by spreading democracy.

Chapter 4 focuses on the role of democracy in extrastate wars. Unlike interstate wars, which involve the regular armed forces of recognized sovereign states (e.g., the Franco-Prussian War or the Falkland Islands War), extrastate wars are armed conflicts between the military forces of recognized sovereign states and nonstate political entities (Small and Singer, 1982). Although these have been primarily colonial and imperial wars, they need not be (e.g., this category of warfare also includes several armed conflicts involving China and Tibet, Ethiopia and Eritrea, and Indonesia and East Timor). The exclusion of extrastate wars from most tests of the DPP leaves us unable to determine the actual applicability of the DPP to the full range of international war. Combining extrastate and interstate wars into a single category of international war, there is no significant relationship between democracy and international war. Focusing on extrastate wars, in particular, I find that, in general, democracies are less likely to become involved in these wars; however, the Western democracies are *more likely* to become involved in them. The findings demonstrate that democracy does not have a uniform impact on different types of war: It increases the probability of interstate war, it neither increases nor decreases the likelihood of international war, and it decreases the likelihood of extrastate war. However, since extrastate warfare is largely a product of a bygone colonial era, it is more likely that for the future, the operative form of international warfare will be interstate warfare, and democracy exacerbates the probability of a state's involvement in—and initiation of—interstate wars. These findings seriously call into question the reliability of foreign policy strategies that attempt to advance peace through the promotion of democracy.

In Chapter 5, I examine the extent to which the democratic peace is applicable to civil wars. Although DPP arguments primarily focus on international conflict, there have been several studies alleging that the DPP is also applicable to civil wars. This claim is all the more relevant since the lion's share of large-scale violence in the post World War II era has resulted from civil wars—especially those in the postcolonial states of the third world. In this chapter, I examine the DPP for civil wars in postcolonial states, which are the most civil war prone states. The findings reveal that there is not a democratic peace in the case of civil wars in postcolonial states. Although both democratic and autocratic states are less likely to experience civil war, these relationships are not statistically significant. I find that states with intermediate levels of democracy—semidemocracies—are the most prone to civil wars. This finding suggests that attempts at democratization will increase the likelihood of civil war if the process does not result in full democratization. Coupled with the findings from the previous chapters, the results indicate that with the exception of extrastate wars, which are largely remnants of a bygone era, the DPP does not appear to be operative for international *or* civil wars.

In Chapter 6, I suggest an alternative explanation of the postwar absence of interstate war between democratic states. This is important because although there is little statistical support for the democratic peace, it is, nonetheless, evident that in the postwar era, democratic states rarely if ever fight each other. Therefore, although the "democratic peace" is not statistically significant, we should address the substantive significance of the absence of war between democracies, and that is what I attempt in this chapter. Specifically, I argue that a combination of factors including bipolarity, alliance membership, and trade links reduced conflict among many jointly democratic and jointly autocratic states. In the postwar era, a "dual-hegemony" system was created wherein the superpowers maintained relative stability within their respective blocs. This situation led many states to become more tightly bound within their alliances, and with trade "following the flag," they linked their economies to each other in such a way as to generate an international security regime among democratic states, which drastically reduced the likelihood of conflict between them. It follows that the "democratic peace" was owed less to joint democracy than to an international security regime that emerged in the bipolar era.

In Chapter 7, I summarize the main findings of the study and briefly discuss their research and policy implications. The main finding resulting from analyses of the relationship between democracy and armed conflict is that democracy is not significantly associated with peace for international or civil wars. There is neither a dyadic democratic peace nor a monadic one. To the extent that any democratic peace may obtain, it does so for extrastate wars, which are more than likely relics of a bygone colonial era; nevertheless, even for these wars, while democracies in general are less likely to become involved in them, the

Western states—especially Western democracies—are more likely to fight them. All of these findings result from analyzes using straightforward research designs, as well as similar data and identical statistical techniques commonly found in research supporting the DPP. They suggest that politico-economic factors particular to the postwar era greatly contributed to the phenomenon that has been mistakenly labeled the "democratic peace." In fact, the results indicate that many who argued that trade more than joint democracy was the main factor in the "democratic peace" were correct (e.g., Polachek, 1997). Further, they imply that foreign policy strategies aimed at increasing the likelihood of peace by spreading democracy are more likely to increase the probability of war.

The findings suggest the need to clearly delineate the separate impact of joint democracy and regime dissimilarity when analyzing the DPP. They call into question the utilization of "weak-link" specifications in analyses of the DPP while challenging researchers to be very careful in drawing inferences from relationships at one level of aggregation to those at another. The clearest policy implication of these findings is that democratic enlargement, as a strategy, is not likely to be effective in reducing the likelihood of wars between or within states, and it is apt to increase the probability of war involvement for individual states. Although Western democracies, following the enlargement strategy, may rationalize their involvement in international wars by suggesting the need to democratize states in order to make them more peaceful, such a rationale is gainsaid by the findings from this study. On the whole, the findings indicate that democracy is hardly a guarantor of peace and in many cases increases the probability of war. To be sure, the findings do not suggest the undesirability of democracy, as a form of government, as much as they remind us that foreign policy is much too complex to simply rely on a single factor to guide it. Instead, we need to devise multifaceted and multidimensional foreign policy strategies to reduce the likelihood of war.

Notes

1. Also see Smith (1994: 92–93) who traces this commitment to democracy to the nineteenth century.

2. Clinton (1996: 9) made it clear that the linchpin of his post–Cold War strategy was to enlarge the community of democratic states because democra-

cies are "far less likely to wage war on one another." There are four key components of this strategy: (1) strengthening the community of democratic states, (2) fostering and consolidating new democracies, (3) countering the aggression of nondemocracies while liberalizing nondemocratic states, and (4) assisting the development of democracy in regions of humanitarian concern to the United States. According to Clinton's National Security Adviser, Anthony Lake (1993: 3), the enlargement of the number of democratic states is central to the foreign policy challenges facing the United States because "it protects our [U.S.] interests and security."

3. Small and Singer (1976: 50) anticipated these theoretical arguments in the first paragraph of their study, where they ponder "whether the allegedly pacific nature of [democracies] is a result of bureaucratic sluggishness or of a more fundamental humaneness on the part of the masses (as opposed to the moral insensitivity of dictatorial leaders)."

4. One may also differentiate between at least two variants of the institutional argument (see Schultz, 1999).

5. This type of rationale is also evident in Weart's (1998: 122) theoretical argument.

6. Morgan and Schwebach's (1992) conclusions should be appreciated in light of the fact that the Polity III dataset, which is the most widely used data set for measuring democracy among DPP researchers, basically measures the degree of executive constraints in a state (see Gleditsch and Ward, 1997). Importantly, if, using these data, one still does not demonstrate that institutional constraints drive the DPP, then clearly there are weaknesses in the institutional constraints explanation of the DPP.

7. The transparency argument also informs Bueno de Mesquita et al.'s (1999) institutionalist explanation of the DPP in which they argue that since state leaders desire to remain in power, they attempt to satisfy a large segment of those who influence the selection process in order to maintain a winning coalition. Since democratic leaders have to satisfy a large electorate (either through the distribution of private or collective goods) instead of a small coterie of officials as in many nondemocracies, they are more likely to provide collective goods to large segments of the society, which, in turn, gives them greater legitimacy while increasing the probability that they will stay in power. The remainder of the argument is similar to the "audience costs" thesis and suffers from the problems associated with it discussed above. In addition, Bueno de Mesquita et al.'s perspective seems to incorrectly assume that losers can switch to rival leaders with relative ease and that the public is attentive to foreign policy decisions and outcomes even in cases of MIDs, which are often very minor disputes that arouse little public attention. Resources are assumed to be explicitly economic and zero-sum, which ignores symbolic resources, which are the everyday currency of politics (e.g., prestige). An important aspect of this thesis, which suggests that autocracies "try less hard" than democracies in war, also seems to ignore Organski and Kugler's (1980) argu-

ments on the war effort of ostensibly "weaker" and nondemocratic states such as the North Vietnamese vis-à-vis that of the United States in the Vietnam War.

8. Kant clearly suggests that the interaction of republican states should occasion international peace (most effectively through a "league of peace"), which implies the dyadic DPP, but the theoretical rationale for the democratic peace also seems to be largely—though not exclusively—grounded in the assumption of the general peacefulness of individual democracies, i.e., the monadic DPP. While Reiter and Stam (1998b) agree that Kant's thesis implies the monadic DPP, Russett (1993) disagrees, although he seems to reverse this view in Oneal and Russett (1997) and Russett and Oneal (2001), which relate support for the monadic DPP to a validation of Kant's thesis. Bueno de Mesquita and Lalman (1992: 155) derive support for the DPP from their rational choice model, which assumes "dovishness" on the part of individual democracies but rejects the monadic DPP.

9. The exception is Rummel, who has steadfastly supported both versions of the DPP.

10. The potential for this problem was anticipated by Ray (1995: 21).

2

Are Democracies Less Likely to Fight Each Other?

I n this chapter I examine the extent to which democracies are less likely to fight each other (i.e., the dyadic DPP), through a replication and extension of one of the most prominent and persuasive studies validating the DPP, that of Oneal and Russett (1997). After replicating the results from the study, I extend the previous analysis utilizing more straightforward measures of joint democracy and dyadic conflict, as well as a control for "political distance," or political dissimilarity. With these modifications and using the identical data and statistical techniques used by Oneal and Russett to support the DPP, I find no significant relationship between joint democracy and the likelihood of international conflict. Instead, I find that having fused political dissimilarity with joint democracy, Oneal and Russett and other DPP advocates incorrectly ascribe to the latter a statistical significance that it does not warrant—especially once one controls for the impact of trade interdependence. I argue that Oneal and Russett's findings are largely the result of questionable research design choices; this calls into question the view that democracies are significantly less likely to fight each other, thereby undermining the empirical support for democratic enlargement strategies. It is important to note that Oneal and Russett arrived at these results using a research design that focused on the post–World War II era, the period in which most cases of joint democracy are found and the era in which DPP advocates suggest the democratic peace is most evident. Therefore, this research design biases the analysis *in favor* of the DPP, and refutation of the DPP for this era is quite persuasive evidence against it.

Were the Classical Liberals Right?

In "The Classical Liberals Were Right: Democracy, Interdependence, and Conflict, 1950–1985," Oneal and Russett (1997) put forth a purportedly definitive empirical substantiation of the dyadic DPP, which holds that democratic states are less likely than nondemocratic states to fight each other. They grounded their analyses in the theoretical assumptions of classical liberalism regarding the conflict-dampening impact of joint democracy and trade.[1] Focusing on the post–World War II era, which is more amenable to statistical analyses of the DPP given the greater number of democratic states as compared to the pre–World War II period, they evaluated the impact of joint democracy on international conflict, controlling for alliance membership, geographic contiguity, economic development, and trade interdependence.[2] Their results led them to conclude that during the Cold War era there was "a separate peace among democratic states" (Oneal and Russett, 1997: 288). Findings such as these would buttress their subsequent claims that joint democracy is almost a sufficient condition for international peace (see Russett and Oneal, 2001).

Although skeptics continue to challenge the theoretical basis of the DPP (see Layne, 1994; Oren, 1995; Gowa, 1999), they have not been able to effectively refute the basic empirical finding that democracies rarely if ever fight each other (see Maoz and Abdolali, 1989; Maoz and Russett, 1993; Ray, 1995; Maoz, 1997; Oneal and Ray, 1997; Thompson and Tucker, 1997ab; Russett and Oneal, 2001).[3] It is the meticulous statistical evidence that has been amassed in support of the DPP—much more than the theoretical explanations of the phenomenon—that has been most persuasive, and Oneal and Russett's (1997) study exemplifies this type of painstaking confirmation. The wellspring of empirical support has not been lost on policymakers. In fact, the DPP has become the centerpiece of the U.S. post–Cold War strategy of "democratic enlargement," which is aimed at expanding the community of democratic states, because, as President Clinton (1996: 9) stated, democracies are "far less likely to wage war on one another." Democratic peace findings seem to provide an empirical substantiation for a "democratic crusade" on the part of the Western democracies while catapulting quantitative approaches to world politics to renewed prominence within Western strategic circles.

The significance of Oneal and Russett's study was recognized immediately after its publication, leading several authors to attempt to replicate the main findings. In one early replication, Beck et al. (1998) found solid and consistent support for Oneal and Russett's central finding that joint democracy reduces the likelihood of interstate conflict.[4] Later, Bennett and Stam (2000) showed that Oneal and Russett's democratic peace findings were robust across even more sophisticated and often more restrictive research design specifications.[5] In light of these earlier replications and extensions, another replication of Oneal and Russett (1997) may seem redundant; however, I raise several concerns with Oneal and Russett's study that have not been addressed in previous replications.

My primary critique centers on Oneal and Russett's reliance on a questionable "weak-link" measure that conflates joint democracy on one hand and political dissimilarity on the other. (I discuss this in detail later in the chapter.) I propose to evaluate Oneal and Russett's (1997) findings using separate and more straightforward measures of these variables. In addition, while Oneal and Russett (1997) code their outcome variable of conflict involvement to include ongoing dispute years, I follow Barbieri (1996) and Bennett and Stam's (2000) suggestion that one should not code subsequent years of the same dispute (or war) as additional cases of conflict. Previous research—including studies conducted by Oneal and Russett—have addressed several of these concerns and found that the "democratic peace" is robust in light of them; however, none of these investigations have examined all of these concerns simultaneously and that is what I intend to do here.

Research Design

As noted, Oneal and Russett's (1997) research design draws on a "weak-link" assumption, which presumably allows one to draw inferences about the relative war-proneness of dyads by focusing on the level of democracy of the least democratic state in the dyad. This approach derives from Dixon's (1993) assertion that by focusing on the weakest link in the dyad, one can better grasp the motive forces compelling the states to conflict (also see Bueno de Mesquita and Lalman, 1992). Oneal and Russett (1997: 274) agree that "the likelihood of conflict [is] primarily a function of the degree of political constraint experienced by the less constrained state in each dyad." To better appreciate the importance of the weak-link specification and its centrality to Oneal and Russett's (1997) study, an aside to trace the evolution of scholarly reliance on this approach in explicating the DPP is warranted.

The Weak-Link Thesis and the Search for a
Continuous Measure of Joint Democracy

Theoretical arguments on the DPP suggest that the greater the extent of shared democracy between two states, the greater the ability of shared democratic norms and institutions to prevent conflict (see Rummel, 1983; Russett, 1993).[6] Since this is an argument with respect to the magnitude of democracy and not simply its presence or absence, it follows that an appropriate operational measure of joint democracy should be scaled as a continuous rather than a discrete (i.e., dichotomous or trichotomous) variable (Henderson, 1999a). Nevertheless, many early studies of the DPP used noncontinuous—mainly dichotomous—measures of democracy. A dichotomous or discrete measure of joint democracy implies that the conflict-dampening impact of joint democracy is only evident above some threshold value, but such thresholds have been largely atheoretical and arbitrary, leading Oneal et al. (1996: 24) to remark that "our confidence in a democratic peace would have to be tempered . . . if the pacific influence of democracy were strong only above a high threshold." Even with more widely accepted measures of regime type garnered from the Polity datasets (e.g., Jaggers and Gurr, 1996), analysts continued to caution against the use of dichotomous measures in evaluating the DPP because "any threshold used to distinguish democratic from non-democratic states in the Polity data is bound to be largely atheoretical, [since] all but the highest and lowest values on the Polity democracy-autocracy scale can be achieved by different combinations on the constituent dimensions making the resulting sums of uncertain meaning" (Oneal and Ray, 1997: 777). It soon became apparent that variables derived from the Polity measures that had been used in important studies of the DPP had some unattractive characteristics.[7]

For example, one of the most widely used continuous measures of joint democracy was Maoz and Russett's (1993) *JOINREG*, which they used in their highly influential *American Political Science Review* article, which demonstrated the greater salience of normative rather than institutional factors in explicating the democratic peace.[8] According to Russett (1993: 76–77), *JOINREG* was constructed to "reflect two things simultaneously: How democratic or undemocratic are the members of the dyad, and how different or similar in their regime types are the two states?" Accordingly, it is a ratio with a numerator that taps the degree of joint democracy between the states and a denominator that gauges the difference between the regime scores. However, *JOINREG* is unreliable as a measure of joint democracy for the very reasons that it was found useful to Russett. That is, since it measures both the average level of democracy and the similarity of the regimes, interpreting results from analyses that used it proved difficult because as Ray (1995: 26) noted, "a pair of states will attain a high score on *[JOINREG]* *either* because they are relatively democratic *or* because they are relatively similar in regime type." A second and even more troubling feature of *JOINREG* is that it does not increase monotonically with increases in the constituent states' democracy scores. That is, in certain cases where a dyad becomes more democratic, its *JOINREG* score decreases markedly (see Oneal and Russett, 1997: 275).[9]

Once these shortcomings were recognized, scholars sought more reliable measures of joint democracy, such as the sum or product of the individual state's regime scores as recorded in the Polity datasets.[10] At the same time, they also began to examine the impact of trade on the democratic peace. In another groundbreaking study, Oneal et al. (1996), still relying on *JOINREG,* found that trade interdependence had a more robust conflict-dampening impact than joint democracy. Their findings presented a quandary for DPP advocates since they also revealed that only a dichotomous democracy variable was significant when controlling for trade interdependence, while continuous democracy variables were not significant in such models. In attempting to address the failure of continuous democracy variables to remain significant in models that controlled for trade, DPP scholars redoubled their efforts to devise a measure that captured both the degree to which two states were democratic and the degree to which they were politically dissimilar (they called the latter attribute "political distance"), while avoiding the problems associated with *JOINREG*. One potential source of problems Ray (1995) observed earlier: Democratic peace scholars were attempting to fuse two attributes, each of which, they believed, had an independent impact on international conflict. Of these two attributes, joint democracy was viewed as reducing the probability of conflict, and political distance was seen as increasing the probability of conflict.

Appreciating the contrasting effects of joint democracy and political distance and seeking to resolve the quandary of Oneal et al.'s (1996) findings, Oneal and Ray (1997) evaluated several indicators of joint democracy to test their robustness in models that included a measure of trade interdependence. When they garnered different results from estimations using a joint democracy variable measured as the sum of the states' regime scores and one measured as the geometric mean of the states' regime scores, they thought they could explain why Oneal et al.'s dichotomous measure of joint democracy had been robust while their continuous measure had not.[11] Oneal and Ray (1997) noted that the geometric mean measure—which was the most robust of the continuous measures they used initially—was more sensitive to changes in the differences in the two states' regime scores and increased more with an increase in the less democratic state's regime score than with a similar increase in the more democratic state's regime score. For Oneal and Ray (p. 764), "this suggests that the prospects for peace improve more when the less democratic nation in a dyad becomes more democratic, which reduces the political distance along the democratic-autocratic continuum separating the two states." On the other hand, their joint democracy variable measured as the sum of the two states' regime scores "is affected equally by an increase in either regime score"; therefore, "its poor performance suggests that a high level of democracy in one state does not compensate for a low level in a strategic partner." They reasoned that "the absolute difference in regime scores—the political distance separating the members of a dyad along the autocracy-democracy continuum—is important for understanding the influence of political regimes on the likelihood of conflict" (p. 764). They concluded that "a discrete measure of joint democracy lends more support for the democratic peace because it identifies those dyads for which political distance is a minimum and the sum of the states' democracy scores is a maximum" (p. 768). They expected pairs of states with these characteristics to be the most peaceful because "the probability of a dispute is not only a function of the average level of democracy in a dyad, but also the political distance separating the states" (p. 768).

Since Oneal and Ray (1997: 771) were clear that scholars should "not rely on a dichotomous measure of regimes because it masks the separate effect of democracy and political distance," they opted for a "weak-link" specification of joint democracy because with such a specification there was "no need . . . to postulate that the effect of democracy on conflict is discontinuous—involving a threshold—or that a club good is involved." In addition, they thought that it captured both the level of democracy of the two states as well as the political distance between them. When they included their weak-link joint democracy variable(s) in models that also included a trade interdependence variable, the coefficient of the joint democracy variable(s) was statistically significant. This finding replicated those of Oneal and Russett (1997), which were published just months prior to Oneal and Ray (1997). Both sets of findings overcame the statistical quandary of Oneal et al.'s (1996) results. Oneal and Ray (1997) explained that the problem with previous continuous joint democracy measures was that analysts did not fully appreciate that "combining states regime scores into a single dyadic measure entails a loss of information, however it is done, [and therefore,] it is preferable simply to identify the higher and lower democracy scores and to use these" (p. 770). They noted that "Maoz and Russett's (1993) instincts were correct; they erred only in combining these two factors into a single variable *[JOINREG]*" (p. 768).

As noted, Oneal and Russett (1997: 274) adopted the weak-link approach for much the same reason as Oneal and Ray, although Oneal and Russett were even more emphatic that the likelihood of a dispute is "a function of the lower democracy score in the dyad" (p. 274) and that "the probability of a dispute is strongly associated with the continuous measure of the political character of the less-democratic state" (p. 288). Therefore, in their basic equation, Oneal and Russett include only the regime score for the less democratic state, while introducing the regime score for the more democratic state when their interest turns to the specific impact of political distance on conflict involvement. In fact, in their subsequent study (i.e., Russett and Oneal, 2001) all of their estimations of the DPP rely on models that include only the democracy score for the less democratic state in the dyad. Clearly, for Oneal and Russett and Oneal and Ray, the weak-link specification was viewed as a huge improvement over previous continuous measures of joint democracy because it was theoretically derived and reliable and because it remained statistically significant in models that controlled for the impact of trade interdependence.

So the adoption of the weak-link specification of joint democracy should be seen as part of a process aimed at generating a more theoretically consistent, reliable, robust, continuous measure of joint democracy that could be utilized to systematically evaluate democratic peace claims. Within this context, Oneal and Russett's (1997) findings served as a reaffirmation and extension of democratic peace research that had faced a serious empirical quandary. The weak-link specification gained greater acceptance, in large part, because it allowed for the substantiation of democratic peace claims; and it is not surprising that in relatively short order it became a standard operationalization for joint democracy in systematic studies of the link between democracy and various international phenomena (e.g., Mousseau, 1998; Bennett and Stam, 2000; Busch, 2000).

Garnering less attention, however, were several theoretical and methodological problems with weak-link assumptions and analyses that drew upon them (more later in the chapter). Several of these problems are manifest in the research design of Oneal and Russett (1997), and they affect scholars' ability to replicate and extend their findings. In the three sections that follow, I address each of these issues in turn.

The Weak-Link Thesis and Joint Democracy

The first research design problem in Oneal and Russett (1997) that I would like to address emerges from the fact that since their weak-link approach assumes that the influence of one state's level of democracy is conditional on that of the other state's, then they should include an interaction term, which should take the value of the product of both states' democracy scores, in their equations that assume the operation of weak-link processes. The coefficient for the interaction term captures the influence of the level of joint democracy between the two states—a dyadic level factor—on the likelihood of conflict, and also partly accounts for the conditional impact of each individual state's level of democracy on the outcome (see Friedrich, 1982). While the inclusion of an interaction term alleviates the specification problem discussed above, in practice it often leads to estimation problems since it is often highly correlated with the individual states' democracy scores and generates serious multicollinearity problems that preclude our fleshing out of either the direct or conditional impact of the primary predictor variables.

Oneal and Russett (1997) do not present analyses using an interaction term in their main findings, but they discuss this issue in a footnote—although they do not address potential or actual multicollinearity problems—and report that such a specification does not seriously affect their findings (p. 283, n. 13). Since their results are purportedly similar, it is not clear why they do not use the more straightforward interaction specification; nevertheless, using data from their study, I found that the correlations among the variables for the less democratic state (Dem_{LO}), the more democratic state (Dem_{HI}), and the interaction term were $-.95$ and $.97$, respectively. Not surprisingly—in light of such pronounced multicollinearity—neither coefficient for Dem_{LO} or Dem_{HI} was even remotely significant in a regression equation including the interaction variable (and the controls found in Oneal and Russett, 1997: table 2, equation 1), with international conflict involvement as the outcome variable.[12] Using a dichotomous interaction variable alleviates a substantial amount of multicollinearity among the variables (the correlations drop to $-.72$ and $.11$), and the principal findings of Oneal and Russett (1997) are supported when it is used in place of the simple product interaction variable; however, such a specification falls prey to the same deficiencies of those that rely on dichotomous measures of joint democracy discussed previously. Further, such a dichotomous specification results in the loss of information that is necessary to determine the direct and conditional impact of the individual states' democracy scores on the likelihood of conflict involvement. Without an interactive variable that is constructed as the product of the two constituent variables, one cannot derive these effects in a straightforward manner; therefore, it is difficult to determine the accuracy of the weak-link assumption's main premise that the likelihood of a dispute is primarily a function of the less democratic state in the dyad. In sum, the weak-link specification used in Oneal and Russett (1997) does not allow us to draw clear inferences regarding the conflict propensity of democratic pairs of states.[13]

Given these concerns regarding the weak-link measure of joint democracy, I extend Oneal and Russett's analyses using several more straightforward indicators of joint democracy: (1) $Dem_{HI} + Dem_{LO}$, which is the sum of the two states' regime scores, after adding 10 to both scores to ensure a positive value (it ranges from 0 to +20); (2) $Dem_{HI} * Dem_{LO}$, which is the product of the two states' regime scores, after adding 10 to both scores to ensure a positive value (it ranges from 0 to + 400); and Dem_{GM}, which is the geometric mean of the joint democracy scores of the two states measured as the square root of the product of the states' regime scores. The latter measure is more useful than a simple arithmetic mean since it takes into consideration the difference in the regime scores. Each of these measures has been used in previous research on the DPP (e.g., see Oneal and Ray, 1997). Using these more straightforward measures of joint democracy, one should be able to circumvent problems associated with weak-link specifications.

The suggestion that scholars use these alternative specifications in explicating the DPP seems inconsistent with the earlier statements of DPP analysts who argued in favor of a measure of joint democracy that reflected both the level of democracy of two states as well as the "political distance" between them. However, since both of these factors are assumed to predict international conflict, it strikes me as a much simpler—and a more methodologically consistent—task to construct one measure of joint democracy and a separate measure of political distance. In this way, one can unambiguously assess the independent impact of each of these factors on international conflict. The alternative specifications of joint democracy annotated above provide half of this requirement; what is left is to provide a variable that measures political distance, and that takes us to the discussion in the next section.

The Weak-Link Thesis and Political Distance

An additional research design problem is associated with Oneal and Russett's (1997) contention that a weak-link specification enables them to determine the impact of political distance on the likelihood of conflict, which is important because they assert that the difference in the regime scores of both states also contributes to the conflict proneness of the dyad. That is, "making a dyad more democratic by increasing the [regime] score of the less democratic state reduces the likelihood of conflict; but raising the level of joint democracy by increasing democracy in the more democratic state, increasing the political distance separating the pair, makes the dyad more prone to conflict" (pp. 281–282). Oneal and Russett's research design conflates both the allegedly conflict-dampening impact of joint democracy and the presumably conflict-exacerbating impact of political distance in the regime variables (or as is often the case, in the single regime variable for the less democratic state), which they focus on in their analyses. Fusing these two contrasting attributes in a single variable makes it difficult to distinguish between the competing processes.[14] To be sure, if political distance—or more accurately, political dissimilarity—is an important factor in international conflict, one should simply include it as a separate variable in the analysis. Such a specification would allow us to better determine the independent impact of political dissimilarity on conflict and to determine whether the effect of joint democracy is robust once one controls for this variable that Oneal and Russett admit is an important predictor to international conflict. Bennett and Stam (2000) employ such an approach in their study. Therefore, I also include a political dissimilarity variable, which is measured as the absolute value of the difference between the two states' regime scores.[15]

One might also conceptualize this argument as one focusing on the salience of political similarity, rather than one regarding the impact of political dissimilarity, but since the original focus of DPP theorists emphasized political distance, which was presumed to increase the likelihood of conflict, then political dissimilarity is a better approximation of what they had in mind. Regardless, the problem is not whether the weak-link specification is capturing two contradictory factors, that is, the degree of joint democracy and political dissimilarity, or two complementary factors—that is, the degree of joint democracy and political similarity; the difficulty arises from conflating two presumably significant and independent factors in a single variable. Therefore, it is important to determine the independent impact of each variable as well as to gauge whether either of them is significant once one explicitly controls for the other. The weak-link specification does not allow us to do this; the specification outlined above does.

Measuring Interstate Conflict Involvement: Including or Excluding Ongoing Dispute Years

Beyond concerns related to weak-link assumptions, Oneal and Russett (1997) rely on a questionable coding of their outcome variable, which allows them to designate subsequent years of multiple-year disputes as additional cases of conflict. Barbieri (1996) maintains that the appropriate specification of the outcome variable in analyses of the DPP should include only the onset of militarized interstate disputes (MIDs) (or wars) and not include ongoing years of disputes as additional cases. While Oneal and Russett (1997) counter that one should include subsequent years of multiple-year disputes since leaders constantly reevaluate and update their decisions with regard to ongoing conflict, Bennett and Stam (2000) articulate the more commonly held view that "factors that lead to the onset of conflict are conceptually distinct from those associated with its duration or termination." They remind us that "existing research supports the contention that what makes conflicts continue or end is quite different from what makes conflicts start" (p. 662). Moreover, most of the research on international conflict from the Correlates of War (COW) project—from which Oneal and Russett (1997) derive their conflict data—substantiates this view (see Vasquez, 1993). For the purposes of this study, the argument is actually moot because Oneal and Russett (1999a) maintain that the democratic peace is no less evident when one excludes ongoing dispute years in the outcome variable. In fact, Beck et al.'s (1998: 1281) replication of Oneal and Russett (1997) reveals that dropping ongoing dispute years does not affect the significance of joint democracy coded in accordance with weak-link specifications, but it does reduce the significance of trade interdependence. Bennett and Stam (2000) found that the conflict-dampening impact of trade was significant and robust when dropping ongoing dispute years (and even using more restrictive research designs) in their study that provided even stronger support for the DPP. Therefore, I utilize such a specification in the data analyses and compare it to results from models that include ongoing years of disputes as are found in Oneal and Russett (1997).[16] With these reconsiderations in mind, I now turn to the data analyses.

Data Analysis

A multivariate logistic regression model is estimated to replicate Oneal and Russett's findings. This is the same statistical method used in Oneal and Russett (1997). The basic model takes the following form: $\Pr(MID_{i,t}) = 1 / (1 + e^{-Z_i})$. $\Pr(MID_{ij,t})$ is the probability that the outcome variable (the onset of a militarized interstate dispute) equals 1; and Z_i is the sum of the product of the coefficient values (β_i) across all observations of the predictor variables $(X_{ij,t})$, that is: $\beta_0 + \beta_1 Democracy_{LO} + \beta_2 Economic\ growth_{LO} + \beta_3 Allies + \beta_4 Contiguity + \beta_5 Capability\ ratio + \beta_6 Trade\ ratio_{LO}$.

Replication and Extension

Equation 1 in Table 2.1 replicates Oneal and Russett's (1997) results found in equation 1 of their table 2 (p. 278), which regresses MID involvement (including ongoing years) on the less democratic state's regime score *(Democracy$_{LO}$)*, the lower economic growth rate of the two states *(Economic growth$_{LO}$)*, whether or not the states are allies *(Allies)*, whether or not the states are contiguous *(Contiguity)*, the ratio of the two states' relative capability scores *(Capability ratio)*, and trade interdependence measured as the lower of the two states' ratio of dyadic trade to GDP *(Trade ratio$_{LO}$)*.[17] The results of Equation 1 are identical to those in equation 1 of Oneal and Russett (1997).[18] In Equations 2–4, I replace the weak-link democracy variable, *Democracy$_{LO}$*, with *Dem$_{HI}$* + *Dem$_{LO}$*, *Dem$_{HI}$* * *Dem$_{LO}$*, and *Dem$_{GM}$*, respectively, and each of these models extends Oneal and Russett's findings and corroborates them completely. The results reveal that Oneal and Russett's (1997) findings

Table 2.1   Replication of Oneal and Russett (1997), with Different Specifications of Joint Democracy, and Including Ongoing Dispute Years, 1950–1985

	Equation 1	Equation 2	Equation 3	Equation 4
Democracy$_{LO}$	−.05*** (.001)	—	—	—
Dem$_{HI}$ + Dem$_{LO}$	—	−.007*** (.003)	—	—
Dem$_{HI}$ * Dem$_{LO}$	—	—	−.002*** (.000)	—
Dem$_{GM}$		—	—	−.028*** (.007)
Economic growth$_L$	−.02*** (.01)	−.03** (.01)	−.03** (.01)	−.024** (.01)
Allies	−.82*** (.08)	−.89*** (.08)	−.89*** (.08)	−.87*** (.08)
Contiguity	1.31*** (.08)	1.31*** (.08)	1.31*** (.08)	1.33*** (.08)
Capability ratio	−.003*** (.000)	−.003*** (.000)	−.003*** (.000)	−.003*** (.000)
Trade ratio$_L$	−66.13*** (13.44)	−92.58*** (13.95)	−92.58*** (13.95)	−82.29*** (13.77)
Constant	−3.29*** (.08)	−2.99*** (.06)	−2.99*** (.06)	−2.80*** (.06)
−2 log likelihood	6,955.14	7,002.43	7,002.43	6,989.43
N	20,990	20,990	20,990	20,990
X^2	764.043***	716.75***	716.75***	729.75***

Note: Standard errors are in parentheses; all p-values are estimated using two-tailed tests. *p ≤ .10, **p ≤ .05 level, ***p ≤ .01 level

are robust across different specifications of joint democracy—just as they claimed; however, when one modifies the analysis further and focuses on the onset of disputes, excluding ongoing dispute years, the results are not as consistent as those in Table 2.1. For example, Equation 5 in Table 2.2, which uses the weak-link specification of the democracy variable, *Democracy$_{LO}$*, is consistent with Oneal and Russett's (1997) original model, but Equations 6–8, which include the alternative specifications of the joint democracy variable, are not as consistent. In fact, in only one of the three equations that use the alternative specifications is the democracy variable significant below the .10 level (i.e.,

Table 2.2   Replication of Oneal and Russett (1997), with Different Specifications of Joint Democracy, and Excluding Ongoing Dispute Years, 1950–1985

	Equation 5	Equation 6	Equation 7	Equation 8
Democracy$_{LO}$	−.03*** (.008)	—	—	—
Dem$_{HI}$ + Dem$_{LO}$	—	−.002 (.004)	—	—
Dem$_{HI}$ * Dem$_{LO}$	—	—	−.001*** (.000)	—
Dem$_{GM}$		—	—	−.009 (.008)
Economic growth$_{LO}$	−.03*** (.01)	−.03*** (.01)	−.03** (.01)	.03*** (.01)
Allies	−.64*** (.09)	−.67*** (.09)	−.66*** (.09)	−.67*** (.09)
Contiguity	1.67*** (.10)	1.74*** (.10)	1.67*** (.10)	1.70*** (.10)
Capability ratio	−.002*** (.001)	−.002*** (.001)	−.002*** (.001)	−.002*** (.001)
Trade ratio$_{LO}$	−43.82*** (12.08)	−64.29*** (12.78)	−45.43*** (12.19)	−56.86*** (12.58)
Constant	−3.99*** (.10)	−3.83*** (.09)	−3.83*** (.09)	−3.75*** (.11)
−2 log likelihood	4,979.55	4,993.66	4,982.50	4,992.51
N	20,990	20,990	20,990	20,990
X^2	560.36***	546.26***	557.41***	547.41***

Note: Standard errors are in parentheses; all p-values are estimated using two-tailed tests. *p ≤ .10, **p ≤ .05 level, ***p ≤ .01 level

Equation 7). This lack of consistency across the models is even more surprising since the other predictor variables (i.e., *Economic growth$_{LO}$, Allies, Contiguity, Capability ratio,* and *Trade ratio$_{LO}$*) are quite robust across the various equations. One may counter that considering that the two alternative specifications of the democracy variable that are not significant have limited ranges (they both have 21-point scales) as compared to *Dem$_{HI}$ * Dem$_{LO}$*, which is significant (and ranges from 0 to 400), then possibly the nonsignificance of *Dem$_{HI}$ + Dem$_{LO}$* and *Dem$_{GM}$* may be due to their failure to adequately capture the scope of democracy and, consequently, its full impact on the outcome variable. This argument, however, does not account for the significance of $Democracy_{LO}$, which also has a 21-point range. Nevertheless, a more direct test of this assumption is provided in subsequent models where we can observe the significance of $Dem_{HI} * Dem_{LO}$, which has the most extensive range of all the joint democracy variables.

Extending the analysis further, the findings reported in Equations 9–12 in Table 2.3 allow us to isolate the impact of political dissimilarity (what Oneal and Russett call political distance) on dispute involvement. When this is done, I find that Oneal and Russett's weak-link democracy variable, $Democracy_{LO}$, as well as each of the alternative democracy variables, is significantly associated with a reduced probability of conflict involvement. These results indicate that, controlling for political dissimilarity, joint democracy reduces the probability of conflict involvement for pairs of states, and these findings are consistent with Oneal and Russett's claims.

The findings reported in Table 2.4, which control for political dissimilarity but exclude ongoing years of disputes in the outcome variable, tell a much different story. For example, Equation 13 in Table 2.4 reveals that the impact of $Democracy_{LO}$ is not significantly associated with the probability of dispute onset. In fact, the coefficients for each of the democracy variables are insignificant across the four models in Table 2.4. These findings undermine the counterargument discussed above that implicates the limited range of the democracy variables for their insignificance because the results in Table 2.4 indicate that $Dem_{HI} * Dem_{LO}$—which is the variable with the greatest range (from 0 to 400)—is also insignificant once one controls for political dissimilarity and excludes ongoing dispute years. More importantly, the results reported in Table 2.4 indicate that by controlling for political dissimilarity and dropping ongoing years of disputes—two straightforward modifications that are widely accepted in the literature on the DPP—the heretofore-significant impact of joint democracy washes out. Oneal and Russett (1997: 279) also claim that "the benefits of the liberals' economic and political prescription were also evident when we re-estimated the coefficients in equation (1) using an indicator of dyadic war as our dependent variable."[19] They state that "the coefficients of Dem_L [the lower democracy score equivalent to my $Democracy_{LO}$] and $Depend_L$ [the lower dyadic trade to GDP ratio, equivalent to my $Trade\ ratio_{LO}$] . . . were *negative and significant at greater than the .001 level*" (emphasis added). In Table 2.5, I attempt to replicate their finding first using the weak-link specification of the

Table 2.3   Replication of Oneal and Russett (1997), with Different Specifications of Joint Democracy, Political Dissimilarity, and Including Ongoing Dispute Years, 1950–1985

	Equation 9	Equation 10	Equation 11	Equation 12
Democracy$_{LO}$	—.035*** (.008)	—	—	—
Dem$_{HI}$ + Dem$_{LO}$	—	–.018*** (.004)	—	—
Dem$_{HI}$ * Dem$_{LO}$	—	—	–.002*** (.000)	—
Dem$_{GM}$	—	—	—	–.024*** (.007)
Economic growth$_{LO}$	–.03*** (.01)	–.03*** (.01)	–.03*** (.01)	–.03*** (.01)
Allies	–.64*** (.09)	–.64*** (.09)	–.72*** (.08)	–.75*** (.08)
Contiguity	1.42*** (.08)	1.42*** (.08)	1.42*** (.08)	1.44*** (.08)
Capability ratio	–.003*** (.000)	–.003*** (.000)	–.003*** (.000)	–.003*** (.000)
Trade ratio$_{LO}$	–68.82*** (13.74)	–68.82*** (13.74)	–67.85*** (13.73)	–74.97*** (13.82)
Political dissimilarity	.02*** (.005)	.02*** (.005)	.03*** (.005)	.04*** (.005)
Constant	–3.57*** (.10)	–3.57*** (.10)	–3.27*** (.10)	–3.28*** (.007)
–2 log likelihood	6,925.64	6,925.64	6,924.56	6,934.34
N	20,990	20,990	20,990	20,990
X^2	793.54***	793.54***	794.62***	784.84***

Note: Standard errors are in parentheses; all p-values are estimated using two-tailed tests.
*p ≤ .10, **p ≤ .05 level, ***p ≤ .01 level

democracy variable, *Democracy$_{LO}$*, without a control for political dissimilarity; next, including a control for political dissimilarity, *Political dissimilarity*; and, in the last two models using *Dem$_{HI}$ * Dem$_{LO}$* and *Dem$_{GM}$*, while excluding ongoing war years in the outcome variables across each of the equations.[20] In none of these models is the coefficient for the respective democracy variable even remotely significant.

Table 2.4 Replication of Oneal and Russett (1997), with Different Specifications of Joint Democracy, Political Dissimilarity, and Excluding Ongoing Dispute Years, 1950–1985

	Equation 13	Equation 14	Equation 15	Equation 16
$Democracy_{LO}$	−.011 (.009)	—	—	—
$Dem_{HI} + Dem_{LO}$	—	−.005 (.005)	—	—
$Dem_{HI} * Dem_{LO}$	—	—	−.001 (.000)	—
Dem_{GM}	—	—	—	−.003 (.008)
Economic growth$_{LO}$	−.04*** (.01)	−.04*** (.01)	−.04*** (.01)	−.04*** (.01)
Allies	−.51*** (.10)	−.51*** (.10)	−.51*** (.10)	−.51*** (.10)
Contiguity	1.80*** (.10)	1.80*** (.10)	1.80*** (.10)	1.82*** (.10)
Capability ratio	−.002*** (.000)	−.002*** (.000)	−.002*** (.000)	−.002*** (.000)
Trade ratio$_{LO}$	−45.13*** (12.28)	−45.13*** (12.28)	−43.77*** (12.24)	−48.83*** (12.37)
Political dissimilarity	.04*** (.007)	.04*** (.007)	.04*** (.006)	.04*** (.006)
Constant	−4.36*** (.12)	−4.36*** (.12)	−4.26*** (.13)	−4.26*** (.13)
−2 log likelihood	4,945.77	4,945.77	4,945.04	4,947.07
N	20,990	20,990	20,990	20,990
X^2	594.14***	594.14***	594.88***	592.84***

Note: Standard errors are in parentheses; all p-values are estimated using two-tailed tests. *p ≤ .10, **p ≤ .05 level, ***p ≤ .01 level

It is clear that using Oneal and Russett's (1997) data there is no statistically significant democratic peace with respect to interstate war. What is most apparent from the results reported in this study is that in light of quite reasonable, modest, and straightforward modifications of Oneal and Russett's (1997) research design, there is no statistically significant relationship between joint democracy and a decreased likelihood of militarized interstate conflict or interstate war.[21]

Table 2.5   Replication of Oneal and Russett (1997), with Different Specifications of Joint Democracy, Political Dissimilarity, and War Onset as the Outcome Variable, 1950–1985

	Equation 17	Equation 18	Equation 19	Equation 20
Democracy$_{LO}$	−.056 (.038)	−.027 (.043)	—	—
Dem$_{HI}$ * Dem$_{LO}$	—	—	−.002 (.002)	—
Dem$_{GM}$	—	—	—	−.01 (.04)
Economic growth$_{LO}$	.02 (.04)	.01 (.04)	.01 (.04)	.01 (.04)
Allies	−1.61*** (.50)	−1.47** (.50)	−1.47** (.50)	−1.48* (.50)
Contiguity	.38*** (.35)	.54 (.35)	.52 (.35)	.56 (.35)
Capability ratio	−.009** (.003)	−.008** (.003)	−.008** (.003)	−.009* (.003)
Trade ratio$_{LO}$	−194.96 (124.11)	−220.51* (130.73)	−212.45 (130.16)	−232.65* (130.79)
Political dissimilarity	—	.047* (.026)	.048* (.024)	.054** (.024)
Constant	−5.59*** (.37)	−6.01*** (.44)	−5.73*** (.46)	−5.73*** (.46)
−2 log likelihood	584.29	580.57	580.19	580.90
N	20,990	20,990	20,990	20,990
X^2	46.37***	50.09***	50.47***	49.76***

Note: Standard errors are in parentheses; all p-values are estimated using two-tailed tests. *p ≤ .10, **p ≤ .05 level, ***p ≤ .01 level

Discussion

Oneal and Russett (1997: 287–288) state that "liberals have claimed that democracy and free trade not only increase individual liberty and prosperity but also ameliorate international conflict," and "our analysis of the Cold War era indicate they were right." Oneal and Russett assert that their findings "clearly reveal the separate peace among democratic states." But a replication and modest extension of their study fails to support their claims. Further, it appears that reliance on weak-link specifications in estimations of the DPP, which is becoming increasingly fashionable in the literature—should be reconsidered, given the methodological critiques and the empirical findings reported above.

Interestingly, although Oneal and Russett (1997) popularized the use of the weak-link specification for systematic analyses of the DPP, their empirical analyses do not directly test weak-link processes. That is, the weak-link thesis implies that the less democratic state in a dyad should initiate—or in some way "generate"—the conflict (p. 247); therefore, studies of the DPP drawing on weak-link assumptions should analyze the relationship between joint democracy and *conflict initiation* rather than *conflict involvement*, which is the focus of Oneal and Russett (1997).[22] Nevertheless, the inability to *directly* test for the presence of weak-link processes in these models is not a major inconsistency because Oneal and Russett's analysis does allow us to *indirectly* test for weak-link processes by evaluating the extent to which the democracy score of the less democratic state exhibits a significant negative impact on the likelihood of international conflict. Moreover, since the DPP addresses both the extent to which democracies become involved in—and initiate—conflict, Oneal and Russett's focus on the former is clearly a relevant query in the evaluation of the DPP.

A larger concern arises from the inability of weak-link assumptions to account for a swath of cases included among Oneal and Russett's (1997) observations. That is, on its face, the weak-link approach does not apply to cases where both states have identical regime scores since in such instances neither state has a lower democracy score, and thus neither is more or less likely to generate conflict. The pattern of conflict among these cases cannot be explicated or accounted for by weak-link explanations. Moreover, these cases are hardly rare, constituting more than 20 percent of the total cases in Oneal and Russett's (1997) study (i.e., 4,390 of 22,990); yet, Oneal and Russett do not provide an explanation for how these cases can be reconciled with their theoretical assumptions nor do they provide coding rules for them. Therefore, for roughly 20 percent of the cases in Oneal and Russett (1997), the authors' theoretical explanation for the processes at work in the democratic peace (i.e., the weak-link thesis) cannot be reconciled with the empirical observations.

One may argue that for two similar democracies, weak-link assumptions imply that neither state will generate conflict: thus the democratic peace. This same logic would have to apply to similar anocracies and similar autocracies, as well, since they also consist of two states with identical regime scores, and thus with no apparent weak link to generate conflict between them. Accordingly, the weak-link thesis would have to assume that similar states do not fight each other, but this is not the same as the DPP (as Oneal and Ray 1997 reminds us), which posits that democratic dyads, more than other types of dyads, exhibit peaceful international relations.[23] Regardless, this argument is not put forward by Oneal and Russett (1997); instead, they conduct analysis on 4,390 cases that could not possibly be explicated using the theoretical argument they enunciate. When I delete these cases from models of the DPP, excluding ongoing dispute years, I find that Oneal and Russett's weak-link democracy variable is reduced to insignificance. In fact, this finding results from the equation without the inclusion of *Political dissimilarity*, so this model is a "strong" version of the weak-link model, and except for the deleted cases is otherwise identical to Equation 2; nevertheless, it refutes the dyadic DPP. These results further reveal the tenuous relationship between joint democracy and peace.

One might contend that the apparent relationship between joint democracy and international conflict is simply a subset of the consistent and robust relationship between political similarity and conflict. Since the findings with respect to the impact of political dissimilarity on conflict indicate that more similar states are less likely to experience disputes and war, it appears that the presumed democratic peace is not significantly different from the "peace" enjoyed by politically similar states, in general, as compared to the more disputatious politically dissimilar states. This is reflected in the equations in Table 2.6, which show that both joint democracies and joint autocracies are significantly associated with a reduced probability of conflict involvement (whether or not ongoing dispute years are included), while joint anocracy is negatively though not significantly associated with international conflict. War onset appears to be an exception to the political similarity thesis, where both joint democracy and joint autocracy are negatively though not significantly associated with war onset while joint anocracy is positively and significantly associated with war onset. Nevertheless, as noted above, joint democracy should be measured as a continuous variable for several reasons: The DPP focuses on the impact of the extent of democracy rather than its presence or absence; there is little theoretical justification for the thresholds between regime types; and the noncontinuous specification results in the loss of quite a bit of information. In addition, subsequent tests reveal that the argument that the "democratic peace" is simply a subset of a peace among politically similar states

Table 2.6   Regression of International Conflict on Democracy, Using Trichotomous Democracy Variables, 1950–1985

	Equation 21 Dispute Involvement	Equation 22 Dispute Onset	Equation 23 War Onset
Coherent democracy	−1.17*** (.01)	−1.08*** (.19)	−1.61 (1.03)
Coherent anocracy	−.17 (.60)	−.07 (.60)	2.90** (1.09)
Coherent autocracy	−.25** (.09)	−.43*** (.11)	−.53 (50)
Economic growth$_{LO}$	−.03*** (.01)	−.04*** (.01)	−.01 (.04)
Allies	−.83*** (.08)	−.83*** (.08)	−1.73*** (.51)
Contiguity	1.36*** (.08)	1.73*** (.10)	.42*** (.35)
Capability ratio	−.003*** (.000)	−.002*** (.000)	−.008** (.003)
Trade ratio$_{LO}$	−64.14*** (13.61)	−35.04*** (11.80)	−211.84* (126.32)
Constant	−2.90*** (.07)	−3.70*** (.09)	−5.10*** (.26)
−2 log likelihood	6,937.49	4,942.06	577.56
N	20,990	20,990	20,990
X^2	781.69***	597.86***	53.09***

Note: Standard errors are in parentheses; all p-values are estimated using two-tailed tests. *p ≤ .10, **p ≤ .05 level, ***p ≤ .01 level

ignores the prominent role of trade interdependence. For example, when I alternated the political dissimilarity and trade variables in the models from Table 2.2 that exclude ongoing dispute years, I found that the weak-link democracy variable, $Democracy_{LO}$, does not lose its statistical significance when *Political dissimilarity* is added to the model, but it does when *Trade ratio*$_{LO}$ is included. In equations where I dropped the trade variable, I found that $Democracy_{LO}$, $Dem_{HI} + Dem_{LO}$, $Dem_{HI} * Dem_{LO}$, and Dem_{GM} remained significant even when controlling for *Political dissimilarity*; however, once the trade variable is included in the model, each of the joint democracy variables becomes insignificant. These findings are reported in Equations 24–27 in Table 2.7.[24] Therefore, in a manner consistent with Oneal et al.'s (1996) previous observations, the negative impact of joint democracy is not robust when it is measured as a continuous variable—in this case, using the weak-link specification—in a model that includes trade interdependence. Ironically, it was just this type of finding that trade washed out the impact of continuous measures of joint democracy that encouraged Oneal and Russett and other DPP researchers to opt for the weak-link specification in the first place.[25]

Given these additional results, one may question whether it is political dissimilarity or trade interdependence that is vitiating the relationship between joint democracy and international conflict. Actually it's a combination of both: The inclusion of the political dissimilarity variable reduces the impact of joint democracy on conflict, and the inclu-

Table 2.7   Replication of Oneal and Russett (1997), Alternating Political Dissimilarity and Trade Interdependence, and Excluding Ongoing Dispute Years, 1950–1985

	Equation 24	Equation 25	Equation 26	Equation 27
Democracy$_{LO}$	−.028*** (.008)	−.011 (.009)	—	—
Dem$_{HI}$ * Dem$_{LO}$	—	—	−.014*** (.004)	−.005 (.005)
Economic growth$_{LO}$	−.039*** (.01)	−.039*** (.011)	−.039*** (.01)	−.039*** (.01)
Allies	−.509*** (.095)	−.507*** (.095)	−.509*** (.095)	−.507*** (.095)
Contiguity	1.72*** (.103)	1.80*** (.104)	1.72*** (.103)	1.80*** (.104)
Capability ratio	−.002*** (.000)	−.002*** (.000)	−.002*** (.000)	−.002*** (.000)
Trade ratio$_{LO}$	—	−45.13*** (12.28)	—	−45.13*** (12.28)
Political dissimilarity	.038*** (.007)	—	.052*** (.006)	—
Constant	−4.49*** (.12)	−4.36*** (.12)	−4.21*** (.14)	−4.49*** (.12)
−2 log likelihood	4,967.14	4,945.77	4,967.14	4,945.77
N	20,990	20,990	20,990	20,990
X^2	572.77***	594.14***	572.77***	594.14***

Note: Standard errors are in parentheses; all p-values are estimated using two-tailed tests.
*p ≤ .10, **p ≤ .05 level, ***p ≤ .01 level

sion of trade interdependence reduces this impact to insignificance. It is important to remember that the weak-link specification is intended to capture both the joint democracy of the dyad and the degree of political dissimilarity between the two states. The inclusion of a political dissimilarity variable allows us to determine the independent impact of this variable on conflict, explicitly, leaving the weak-link democracy variable to account for the impact of democracy qua democracy on international conflict. As noted, one may be better able to appreciate this point if one focuses on political similarity rather than political dissimilarity. The former reduces conflict and the latter increases it; therefore, it may be easier to think of the weak-link specification as combining the complementary conflict-dampening impact of joint democracy and political similarity in a single variable. Once the significant conflict-dampening impact of political similarity is excised from the weak-link democracy variable (which is, in effect, what I've done in Equations 3–5 in this study), what is left is the singular effect of joint democracy on conflict. In this specification, the impact of joint democracy is substantially reduced because it can no longer tap into the significant conflict-dampening impact of political similarity, which is now captured in a separate independent variable. It appears that the actual impact of joint democracy on international conflict is quite weak; therefore, once one controls for trade interdependence and excludes subsequent years of ongoing disputes, the joint democracy variable is no longer significant. In effect, what results from using this framework is a weak-link joint democracy variable that performs identically to the continuous joint democracy variables used in earlier studies whose impact was vitiated by that of trade interdependence.

The nonsignificance of joint democracy obtains, in large part, because the problem with earlier studies of the DPP, which showed that largely atheoretically derived dichotomous variables of joint democracy outperformed more theoretically consistent continuous joint democracy variables, may not have been fully appreciated. The common assumption was that the inability of the continuous variables to remain significant once one controlled for trade was mainly due to the unreliability of the *JOINREG* measure. Once the weak-link specification was shown to be robust, DPP scholars seemed to stop analyzing why continuous variables other than *JOINREG* (e.g., the sum and product of the two states' regime scores) also were not robust when trade was introduced as a control. The findings from the present study suggest that these other indicators were not inconsistent because they were unreliable measures of joint democracy, but it is more likely that they were quite reliable measures of joint democracy but did not adequately capture the extent of similarity between the two states. Since only the similarity factor is statistically significant, the variables that focused specifically on joint democracy could not overcome the vitiating impact of trade interdependence.

On the other hand, the extent to which continuous joint democracy variables such as the weak-link variable(s) have been significant may be largely due to the fact that they capture aspects of regime similarity, especially at the two extremes of their ranges (i.e., at the highest level of democracy or the highest level of autocracy where Dem_{HI} and Dem_{LO} are at their respective maximum values of democracy/autocracy). That is, where Dem_{HI} and Dem_{LO} both have values of +10, or where Dem_{HI} and Dem_{LO} both have values of –10, they are not simply measuring the regime score of the two states but are also capturing the degree of similarity between the two states (i.e., either full democracies or full autocracies).[26] Once one includes a political similarity variable in the same model with the two joint democracy variables (actually, we include only Dem_{LO} in such models so that we do not create a linear combination among the predictors, which would preclude estimation), the greater conflict-dampening impact of political similarity is excised from the joint democracy measure, and what is left is the less significant relationship between regime type and the probability of conflict. One might conjecture that regime type is largely significant to the extent that it also measures political similarity, but when one evaluates the effect of regime type qua regime type—in this case, joint democracy—one finds that it is not significant. In sum, earlier tests of the DPP that used reliable, continuous measures of joint democracy failed because the DPP failed: Joint democracy simply is not a significant factor in reducing the likelihood of international conflict once one controls for political (dis)similarity and trade interdependence and excludes subsequent years of ongoing disputes. Oneal and Russett's (1997) data bear this out.

Conclusion

In this chapter, I've replicated and extended the findings of Oneal and Russett (1997), which is one of the most important studies of the DPP. After replicating Oneal and Russett's (1997) findings, I reexamined them in light of several straightforward modifications of their basic research design. Importantly, the modifications that I presented here have each been used in previous studies of the DPP (including several by Oneal and Russett); however, previous studies have not examined each of these modifications in combination.[27] The results demonstrate that Oneal and Russett's (1997) findings in support of the DPP are not robust and that joint democracy does not reduce the probability of international conflict for pairs of states during the postwar era. It is important to remind the reader that the Oneal and Russett study is not simply an isolated analysis of the DPP, but is the seminal treatment of the DPP that establishes the significance of the conflict-dampening impact of joint democracy (coded as a continuous variable) when controlling for trade—no other study up to that time had been successful in accomplishing this. Further, Oneal and Russett's research design has become one of the most widely used, cited, and respected approaches to the analysis of the DPP. It also is the empirical bedrock on which their later studies rest, including the most recent one (Russett and Oneal, 2001).[28] It follows that in refuting the findings of Oneal and Russett (1997), we have refuted one of the fundamental supports of the DPP. This is by far the most important research implication of these findings.

In addition, the results from this chapter suggest that the arguments of those who have maintained that the democratic peace is epiphenomenal of other factors such as trade interdependence (Polachek, 1997) should be reconsidered. For that matter, theoretical arguments that center on any of the control variables whose impact is consistent throughout the models presented here should be reconsidered. The results also call into question the accuracy of deductive models that derive the DPP from their rational choice assumptions (e.g., Bueno de Mesquita and Lalman, 1992; Bueno de Mesquita et al., 1999). The most important policy implication of the findings is that the post–Cold War strategy of "democratic enlargement," which is aimed at ensuring peace by enlarging the community of democratic states, is quite a thin reed upon which to rest a state's foreign policy—much less the hope for international peace. Having refuted the dyadic DPP, in the next chapter I analyze the extent to which the monadic DPP obtains for individual democracies.

Notes

1. Subsequently, Oneal and Russett (1998, 1999b) included IGO membership in their "Kantian Triad," which they more fully explicate in Russett

and Oneal (2001). Both of these subsequent analyses are grounded in the theoretical and empirical approach in Oneal and Russett (1997).

2. They focus on dyads consisting of contiguous states or at least one major power.

3. Probably the two studies that come closest to invalidating the empirical finding of a statistically significant negative relationship between joint democracy and war are James et al. (1999) and Gartzke (2000), but Oneal and Russett (2000) and Russett and Oneal (2001) respond convincingly to their critiques on both theoretical and empirical grounds. Harder to refute have been the theoretical and empirical analyses of scholars such as Polachek (1997), whose arguments are grounded in macroeconomic theory and econometric modeling; however, his use of very different research designs and reliance on COPDAB data, which restricts the temporal coverage of his analyses, limits the inferences one may draw from his findings. Nevertheless, the findings in this study provide support for Polachek's arguments.

4. However, the impact of trade interdependence was vitiated by the autocorrelation controls.

5. Bennett and Stam's (2000) more extensive analyses reveal greater support than Beck et al. (1998) for the view that trade reduces the likelihood of conflict, but trade was not always significant, depending on the estimator choices employed by the authors (including Beck et al.'s diagnostic). Oneal and Russett (1999a) found support for the conflict-dampening impact of both democracy and trade interdependence in a subsequent study using alternative specifications of these variables.

6. Russett (1993: 77) states, "Our hypothesis . . . says that the more democratic both members of the pair are the less likely they are to become embroiled in a militarized dispute." Rummel (1983) makes a similar point.

7. With respect to the use of continuous measures in coding democracy, one should keep in mind that the Polity dataset is problematic because its indices of democracy are largely ordinal.

8. Beyond the analyses that resurrected the systematic study of the DPP (e.g., Small and Singer, 1976; Rummel, 1979, 1983; Chan, 1984; Weede, 1984), prior to Maoz and Russett (1993), the most exhaustive and compelling findings supportive of the DPP were Maoz and Abdolali (1989) and Bremer (1993); however, these two studies relied on trichotomous and dichotomous indicators of joint democracy, instead of continuous measures.

9. *JOINREG* is measured as the ratio of the sum of the two states' regime scores and the difference of the two states' regime scores plus 1: (Democracy$_A$ + Democracy$_B$) / (Democracy$_A$ − Democracy$_B$ + 1). As Oneal and Russett (1997: 274) point out, if one takes a pair of states whose regime scores are both 50 (well above the democracy threshold of Maoz and Russett [1993], which is +30), then *JOINREG* is (50 + 50) / (50 − 50 + 1), or 100. If one state becomes more democratic and now scores 70, while the other state remains at 50, *JOINREG* for this more democratic dyad now equals (70 + 50) / (70 − 50 + 1), or

5.7. The continuous measure of joint democracy *decreases* substantially as one of the two states—and, therefore, the dyad—becomes *more democratic*. This critique was originally put forward by Rummel.

10. Maoz and Russett (1993) and Oneal et al. (1996) also used a measure of the difference of the regime scores for the two states multiplied by a "power concentration" (PCON) value, which gauges the extent that a government exercises effective control over its citizenry. Oneal and Russett (1997: 274) avoid this measure mainly because "not even the originators of the data" have used it "as a defining characteristic of democracy," but Maoz (1997) uses it in his analyses of the DPP.

11. The geometric mean is measured as the nth root of the product of n values. Unlike a simple arithmetic mean (i.e., an average), it takes into consideration the difference in the values.

12. Oneal and Ray (1997: 765) note that the coefficient for their joint democracy interaction term was not significant, and I presume that this is due to multicollinearity problems. In a later study, Oneal and Russett (1998: table 2) report findings on the DPP using an interaction specification, and the coefficient for Dem_{LO} is not significant in any of their results.

13. To better appreciate why the dichotomous specification of the joint democracy variable precludes our ability to estimate the direct and conditional effects of Dem_{HI} or Dem_{LO}, consider a logistic regression equation: logit (Y) = α + $\beta_1 X_1$ + $\beta_2 X_2$ + . . . + $\beta_k X_k$, where α is a constant; β_1 and β_2 are the multiple regression coefficients that represent the independent effect of each respective predictor variable, X_1 and X_2, on the outcome variable; and X_1 and X_2 are values of Dem_{HI} and Dem_{LO}, respectively. The effect of Dem_{HI} and Dem_{LO} on the outcome is measured by their respective β coefficients; however, when an interactive variable, $X_1 X_2$, is introduced in the model: logit (Y) = α + $\beta_1 X_1$ + $\beta_2 X_2$ + $\beta_3 X_1 X_2$ . . . + $\beta_k X_k$, the effects of X_1 and X_2 are only partially captured by their β coefficients. Here, β_1 and β_2 only represent the effects of X_1 and X_2 on the outcome variable when the value of the other predictor is 0. One must also consider the conditional effect of each predictor on the outcome, measured as the product of the β coefficient of the interactive variable and the value of the other state's democracy score. More formally, given an interactive specification, the effect of X_1 on logit (Y) = $(\beta_1 + \beta_3 X_2)$; and the effect of X_2 on logit (Y) = $(\beta_2 + \beta_3 X_1)$. With a dichotomous interaction variable, X_3, which takes the value of 1 if the dyad is jointly democratic and 0 otherwise, the interpretation of the conditional effects is not as straightforward because by restricting the interactive variable to two values (i.e., 0 or 1) we lose the variation in the interaction of X_1 and X_2 that was evident in the continuous interaction variable, which ranged from -100 to $+100$. We are left with a specification that gauges the direct effect of X_1 and X_2 on the outcome, controlling for the impact of joint democracy (i.e., X_3) measured dichotomously; however, we are unable to capture the conditional effects of X_1 and X_2 as either variable varies across the range of its possible values. To be sure, the continuous interactive specification provides a much more straightforward interpretation.

14. Similarly, fusing the impact of three factors (dyadic democracy, monadic democracy, and political distance) using two variables (i.e., Dem_{LO} and Dem_{HI}) makes it difficult to tease out their independent effects.

15. Results using a dichotomous measure of political dissimilarity, *Mixed dyads*, which is coded 1 for states that are neither coherent democracies, coherent anocracies, nor coherent autocracies, and 0 otherwise, are consistent with those reported above, although the caveats against the use of discrete joint democracy measures apply here, as well. Coherent democracies have regime scores > +6, coherent anocracies range from +3 to –3, and coherent autocracies have scores < –6.

16. Technically, in the models that follow, dropping ongoing dispute years amounts to not coding subsequent years of the same dispute as additional dispute cases.

17. See Oneal and Russett (1997: 277) for the coding rules for the variables in the original model. I also reestimated the models using the GEE diagnostic, which Oneal and Russett (1999a: 427) and Russett and Oneal (2001) favor as a technique to control for spatial and temporal dependence. Results garnered from using this specification are consistent with those reported throughout this chapter, and they corroborate the main finding that joint democracy does not reduce the probability of international conflict when one controls for political dissimilarity and trade and drops ongoing years of disputes. The only difference is the coefficient for the political dissimilarity variable in Equation C, which is not significant (p = .14) but it is in the expected direction; more importantly, it is highly significant (p = .005) and in the expected direction in Equation D, which contradicts the democratic peace finding. See the Appendix for a table that details this reestimation.

18. Models were also estimated including the value of the more democratic state's regime score, $Democracy_{HI}$, and the results were consistent with weak-link assumptions. $Democracy_{HI}$ was not included in models that included *Political dissimilarity* because that would create a linear combination among the predictors and preclude estimation, since the latter is coded as the absolute value of the difference between $Democracy_{LO}$ and $Democracy_{HI}$.

19. Oneal and Russett's equation (1) is identical to Equation 1 in this study.

20. The model including $Dem_{HI} + Dem_{LO}$ was consistent with that using $Dem_{HI} * Dem_{LO}$ and is not presented in order to preserve space.

21. The tenuous nature of the joint democracy variable and its inability to attain statistical significance in our research design reminds us of Ray's (1997: 14) prescient observation that the relationship between joint democracy and peace "is in fact so modest in strength . . . that it is something of a minor miracle that it has yet to be eliminated by most of the 'controls' to which it has been introduced."

22. A direct test of weak-link assumptions on the DPP requires an examination of directed dyads, which distinguish initiators from targets, rather than nondirected dyads, which do not distinguish between initiators and targets,

such as those that are the focus of Oneal and Russett (1997) and most studies of the DPP. Bennett and Stam (2000) focus on directed dyads using a weak-link specification and find support for Oneal and Russett's main findings; however, their results are not directly comparable to mine. (See note 27.)

23. This point speaks to problems in the causal logic of the weak-link assumption and an analogy might usefully illuminate the rationale behind it. Imagine a theoretical argument that posits that in accidents between two drivers, the one with the greater number of points on his or her driving record is more likely to have been responsible. Such an argument cannot be used to explain cases where both drivers have the same number of points. That is, such a "theory" by definition can only address cases where the records of the drivers are not identical. Similarly, the "weak-link" thesis is only applicable, by definition, to those cases where a "weak link" is observable, and that simply is not evident in cases where regime scores are identical.

24. The findings in Table 2.7 are presented for both $Democracy_{LO}$ and $Dem_{HI} * Dem_{LO}$; although the results are consistent when either $Dem_{HI} + Dem_{LO}$ or Dem_{GM} are included, the latter two estimations are not included in order to conserve space.

25. Interestingly, Oneal et al. (1996: 251, n. 14) downplayed the significance of their findings that continuous measures of joint democracy were not robust when controlling for trade interdependence (they stated that this important point should not be "unduly emphasized"), because they acknowledged in a subsequent paper, which would turn out to be "The Classical Liberals Were Right," that using a continuous measure of joint democracy (i.e., the weak-link specification) allowed them to find strong support for the DPP.

26. Although one can make this case for any point along the democracy-autocracy continuum where the regime scores for the two states are identical, the points of full democracy and full autocracy are important because it is mainly by differentiating between the conflict proneness of democracies and autocracies that scholars have argued that joint democracies are less conflict-prone than joint autocracies, which for some provides a substantiation of the DPP.

27. For example, Oneal and Russett (1999a) have used a sum of regime scores measure of joint democracy and also utilized the outcome variable that excludes ongoing dispute years. The only exception is the political (dis)similarity variable, which they discuss but do not use explicitly because they presume that their weak-link specification provides an indirect check on the impact of this variable. Bennett and Stam (2000) include a "regime dissimilarity" measure equivalent to the one used here, and their results support Oneal and Russett's findings; however, they do not report results using this specification for nondirected dyads—such as those used in this study—so their results are not comparable to those reported here (see pp. 680–683).

28. Although Russett and Oneal (2001) ostensibly provide evidence for the democratic peace back to the nineteenth century, there is a dearth of reliable trade data for this time period; therefore, the main argument put forth in

this chapter cannot be adequately tested using their research design. Further, there are several inexplicable alterations in the research design found in that study that may affect their findings. The most obvious one is their choice to exclude the economic growth variable from their models although both Russett (1993: 28, 82) and Oneal and Russett (1997) put forth solid theoretical arguments for its inclusion. According to Oneal and Russett (1997: 276–277) it is important to control for economic growth because "states enjoying economic success are apt to be disinclined to fight. They are beneficiaries of the status quo; and *as the liberals have emphasized*, conflict is inconsistent with modern financial and commercial relations" (emphasis added). But Oneal and Russett (1999c: 220) are less enthusiastic about the inclusion of economic growth as a control in the analysis of the DPP, and in discussing economic growth they frame it in this way: "A related hypothesis, *less often articulated in classical liberal thinking*, is that a state enjoying a high rate of economic growth will be less inclined to fight others" (emphasis added). Regardless, there is a straightforward argument that growth more than democracy accounts for the absence of war between democratic states, and economic growth should be used as a control in analyses of the DPP. Interestingly, the findings in this chapter actually are not inconsistent with the view that growth, more than democracy, accounts for the democratic peace (see also Mousseau, 2000).

3

Are Democracies More Peaceful than Nondemocracies?

In this chapter, I test the monadic DPP, which posits that individual democratic states are more peaceful than nondemocratic states. As noted in Chapter 1, earlier findings on the DPP indicated that democracies are no more or less war prone, in general, than nondemocracies. The comparable warlike record of democracies and nondemocracies seemed to pose a challenge to the theoretical basis of the DPP. This apparent inconsistency poses a problem for democratic peace scholars with respect to building a consistent theoretical argument regarding democracy and war. In addition, in the policy domain, the inconsistency undercuts the "democratic crusade," an effort ostensibly led by Western democracies to promote peace abroad (see Diamond, 1992).[1] Of course if democracies are more peaceful than nondemocracies, then the spread of democracy would be a desirable mechanism for peace. But if democracies are not generally more peaceful than nondemocracies, then the spread of democracy would promote egalitarianism, but it would not reduce the likelihood of war involvement for democratic states. However, if democracies are *more* war prone than nondemocracies, then the spread of democracy to nondemocratic states would be an undesirable and ineffective mechanism to encourage peace and it would increase the probability of those states becoming involved in interstate war. To determine whether democracy is likely to engender war or peace for individual states, we need to examine the relationship between democracy and war at the state level.

Recently, scholars have begun to challenge earlier findings on the DPP and have presented evidence that democracies are, indeed, more peaceful than nondemocracies, thereby substantiating the monadic level DPP. Indeed, Oneal and Russett (1997: 288) conclude that "not only was there a separate peace among democratic states but *democracies were more peaceful than autocracies generally*" (emphasis added). They draw the same conclusions from subsequent analyses of the DPP (Oneal and Russett, 1999c: 223; Russett and Oneal, 2001). Oneal and Ray (1997) reach a similar conclusion from their empirical analyses. These studies, which confirm the monadic DPP, appear to have filled the breach in the theoretical arguments of democratic peace theorists created by the earlier findings that although democracies did not fight each other, they were just as war prone as nondemocracies. However, the findings in support of the monadic DPP suffer from several problems, which seriously affect their reliability. In the next section, I will briefly review some of this research and show how much of it suffers from level of analysis problems that severely limit its applicability to the monadic DPP. I also show how many of these studies suffer because they rely on weak-link specifications, the shortcomings of which I discuss in Chapter 2. To alleviate these problems, I provide a research design that focuses squarely on state-level processes and straightforward measures of democracy. I then present my findings and briefly discuss their research and policy implications. I conclude with a summary of the main points of the chapter.

Is There a Monadic Level Democratic Peace?

The monadic version of the DPP has received varying degrees of support in the literature. For example, Haas (1965: 319) finds "a slight but consistent tendency for democratic countries to have less foreign conflict than undemocratic political systems." His findings are consistent with those of Salmore and Hermann (1969), Zinnes and Wilkenfeld (1971), and East and Hermann (1974). East and Gregg (1967) also find that "freer" states exhibited less foreign conflict behavior than more authoritarian states.

The most emphatic proponent of the monadic level DPP has been Rummel (1979, 1983, 1995), who insists that democracies are less violent in their international relations than nondemocracies; however, this conclusion is at odds with his earlier findings (see Rummel, 1968: 207) and with most early studies of the relationship between a state's regime type and its propensity for war. For example, Wright (1942: 841) finds no statistical support for the view that "democracies have been less often involved in war than autocracies." Gregg and Banks (1965) find no significant relationship between democracy and foreign conflict behavior. Russett and Monsen (1975: 27) also conclude that "polyarchy has no independent effect on war-proneness." Similarly, Small and Singer (1976), in an analysis of interstate wars from 1816 to 1965, find no support for the monadic level DPP, nor does Chan (1984) or Weede (1984).

More recently, however, the monadic DPP has been resurrected and has received increased support. For example, Geller's (1985) analysis reveals that states with more constrained regimes, such as democracies, are likely to experience less foreign conflict. Bueno de Mesquita and Lalman (1992: 152–153) make a similar argument with respect to the role of constraints and find that even the presence of a single democracy in a dyad (i.e., a pair of states) reduced the likelihood of a crisis escalating to war. These findings confirmed those uncovered previously by Maoz and Abdolali (1989) as well as the subsequent findings of Hewitt and Wilkenfeld (1996). Morgan and Schwebach (1992: 318) also find that more constrained states, such as democracies, are less belligerent, regardless of the "domestic structure of the opponent." Bremer (1992: 329) agrees that "the presence of a [single] democracy in a dyad significantly reduces its war propensity," concluding, "It appears that the contention of some that both states must be democratic before the war-inhibiting effect of democracy is felt is unsupported." Ray (1995, 1997) echoes this view and provides detailed support for the monadic version of the DPP in the literature. In addition, although Rousseau et al. (1996: 526) find evidence of the monadic DPP "actually quite thin," they insist that "democracies are less likely to initiate crises with all other types of states." Huth (1996: 187) seems more convinced of the accuracy of the monadic DPP, and his findings reveal that "increasing levels of democracy reduce escalation and promote peaceful conflict resolution consistently, regardless of who the adversary was in a territorial dispute." Similarly, Leeds and Davis (1999: 17) find that "regardless of the characteristic of the dyadic partner, states with more democratic characteristics engage in higher levels of international cooperation and lower levels of international conflict."

Benoit (1996: 654) also provides support for the monadic DPP and states that "democracies were significantly less likely, on average, to be involved in international wars during the 1960s and 1970s than less free states."

Two of the clearest and most unequivocal endorsements of the monadic DPP are found in Oneal and Ray (1997) and Oneal and Russett (1997). For example, Oneal and Ray (1997: 751) assert that the findings from their dyadic level analysis of regime type and dispute involvement from 1950 to 1985 reveal that "democratic states are more peaceful than autocracies at the *national* level of analysis" (emphasis added). In addition, Oneal and Russett (1997: 388–389) are emphatic that their evidence "contravenes the conventional wisdom that democracies fight as often as nondemocracies," and they add that "during the Cold War era at least, not only was there a separate peace among democratic states but *democracies were more peaceful than autocracies generally*" (emphasis added). All told, although earlier research seemed to challenge the monadic DPP, more recent research provides what appears to be strong support for it. In fact, some of the most recent research such as Oneal and Ray (1997), Oneal and Russett (1997), and Russett and Oneal (2001) provide what the authors contend is "clear support" for the view that democracies are more peaceful than other types of states. However, a closer look at the research designs of several of these studies reveals that the evidence used to support the monadic DPP is not without its problems.

Problems with Monadic Level DPP Findings

Several concerns arise from a review of the major studies of the proponents of the monadic DPP. First, as the previous section indicates, these studies offer varying degrees of support for the monadic DPP, and the analyses cover a range of international outcomes not all of which are international wars—the primary class of cases to which the DPP is most clearly applicable. Second, there are methodological concerns with the research designs of many of the studies that are most supportive of the monadic DPP insofar as they rely on dyadic level observations (i.e., those that focus on interactions between two states) to infer to monadic level processes (i.e., those that focus on the behavior of single states) in apparent disregard of potential level of analysis problems. For example, Bremer (1992) and Morgan and Schwebach (1992)—

among others—assume that, given a dyad, if one can observe changes in the regime characteristics of one of the states in the pair, then one may reasonably infer that the observed relationship is operative at the monadic level; however, such an inference may violate level of analysis assumptions because a monadic level specification should not proceed from the condition, "given a dyad."

Studies such as Dixon (1993, 1994), Oneal and Ray (1997), Oneal and Russett (1997, 1999b), and Russett and Oneal (2001) are characterized by similar problems insofar as they rely on a "weak-link" research design, which presumably allows the analyst to draw inferences about the relative war-proneness of individual democracies by focusing on the democracy score of the least democratic state in the dyad. Beyond the problems associated with the weak-link specification and estimations of the dyadic DPP, problems emerge from relying on weak-link specifications in examining the monadic DPP. First, since the weak-link approach assumes that the influence of one state's level of democracy is conditional on the other state's level of democracy, then one should include an interaction term, which would take the value of the product of both states' democracy scores, in equations that assume the operation of weak-link processes. The coefficient for this term captures the influence of dyadic level forces on the likelihood of conflict and also accounts for the conditional impact of the two state level variables on the outcome (see Friedrich, 1982). As reported in Chapter 2, I was unable to estimate such an equation using Oneal and Russett's (1997) data; therefore, I was unable to determine the impact of the individual states' level of democracy on their likelihood of international conflict involvement. Without an interactive variable that is constructed as the product of the two constituent variables, one cannot derive, in a straightforward manner, the direct and indirect impact of the individual states' level of democracy on the probability of conflict involvement. It follows that the weak-link specification used in Oneal and Russett (1997) does not allow us to draw clear inferences regarding the conflict propensity of individual democracies and is, therefore, inadequate for examining the monadic DPP.

Second, as noted in Chapter 2, weak-link specifications conflate both the allegedly conflict-dampening impact of monadic level democracy and the conflict-exacerbating impact of political distance in the regime variables (or, as is often the case, in the single regime variable for the less democratic state). Fusing these two conflicting attributes in a single variable makes it difficult to distinguish between dyadic and monadic level processes. In this way, weak-link specifications create level of analysis problems. To be sure, if political distance is an important contributor to international conflict, one should simply include it as a separate variable in the analysis. Such a specification would allow scholars to better determine the impact of political distance on conflict; but, again, as a dyadic level factor, it does little to shed light on the monadic DPP.

Third, and finally, the implication that interstate conflict arises from "the freedom for military action of the less-constrained state" assumes that the less democratic state in a dyad should initiate conflict; however, the statistical tests used to examine the democratic peace in most of the studies that rely on the weak-link thesis do not focus on conflict initiation but rather on a state's involvement in international conflict (Oneal and Russett, 1997: 288). Interestingly, early analysts of the monadic DPP often focused on conflict initiation without clouding their estimations by reliance on weak-link assumptions. As I will show, many of these studies found no evidence of a monadic DPP (e.g., Small and Singer, 1976; Chan, 1984). To be sure, there are much more straightforward ways of testing the DPP with respect to conflict initiation that are not hamstrung by the theoretical and methodological issues affecting weak-link specifications, to wit: one that simply provides an explicit test of the relationship between a state's democracy score and its probability of becoming involved in—and initiating—interstate conflict.

All told, Oneal and Ray (1997), Oneal and Russett (1997), and Russett and Oneal (2001) argue that using the weak-link specification, they find "clear support" for the monadic level democratic peace; however, I maintain that reliance on weak-link specifications makes it very difficult to analyze—much less provide clear support for—the monadic DPP. Therefore, my analyses do not rely on weak-link specifications but instead focus squarely on the relationship between a single state's level of democracy and its likelihood of becoming involved in international conflict. As in the previous chapter, I analyze this relationship for all states during the postwar era—the period within which the democratic peace is most evident and that for which the most unambiguous claims in support of the monadic DPP have been advanced (e.g., Oneal and Russett, 1997; Oneal and Ray, 1997; Leeds and Davis, 1999). In the following section I will discuss the research design used in the subsequent analyses because it is understandably somewhat different from the one used in the previous chapter, which focused on dyadic level relationships.

Research Design

Outcome Variable: The Onset of Interstate War

In this chapter, I examine cases of interstate war from 1946 to 1992. The unit of analysis is the state-year, which is the annual observation for each of the 159 states in the dataset. There are a total of 4,727 state-years for which we have complete data. The outcome variable is the onset of interstate war, which is a dichotomous variable that is coded as "1" if the state experiences an interstate war onset in that year and "0" if it did not. War data are from Singer and Small (1995).

Predictor Variable: Democratic Regime Type

The primary predictor variable, *Democracy*, is measured as the difference between the democracy and autocracy scores of the state, using the codings from the Polity III dataset (Jaggers and Gurr, 1996), and assumes values from −10 (most autocratic) to +10 (most democratic). This is a clearly monadic level specification and does not draw on weak-link assumptions and, therefore, does not suffer from the limitations associated with that approach.

Control Variables: Political, Economic, and Cultural Factors

It is also important to control for the various political, economic, and cultural factors that have been found to significantly affect the war proneness of states in order to limit the likelihood of drawing spurious inferences from simple bivariate results. Although much of the recent data-based research on interstate war has focused on dyadic level relationships, several state level factors have been shown to be important correlates of interstate war (see Geller and Singer, 1998). Moreover, since these controls have been shown to affect the likelihood of war, we need to determine the extent to which they may vitiate the relationship between democracy and war, which is the central focus of my study. These political, economic, and cultural variables will serve as the control variables in my analysis of the monadic DPP.

Beginning with political factors, analysts have long observed that major powers are more likely to become involved in war (Small and Singer, 1982). Moreover, scholars have demonstrated the importance of controlling for major-power status when evaluating the DPP (see

Morgan and Campbell, 1991; Morgan and Schwebach, 1992). In this study, major-power status is designated following COW criteria and includes China since 1949 as well as France, Russia/USSR, the United Kingdom, and the United States since 1946, respectively. The variable, *Major power*, takes the value of "1" for those states that are major powers in the given year and otherwise is coded "0."

There is also evidence that states undergoing political transitions are likely to become involved in interstate conflict (see Mansfield and Snyder, 1995; Enterline, 1996; Ward and Gleditsch, 1998; Thompson and Tucker, 1997ab); therefore, I include a political transition variable, *Transition*, in the data analysis. *Transition* is a continuous variable that is measured as the difference in a state's regime score on the Polity III scale from one year to the next. There is also support for the view that highly militarized states are more likely to fight (Weede, 1970; Kemp, 1977; Wayman et al., 1983). The militarization variable, *Militarization*, is measured as the log of the ratio of a state's military personnel to its total population. Data for this variable is from the COW Material Capabilities dataset (Singer and Small, 1995).

Turning to economic factors, more developed states have been found to be less war-prone than less developed states. In our analysis, a state's level of development, *Development*, is measured as the log of the ratio of the state's energy consumption and its total population. Data for this variable is also from the COW Material Capabilities dataset (Singer and Small, 1995). In addition, Russett's (1990) empirical analysis found significant but weak support for the view that economic downturns are associated with an increased likelihood of interstate war. Therefore, I also control for the presence of economic downturns as a factor affecting the likelihood of interstate war involvement. An economic downturn, *Downturn*, is a dichotomous variable that takes the value of "1" in cases where the annual percentage change in *Development* is negative for three consecutive years, and "0" otherwise.

Finally, among the cultural factors that are implicated in interstate wars, Huntington (1996) suggests that states belonging to certain civilizations are more war prone than others. Although the dyadic level aspect of Huntington's thesis has been empirically challenged (Russett et al., 2000; Henderson and Tucker, 2001), there is partial support for aspects of his thesis at the monadic level (e.g., Davis and Moore, 1997); therefore, it is useful to provide a "civilization membership" control variable in our study. A provocative sub-proposition of Huntington's "clash of civilizations" thesis implicates Islamic states in interstate violence, so it is also useful to control for the ostensible war-proneness of these states. Moreover, the focus on civilization membership is important since critics of the DPP argue that conceptualizations of democracy among democratic peace advocates largely reflect the shared identity and cultural affinity of Western states, which—it is surmised—has led to the decreased violence between these states, which has been incorrectly attributed to joint democracy (e.g., Cohen, 1994; Oren, 1995). Therefore, by controlling for Western civilization membership we can better determine the extent to which democracy qua democracy (as opposed to Western civilization membership) decreases the likelihood of war. Civilization membership follows closely Huntington's (1996) classification and the criteria outlined in Henderson and Tucker (2001), and it includes separate variables for the Sinic, Japanese, Hindu, Islamic, Orthodox, Western, Latin American, African, and Buddhist civilizations. States that do not fall within these categories are classified as *Other.* Each state is classified by its civilization type using a dummy variable that takes the value of "1" for states that are members of the respective civilization and "0" otherwise. I do not include all of the civilization variables in the same equation since that would create a perfect linear combination and preclude estimation; therefore, I exclude *African* so that it can be used as the baseline by which to determine the impact of the other civilization variables.

Data Analysis

A multivariate logistic regression model is estimated to evaluate the monadic DPP. The basic model takes the following form: $\Pr(Interstate\ war_{i,t}) = 1 / (1 + e^{-Z_i})$. $\Pr(Interstate\ war_{i,t})$ is the probability that the outcome variable (the onset of interstate war) equals 1; and Z_i is the sum of the product of the coefficient values (β_i) across all observations of the predictor variables $(X_{i,t})$, that is: $\beta_0 + \beta_1 Democracy + \beta_2 Major\ power + \beta_3 Transition + \beta_4 Militarization + \beta_5 Development + \beta_6 Downturn + \beta_7 Civilization_i \ldots n-1.$[2]

Findings

Turning to the initial findings, which are reported in the first column of Table 3.1 (Equation 1), the results indicate that each of the models per-

Table 3.1 Logistic Regression of Factors Associated with Interstate War, 1946–1992

	Equation 1	Equation 2
Democracy	.06*** (.02)	.05** (.02)
Major power	1.94*** (.35)	2.00*** (.38)
Transition	−.03 (.06)	−.02 (.06)
Militarization	1.42*** (.29)	1.20*** (.30)
Development	−.36* (.20)	−.19 (.21)
Downturn	−.13 (.29)	−.25 (.30)
Buddhist	—	.16 (1.02)
Hindu	—	2.10** (.94)
Islamic	.90*** (.27)	1.60** (.76)
Japanese	—	−3.06 (9.70)
Latin American	—	−.08 (.89)
Orthodox	—	−.53 (1.10)
Other	—	1.43* (.85)
Sinic	—	1.32 (.84)
Western	−.74* (.40)	−.09 (.87)
Constant	−1.23* (.64)	−2.32** (1.06)
−2 log likelihood	758.78	738.95
N	4,727	4,727
X^2	68.90***	88.53***

Note: Standard errors are in parentheses; all p-values are estimated using two-tailed tests.
*p ≤ .10, **p ≤ .05 level, ***p ≤ .01 level

forms well as evident from their goodness of fit statistics. As for the associations among the predictor variables and the likelihood of inter-state war, I find that major power, poor, militarized, and Islamic states are more likely to be involved in interstate war, while Western countries are significantly less likely to be involved in interstate war. These findings are consistent with previous research on state level factors in war (see Geller and Singer, 1998) and also provide support for aspects of Huntington's (1996) thesis. Only the coefficients for *Transition* and *Downturns* are not significant. Most important among the findings is that democracies are *more likely* to be involved in interstate war, which not only contradicts the monadic DPP but literally turns it on its head.

When I include the complete list of civilization variables (with *African* states as the baseline) in Equation 2, the greater war-proneness of democratic states is again evident. Further, I find that the pacificity of *Western* states evinced in Equation 1 is clearly not robust. In addition, it is clear that *Islamic* states are not singularly bellicose but that *Hindu* and *Other* (mainly Israel) states are also more prone to war, which suggests that Huntington's (1996) assertion of the singular belli-cosity of Islamic states is misplaced, at best. The findings with respect to the civilization variables in Equation 2 largely reflect the heightened degree of interstate war in South Asia and the Middle East since World War II. To be sure, democracies from these regions, primarily India and Israel, have been heavily involved in wars in the post–World War II era.

In an attempt to determine the war-proneness of particular democ-racies, I also disaggregated the democracy variable by civilization membership. I found that *Western* democracies were significantly less likely to become involved in interstate wars, but *Hindu* democracies (predominantly India) and the *Other* democracies (predominantly Israel) were significantly more likely to be involved in interstate wars. The finding with respect to *Western* democracies may offer some sup-port for those who argue that the pacific impact of democracy is found especially within Western liberal democracies (e.g., see Owen, 1994), and they might also provide succor to democratic enlargement advo-cates; however, it is important to remember that although Western democracies are less likely to become involved in wars, the findings do not encourage a sanguine view of the prospect of peace emerging from the implementation of a democratic enlargement strategy because democratic states, in general, are *more prone* to become involved in militarized disputes and interstate wars. The best example of democratic involvement in war is provided by the experiences of the *Hindu* and *Other* democracies (primarily India and Israel, respectively), which are consistent with the intuitive assessment outlined above regarding the involvement of democracies in South Asian and Middle Eastern wars. All told, the findings up to this point clearly refute the monadic DPP. It seems evident that, controlling for a host of political, economic, and cultural factors, democracies are *more likely* to become involved in interstate war than nondemocracies.

There are three strong critiques of the analysis thus far: One centers on the operationalization of the primary predictor variable, *Democracy*, and the other two focus on alternative choices of outcome variables. Taking the initial critique first, some may question the use of a continuous operationalization of the regime variable in the analyses reported here; however, as noted in Chapter 2, researchers of the DPP generally agree that indicators of democracy in systematic research should be scaled as continuous variables because the DPP suggests that the *greater the extent* of democracy the *greater* the ability of democratic norms and institutions to prevent war, which is "clearly an argument with respect to the *extent* of democracy and not simply its presence or absence" (Henderson, 1999a: 219, emphasis in original). Nevertheless, I reestimated the basic equation (i.e., Equation 1) using a dichotomous measure of democracy to test the sensitivity of the findings to a different specification of the primary predictor variable (see Table 3.2). Actually, I use a trichotomous measure that distinguishes among democracies, anocracies, and autocracies, with autocracies excluded from the equation to serve as a baseline. Democracies have regime scores greater than +6, anocracies range from +6 to –6, and autocracies have scores less than –6.[3]

The findings from Equation 3, which uses the noncontinuous specification, are generally consistent with those from Equation 1, which uses a continuous measure of democracy.[4] Specifically, the results indicate that democracies are significantly more likely to be involved in interstate wars. In fact, these findings comport with a comparison of the difference across regime types in the proportion of total state-years to total war-years. For example, although democracies constitute 29 percent of the total state-years in the population of cases in our study, they account for 34 percent of the war-years; anocracies constitute 25 percent of the state-years and 23 percent of the war-years, while autocracies constitute 46 percent of the state-years and 43 percent of the war-years. These distributions indicate that democracies are involved in war

Table 3.2 Logistic Regression of Factors Associated with Interstate War, Using a Dichotomous Democracy Measure, 1946–1992

	Equation 3
Democracy	.89*** (.33)
Anocracy	.44 (.30)
Major power	1.93*** (.35)
Transition	−.03 (.06)
Militarization	1.40*** (.30)
Development	−.32* (.19)
Downturn	−.12 (.29)
Islamic	.86*** (.27)
Western	−.64 (.40)
Constant	−1.71*** (.63)
−2 log likelihood	760.87
N	4,727
X^2	66.61***

Note: Standard errors are in parentheses; all p-values are estimated using two-tailed tests.
*$p \leq .10$, **$p \leq .05$ level, ***$p \leq .01$ level

in excess of their proportion in the population of states—and much more so than are anocracies and autocracies. Therefore, it is not surprising that—using autocracies as a baseline—we find that democracies are more likely to become involved in interstate war. In sum, regardless of whether one uses a continuous or a noncontinuous specification of the democracy variable, democracies have been more war prone than nondemocracies in the postwar era.

Turning to the second critique, one may argue that the greater probability of war involvement on the part of democratic states reflects the greater adherence of democratic states to collective security requirements or their greater willingness to support democratic allies in ongoing wars. If this hypothetical relationship were borne out empirically, then focusing on war involvement would make democracies appear more bellicose than they are in actuality. According to the logic of this critique, the more appropriate focus of an inquiry into the relative war-proneness of democracies is not "war involvement" but "war initiation." However, the problem with this critique is that the literature on the DPP suggests that democracies are no less likely to initiate wars or to fight on the side of the initiators than nondemocracies (Small and Singer, 1976; Chan, 1984). In fact, previous research indicates that democracies appear to be more likely to initiate war against autocracies than are autocracies to initiate wars against them (Bennett and Stam, 1998). On the other hand, Oneal and Russett (1999a) argue that the conflict-dampening impact of democracy—which they maintain is manifest at both the dyadic and monadic levels—is no less evident when using the onset of an international dispute as the outcome variable. Therefore, I reestimate Equation 1 using war initiation as the outcome variable.[5]

Equation 4 in Table 3.3 shows the result of estimations using this specification of the model, and the findings are consistent with those of Equations 1–3, which specify war involvement as the outcome variable and indicate that there is a significant positive relationship between democratic regime type and war initiation in the postwar era. Equation 5 in Table 3.3 shows that the significant positive relationship between democracy and war initiation is not vitiated by use of a noncontinuous measure of regime type. That is, in Equation 5, as in Equation 3, using a trichotomous measure that distinguishes among democracies, anocracies, and autocracies, with autocracies excluded from the equation to serve as a baseline, I find that democracies are more likely to initiate war. As before, in order to determine the war-proneness of particular democracies, I disaggregated the democracy variable by civilization membership. Again, I found that the Western democracies were significantly less likely to initiate interstate wars but that the Hindu democracies (predominantly India) and the *Other* democracies (predominantly Israel) were significantly more likely to initiate them. In sum, the findings reveal that the view that the greater war involvement of democratic states simply reflects their defensive reaction to aggression from nondemocratic states is not only unfounded but essentially backwards—democratic states are significantly *more likely* to initiate wars than other states.

The third critique suggests that the inconsistency between the findings of the present study and those of previous works focusing on the

Table 3.3   Logistic Regression of Factors Associated with Interstate War Initiation, 1946–1992

	Equation 4	Equation 5
Democracy	.10***	1.46***
	(.03)	(.56)
Anocracy	—	.54
		(.54)
Major power	3.15***	3.02***
	(.64)	(.63)
Transition	−.07	−.06
	(.09)	(.09)
Militarization	1.56***	1.50***
	(.49)	(.49)
Development	−.58*	−.49
	(.33)	(.32)
Downturn	−.13	−.57
	(.29)	(.55)
Buddhist	—	—
Hindu	—	—
Islamic	.69	.62
	(.47)	(.47)
Japanese	—	—
Latin American	—	—
Orthodox	—	—
Other	—	—
Sinic	—	—
Western	−3.81***	−3.60***
	(1.17)	(1.16)
Constant	−1.88*	−2.64***
	(1.04)	(1.06)
−2 log likelihood	278.79	281.55
N	4,727	4,727
X^2	43.62***	40.86***

Note: Standard errors are in parentheses; all p-values are estimated using two-tailed tests.
*$p \leq .10$, **$p \leq .05$ level, ***$p \leq .01$ level

monadic level DPP derives largely from the differences among outcome variables. That is, while the present study focuses on interstate war as an outcome, both Oneal and Ray (1997) and Oneal and Russett (1997) focus on militarized interstate disputes (MIDs)—although the latter insist that their findings are consistent using interstate war involvement as the outcome variable. It is plausible that although democracies may be more conflict prone with respect to their involvement in wars, they may also inhibit conflict with respect to their involvement in MIDs. I tested this contention by reestimating the basic equations and specifying "initiation of militarized dispute" as the outcome variable. The results are reported in Equations 6 and 7 in Table 3.4, and they reveal that even when we focus on MIDs, the basic relationship remains: Democratic states are more likely to initiate interstate conflict. Coupled with the earlier findings, it is clear that democracies are not more peaceful than nondemocracies; in fact, they are *more* conflict-prone than nondemocracies.

As before, in order to determine the conflict-proneness of particular democracies, I disaggregated the democracy variable by civilization membership. Again, I found that the *Western* democracies were significantly less likely to initiate MIDs, but the *Hindu* democracies (predominantly India) and the *Other* democracies (predominantly Israel) were significantly more likely to initiate them. Given these consistent findings that the Western democracies are less conflict-prone and that the lion's share of democratic conflict is prosecuted by India and Israel, one may contend that the findings actually do reveal a monadic democratic peace for the Western democracies. However, it is important to remember that neither the monadic nor the dyadic DPP suggests that *only* Western democracies are more peaceful than nondemocracies; in fact, this is a critique of the DPP by scholars such as Cohen (1994) and by implication Huntington (1996), which has been roundly criticized and empirically challenged by DPP advocates such as Maoz (1997) and Russett et al. (2000). In a slightly different variant of the previous argument, one may insist that there is a democratic peace for most democratic states except for those in the Hindu and Jewish civilizations (i.e., other than India and Israel), but, again, the monadic DPP does not suggest that democracies other than India and Israel are peaceful, it contends that democracies— in general—are more peaceful than nondemocracies. The findings in this chapter clearly contradict that assertion.

Discussion

My findings refute the monadic level DPP, which suggests that democracies are more peaceful than nondemocracies, and they reveal that

Table 3.4 Logistic Regression of Factors Associated with Militarized Dispute Initiation, 1946–1992

	Equation 6	Equation 7
Democracy	.03***	.41***
	(.01)	(.13)
Anocracy	—	.21**
		(.10)
Major power	2.62***	2.62***
	(.17)	(.17)
Transition	−.03	−.03
	(.02)	(.02)
Militarization	1.27***	1.25***
	(.10)	(.10)
Development	−.32***	−.29***
	(.07)	(.07)
Downturn	.35***	.36***
	(.10)	(.10)
Buddhist	—	—
Hindu	—	—
Islamic	.35***	.32***
	(.10)	(.10)
Japanese	—	—
Latin American	—	—
Orthodox	—	—
Other	—	—
Sinic	—	—
Western	−1.34***	−1.28***
	(.16)	(.16)
Constant	1.55***	.88***
	(.24)	(.23)
−2 log likelihood	3,777.21	3,783.56
N	4,727	4,727
X^2	534.04***	527.69***

Note: Standard errors are in parentheses; all p-values are estimated using two-tailed tests.
*p ≤ .10, **p ≤ .05 level, ***p ≤ .01 level

democracies are more likely than nondemocracies to be involved in—and to initiate—interstate wars and MIDs. Wedding these findings to those in Chapter 2, it appears that the spread of democracy may precipitate an increase in the likelihood of wars as individual states become democratic and, subsequently, more war-prone. Further, casting these findings in the light of recent studies of the DPP highlights some daunting prospects for global peace. For example, recent empirical findings indicate that regime changes are much more likely to occur during or following wars and that losing states are much more likely to experience regime change (Bueno de Mesquita et al., 1992). Since democracies are more likely to win wars as compared to nondemocracies (Lake, 1992; Stam, 1996; Reiter and Stam, 1998a), it follows that nondemocracies are more likely to experience regime change, which in some cases may result in their full democratization. The result is that war involvement may actually increase the proportion of democratic states in the system and, subsequently, increase the likelihood of warfare for those newly democratic states. From this perspective, the spread of democracy will create more of the most war-prone states, thereby increasing the likelihood of war involvement and initiation for those states. These relationships hardly encourage a sanguine view of the prospects for peace with a democratic enlargement strategy.

One may ask how to reconcile the monadic DPP findings reported here with previous monadic level DPP results. Well, this is a problem only if one ignores two important factors: (1) earlier monadic level DPP research, and (2) the impact of level of analysis problems. First, it is important to remember that the findings reported here are actually consistent with early monadic level findings such as Chan's (1984: 632), which reveal that for the period from 1816 to 1945 and from 1946 to 1972, democratic states were actually more war-prone than nondemocratic states. Weede (1984) also finds a positive though nonsignificant relationship between democracy and war at the state level from 1960 to 1974. Chan (1984: 632) is clear that "contrary to the view that freedom discourages war, the evidence points in the direction that it is associated with more war." My findings corroborate and extend Chan's (1984) results and, therefore, are not totally inconsistent with earlier research on the DPP—especially that which carefully distinguishes between the interaction of *pairs of states* and the behavior of *individual states*.

In contrast, the results presented here contradict Benoit's (1996: 654) findings that "democracies fought fewer wars *on average* than less-free regimes" (emphasis in original). Although Benoit's (1996) study is largely unfettered by the research design problems of many of the monadic DPP studies discussed earlier, it is not without its own problems. For instance, his research design includes both interstate and extrastate wars, and his sensitivity tests with respect to the inclusion of the latter wars suggest that they affect—if only marginally—the significance of the relationship between democracy and war involvement (see his note 12). Since the relationship between democracy and war is quite different depending on whether one focuses on interstate or extrastate war (as will be shown in Chapter 4), it follows that Benoit's findings of a monadic level democratic peace may be partly owed to his inclusion of extrastate wars in his analysis. More importantly, since Benoit's study—as compared to the present one—focuses on a limited time period (from 1960 to 1980), which ignores several wars involving democratic states included in the present analysis, such as the Korean War, the Sinai War, the Falklands/Malvinas War, the Lebanese War, and the Gulf War, then it is likely that Benoit's findings are skewed by its limited temporal focus. Specifically, in my estimation, the temporal domain of Benoit's study is heavily influenced by the negative relationship between democracy and war involvement during the period from 1973 to 1980 (as revealed in Chan's 1984 study and my own analysis not reported here) and especially from 1976 to 1980 (as revealed by Rummel, 1983).

Second, the difference between my strictly monadic level DPP finding and previous findings that inferred monadic level processes from dyadic level observations is hardly anomalous as long as one does not ignore level of analysis problems and presume that relationships that obtain at one level are operative at another.[6] For example, since the end of the Korean War, major powers have not fought each other in interstate war (a dyadic level phenomenon); however, in the same period individual major powers have been more likely to engage in interstate war (a monadic level phenomenon). If one assumed that since major powers did not fight each other, then they were less likely to fight, in general, one would be making an inferential error indicative of a level-of-analysis problem. These types of inconsistent relationships across levels are evident in many political phenomena in world politics. For example, while Wallace (1973) and Midlarsky (1975) find a strong relationship between status inconsistency and war involvement at the system level, Ray (1974) and Gochman (1980) find that status-inconsistent states are no more likely to be involved in war than status-consistent ones. It appears that many recent advocates of the monadic level DPP seem to have been insufficiently attentive to level of analysis problems in their declaration that democracies are more peaceful than nondemocracies. Relying largely on dyadic level specifications to draw inferences about monadic level relationships, they've failed to capture the actual conflict exacerbating relationship between democracy and war that is uncovered once one focuses on explicitly state level processes.[7]

It is important to remember that concerns with level of analysis problems do not preclude our drawing logical inferences from results at one level to those one can *expect* to observe at another; they only caution us not to assume that processes operative at one level are, ipso facto, operative at another. When put to the test, scholars often find that many such assumptions are not borne out empirically. In that vein, I contend that the research cited earlier demonstrates that by simply inferring to the system level relationships that are observed at the dyadic level, democratic enlargement strategy suffers from a level of analysis problem.

To be sure, I do not contend that democracy is an undesirable form of government or that the promotion of democracy should be abandoned. My intention is simply to point out that the notion that by promoting democracy one can facilitate—much less ensure—peace seems severely flawed. The findings in this chapter indicate that democracy, in itself, not only fails as a guarantor of international peace but actually increases the likelihood of interstate war. Given this conclusion, one has to question the effectiveness of a democratic enlargement strategy, whose aim is to pursue peace by assisting in the creation of what is the most bellicose type of states, democracies. To my mind, in order to better understand the motivation for war and the conditions that give rise to peace, scholars should focus on the interplay of political, economic, and cultural factors as they inform the decisions of leaders and their fellow citizens to go to war.

Conclusion

In this chapter, I have examined the relationship between democracy and interstate war in the postwar era. By focusing explicitly on state level factors in an era when the democratic peace is thought to be clearly evident, I've provided a clearer test of the claim that democratic states are more peaceful than nondemocratic states. Controlling for a host of political, economic, and cultural factors that have been implicated in the onset of interstate war, the results indicate that democracies are more war-prone than nondemocracies (whether democracy is coded as a continuous variable or not) and that democracies are more likely to initiate interstate wars.

These results suggest several research and policy implications. First, analysts of the monadic level DPP should use explicitly state level specifications of their variables in order to avoid level of analysis problems.[8] Second, the results seriously call into question the empirical underpinnings of the democratic enlargement strategy. Some might interpret the finding that *Western* democracies are less likely to initiate disputes and wars as vindication of the view that these states should embark on a crusade to spread democracy; however, my findings indicate that democratic enlargement is more likely to fuel increased interstate war involvement because the spread of democracy will generate more democratic states, which are more likely to become involved in— and to initiate—interstate wars. These conclusions cast an ominous shadow over otherwise positive developments such as the democratic transformation of states in the present wave of democratization. They certainly raise concerns about the efficacy of recent enlargement initiatives, such as the expansion of NATO, to include several newly democratized Eastern European states. Eastern Europe remains a volatile region, and the presence of democracy in the new NATO members of Poland, the Czech Republic, and Hungary may exacerbate the propensity to international conflict among these states and draw their NATO allies into a larger regional conflict. Layne (1994: 47) argues that "there is little wisdom in [the United States] assuming such potentially risky undertakings on the basis of dubious assumptions about the pacifying effects of democracy." The findings from this study provide empirical support for Layne's skepticism. It appears that for all of its positive value as an egalitarian form of government, one of the key threats to peace for individual states is the presence of a democratic regime.

Notes

1. Although Clinton administration officials publicly shunned calls for a "democratic crusade," Layne (1994: 46) avers that interventionism is implicit in the logic of the DPP because "if democracies are peaceful but nondemocratic states are 'troublemakers' the conclusion is inescapable: the former will be truly secure only when the latter have been transformed into democracies, too." In spite of that, Lake (1993: 4) argues that enlargement "is not a democratic crusade [but] a pragmatic commitment to see freedom take hold where that will help us [the United States] most." Nevertheless, he details how the

United States "must target" its efforts "to assist states that affect our strategic interests" using methods that range from trade, aid, and diplomacy to military containment of "backlash states." While Lake disaffirmed the impulse to crusade, he outlines U.S. enlargement interests in the Western hemisphere, Central and Eastern Europe, Asia and the Pacific, and sub-Saharan Africa.

2. I checked for autocorrelation (up to 16 lags in the ACF and PACF series) using the Box Ljung Q statistic for the models and it was not pronounced. Using the GEE autocorrelation diagnostic, I found that the estimates were consistent with those reported here. Beck et al.'s (1998) *Peaceyrs* diagnostic revealed an absence of autocorrelation (e.g., in the original model the coefficient for *Peaceyrs* is –6.63 with a standard error of 8.11). I conclude that the findings are robust with respect to autocorrelation.

3. The coding of anocracy is not identical to the one used in Chapter 2, which focused on "coherent anocracy," a subset of the broader category of "anocracy." Unlike the coding for coherent democracy and coherent autocracy, there is not a generally accepted threshold for coherent anocracy in the DPP literature. Using the identical coding of coherent democracy as found in the analyses in Chapter 2 yields similar results as those reported in this chapter (i.e., Tables 3.2–3.4).

4. The exception is that the coefficient for *Western* is not significant.

5. Initiation data are from Bueno de Mesquita (1981), updated by the author.

6. The main difference between my findings that reject the monadic DPP and those of Leeds and Davis (1999) and Bennett and Stam (2000), who support it (without suffering from level of analysis problems), is likely due to their inattention to civilization factors. By controlling for civilization factors, one can more readily discern the impact of democracy qua democracy at the state level. Western democracies make up 60 percent of all democratic state-years, and while their rate of war involvement is equal to that for all democracies, their rate of war and MID initiation is less than that for democracies in general. Controlling for Western civilization allows us to flesh out the greater propensity to conflict among non-Western democratic states and, subsequently, democracies in general.

7. Democratic enlargement strategists assume a negative monotonic relationship between the spread of democracy and the probability of war in the global system; in contrast, Gleditsch and Hegre (1997) suggest an inverted U relationship between the two. Ray (1997) and Maoz (2000) disagree with the inverted U thesis. Crescenzi and Enterline (1999) do not find evidence for the inverted U relationship over the period 1816 to 1992, but they find a negative relationship from 1936 to 1992.

8. Only after scholars have ascertained the actual relationship between democracy and war at the state level can we effectively wed it to research focusing on dyadic, regional, and system level processes and provide an integrated model of the DPP, such as attempted by Maoz (2000).

4

The Democratic Peace and Extrastate Wars

As we have seen from the discussion up to this point, most studies of the DPP focus mainly on one type of international war, interstate war (i.e., war between at least two states); however, there is another major form of international war that is extrastate, or extrasystemic—in other words, war between states and nonstate actors, such as colonial and imperial wars. Findings from Chapter 3, which empirically refute the monadic DPP, do not address the issue of whether the democratic peace obtains for extrastate wars. Therefore, in this chapter, I analyze the relationship between democracy and extrastate war for all states during the postwar era from 1946 to 1992—the period for which the most unambiguous claims in support of the monadic level DPP have been advanced.

Earlier research on the relationship between democracy and international war often included analyses of extrastate wars (e.g., Small and Singer, 1976; Chan, 1984; Weede, 1984), and these studies found no evidence that democracies were more peaceful than nondemocracies. By comparison, recent studies of the DPP largely ignore data on extrastate wars. These data have been available since publication of Small and Singer's *Resort to Arms* in 1982, a widely accepted source for interstate war data. Interestingly, it is the more recent studies that have emphatically proclaimed that democracies are more peaceful than nondemocracies (e.g., Oneal and Ray, 1997; Oneal and Russett, 1997, 1999c; Leeds and Davis, 1999; Russett and Oneal, 2001). The key concern of this chapter is to what extent democratic states are more peaceful with respect to extrastate wars. Additionally, I hope to better determine the extent to which democracies are more peaceful across the full range of international wars, including both interstate and extrastate wars. With its focus on extrastate wars, this chapter fills a lacuna in recent research on the democratic peace, and it has important implications for foreign policy.

The chapter proceeds in several parts. In the next section, I will discuss the relationship between democracy and extrastate war as suggested by DPP arguments. Following that, I provide an empirical analysis of the relationship between democracy and war, controlling for several political, economic, and cultural factors. After presenting the results, I discuss their research and policy implications. Finally, I conclude with a brief summary of the main points of the chapter.

Democratic Imperialism and Democratic Peace

The theoretical rationale for democratic involvement in extrastate wars draws mainly from the arguments regarding the prospects for democratic imperialism. Doyle (1997) argues that liberalism, the political philosophy in which the DPP is embedded, is ambivalent with respect to imperialism and the wars it spawns. While "liberal cosmopolitanism" is said to "eschew imperialist intervention in states," other liberal approaches do not support the view "that all peoples are sufficiently 'civilized' to be fit for national independence" (p. 399). Such societies were viewed as incapable of "the 'reciprocity' on which all legal equality rests partly because of political chaos, partly because these peoples (like children) are incapable of postponing gratification. Moreover, they would benefit from the tutelage and commercial development imperial rule could provide" (p. 399). To be sure, Wilsonian idealism, the paradigmatic expression of classical liberalism in world politics, in practice legitimized imperialism and colonialism for the predominantly "democratic" victors of World War I, who had subjugated much of Africa and Asia while proclaiming the right of Europeans to be free from imperialism in recognition of their rights of national self-determination. It is clear that Western liberalism, at least in the past two centuries, has been schizophrenic regarding imperialism: The domination of whites was clearly illegitimate, to be vigorously and even violently resisted (e.g., in "wars to make the world safe for democracy"), while the subjugation of nonwhites could be quite legitimate and even laudable. This perspective, therefore, rarely warranted the violent overthrow of even the most oppressive white imperialists, who were viewed in this racist rationalization as bearers of civilization, justice, Christianity, and so on.

This classical liberal hypocrisy informs the democratic peace by reminding us that under certain conditions, democratic leaders prosecute wars to achieve the objectives of imperialist policies. Their imperialist policies result, in part, from the perception that opponents are inferior according to racial and cultural criteria. This mind-set mitigates the conflict-dampening impact of democratic government and may allow democratic decisionmakers to pursue aggressive foreign policies against even arguably democratic foes. For example, Owen (1994: 95) maintains that the basic premise of the cultural/normative variant of the DPP is that "liberalism [is] more tolerant of its own kind." That is, when citizens and elites within liberal societies recognize their potential rival as a liberal regime, they oppose war between their states. Oren (1995: 151) argues that "the democratic peace proposition is not about democracy *per se;* rather, it should be understood as a special case of an argument about peace among polities that are similar relative to some normative benchmarks." What is "special" about the benchmarks that indicate "democracy," for Oren, is that they represent "our kind."[1]

The designation of "our kind," in my view, often transcends regime type and may draw instead on the cultural characteristics of the rival society (see Henderson, 1998a). Therefore, the conflict-dampening impact of democracy that Owen ascribes to liberal regimes often rests on whether the political elite perceive the adversary as similar to themselves. Specifically, among culturally dissimilar disputants, the reduction of conflict occasioned by joint democracy may be undermined by racist or ethnocentric animus on the part of decisionmakers. This view seems consistent with those of such staunch democratic peace advocates as Weart (1998: 242), who is convinced that the major influence that "may undermine peace between approximately republican regimes" is the misperception of leaders, which biases them against those who are politically, economically, or culturally different. He opines that the

> weak point . . . that threatens peace between any regimes, democracies or not [is that] people may identify so strongly with their nationality (with its territory, language, ethnic stock, religion, and so forth) that this loyalty outweighs even the solidarity among fellow democrats. They may then see foreigners as an alien and untrustworthy outgroup regardless of their form of government. (p. 221)

The result of this process often takes the form of "aggressive imperialism" on the part of a strong democracy that attempts to "enforce its hegemony over other peoples." Weart suggests that such aggressive imperialism has been facilitated by the fact that in the colonies "the distinction between the domestic citizen and the foreign potential enemy was already blurred" (p. 239). He avers that "republics in general, with their ideals of equality and tolerance, tend to define their in-group of citizens as those who follow republican practices" (p. 237); however, "approximately republican regimes may turn to violence exactly at the point where the principles of equality and toleration are not fully established domestically" (p. 239). That is, in the cases of democratic imperialism, "the readiness of leaders to use force abroad was almost predictable in view of how they coerced people, if not exactly at home, then certainly under their domination" (p. 239). Nevertheless, Weart (1998: 242) insists, "No matter how severe the differences between rival republics, their style of diplomacy contributes to a mutual trust which moves them toward alliance rather than war."

Russett has also addressed the impact of racism on perceptions of an adversary's regime type, and his views seem quite similar to those of Weart. For example, in reviewing the Second Philippines War of 1899 as a potential "candidate war between democracies," Russett (1993: 17) suggests that "Western ethnocentric attitudes at the time" prevented normative or institutional constraints from exerting a dampening effect on U.S. foreign policy in the face of an arguably democratic though culturally dissimilar adversary.[2] He observes that the impact of the West's racism on its colonial subjects was such that "Europeans' ethnocentric views of those peoples carried the *assumption* that they did not have institutions of self-government. Not only were they available for imperial aggrandizement, they could be considered candidates for betterment[?] and even 'liberation'—the white man's burden, or *mission civilatrice*. . . . Their governments or tribal leaders could not, in this ethnocentric view, be just or consensual, and thus one need have few compunctions about conquering these legitimate candidates for 'liberal' imperialism" (pp. 34–35, emphasis in original).

Hunt (1987: 91) reminds us that the Second Philippines War is not exceptional in this regard; in fact, he argues that decisionmakers in the United States—one of the most enduring democracies—"fixed race at the center of their world view" (also see Dower, 1986). Further, "public policy in general and foreign policy in particular had from the start of the national experience reflected the central role that race thinking played." For Hunt, the overall pattern was clear enough in that U.S. elites "shared a loyalty to race as an essential category for understanding other peoples and as a fundamental basis for judging them" (p. 91). He also takes issue with Russett's (1993: 35) contention that "when Western forms of self-government did begin to take root on a local basis in many of the colonies, the extremes of pseudo-Darwinian racism lost their legitimacy" because such attitudes have not disappeared with respect to the West's treatment of the former colonized world (pp. 171–198). Nevertheless, for many democratic peace theorists, pervasive white racism in the domestic and foreign policies of Western imperialist states does not disqualify them from being classified as democratic.

Probably the most egregious example of this is found in the designation of Belgium as a democracy (usually from 1830 on—with the exception of the few years when it was occupied, see Doyle 1983ab), even as Belgian King Leopold II committed what Hochschild (1998: 3) labels "one of the great mass killings of recent history," in the Rubber Terror of the Belgian Congo. During this conflict, an estimated 10,000,000 Africans were killed between 1880 and 1920—truly a holocaust in Central Africa. Further, the author maintains that only the scale of the killing subsided when the "democratic" Belgian government took over control of the colony.[3] Democratic France followed similar policies in their equatorial African territories with some indigenous population losses estimated at roughly 50 percent, but these factors hardly affect the designation of France's democratic status. Britain's colonial subjugation of African and Asian peoples also does not seem to affect its democratic standing among DPP researchers. Moreover, the democracy score of the United States is consistent from the eighteenth century on according to Doyle (1983ab), and it never registers below +8—a coherent democracy—on the Polity III scale. In fact, it is coded +10—the highest level of democracy—from 1871 on. Yet Karnow (1989: 194) notes that in just one of several cases of U.S. imperialist wars, in the Second Philippines War of 1899–1902, 4,000 U.S. troops, 20,000 *insurrectos*, and roughly 200,000 civilians were killed. In this arguably joint democratic war, there was almost a ten-to-one ratio of civilian to military deaths—with civilian deaths representing 89 percent of the total—surpassing even that of the Vietnam War (Henderson and Singer, in press). In each of these cases and potentially others, racist states coded as democracies prosecuted imperialist wars against polities that may also have been democratic, but with the exception of the latter, these cases are rarely mentioned in democratic peace tracts as candidate cases of joint democratic conflict. This reflects, in large part, two aspects of Eurocentric world politics: (1) the view that colonized people do not have a history of organized armed resistance to Western imperialism and (2) the enduring view that colonized people could not possibly have a history of egalitarian forms of governance.

The latter point seems to inform Weart's (1998) and Russett's (1993) view that even given their biased perceptions of certain peoples, democratic leaders have not prosecuted international warfare against other democracies. Such a view ignores extrastate wars between Western democracies and potentially egalitarian polities. For example, the conflicts related to the Belgian subjugation of the indigenous societies of the Democratic Republic of Congo may provide candidate cases of joint democratic conflict especially in light of the research by African scholars, such as Ernest Wamba-Dia-Wamba (1985), who have been documenting indigenous representative institutions such as *palaver* found in several societies in Africa's interlacustrine region.[4] A discussion of these types of candidate cases is noticeably absent from most DPP research, including Russett (1993), Ray (1995), Russett and Oneal (2001), and Weart's 1998 study—the latter claims to have documented the entire population of approximate cases of joint democratic war.[5]

The reasoning behind the argument that pervasive white racism on the part of Western "democracies" does not disqualify them as democracies is not dissimilar from the rationalizations proffered by democratic peace advocates to explain away cases where democracies use covert warfare against other democracies (see Forsythe, 1992; James and Mitchell, 1995). For example, Weart (1998) characterizes the U.S.-assisted overthrow and assassination of Chile's democratically elected leader, Salvador Allende, in a military coup in 1973 as a clear example "of one democratic government deliberately working to destroy another" (p. 227). Russett (1993: 123) views the Allende regime similarly and points out that "had war erupted between the United States and Chile we would have had to reexamine any generalization that democracies do not make war on each other." Both authors also agree that U.S. intervention to overthrow the Arbenz regime in Guatemala involved aggression by one democracy against another democratically elected government. What is interesting, though, is that both authors contend that these covert uses of force by the United States against, arguably, other democratic states do not challenge the democratic peace thesis; in fact, they maintain that such cases actually support the DPP.

For example, Russett (1993) maintains that it is largely a reflection of the high level of democracy in the aggressive state that leaders resort to covert uses of force in the first place! He states that in such cases, "the normative restraints of democracy were sufficient to drive the operations underground amid circumstances when the administration otherwise might well have undertaken an overt intervention" (p. 124). For him, "When a democracy does use or threaten to use force against another, it will be at a target that is perceived to be unstably democratic" (p. 123). But, even Weart (1998)—a fellow proponent of the DPP—acknowledges that perceptions of the stability of a state or its democratic character often rest on one's perception of the people who govern that state, especially when they are viewed as culturally inferior. For example, in considering Eisenhower's overthrow of the Arbenz regime in Guatemala, he probes, "Could democracy be maintained among people who had been mired for centuries in ignorance and subservience, a nation moreover composed largely of 'primitive' peasants with dark skins? The sad history of Latin politics combined with racist prejudices to paint a picture of natives prone to anarchy and easily misled by scoundrels" (p. 222).

While in some ways more nuanced in his treatment of the impact of racism on the foreign policies of democratic states as compared to Russett (1993), Weart (1998) is even more imaginative in the rationalization he offers to reconcile the use of covert force by democratic states against other democracies with the DPP. Simply put, he argues that this type of covert action usually occurs when undemocratic subcultures ascend within the foreign policy hierarchy of democratic states such as occurred during the Nixon administration in the United States. Weart suggests that during that time "there was a symmetry between the U.S. government's actions in Chile and its actions at home. In precisely these years Nixon also secretly dispatched agents to molest U.S. citizens, under the conviction that his opponents were aiding the advance of Communism. . . . Subversion in Chile was no departure for an administration that condoned breaking into the offices of political rivals in Washington itself" (p. 227). In such a context "diplomacy, in the traditional sense of exchanges of notes between envoys, was beside the point. Suspicious leaders turned less to diplomats than to corporations, intelligence agencies, and military units. It is no contradiction to the thesis that political culture affects negotiations, *but exactly in accordance with it,* that the resulting 'diplomacy' was in a style far from cooperative. . . . One side, ambiguous in its democracy, is branded an enemy by *leaders who are already abnormally repressive of similar opponents at home"* (pp. 228–229, emphasis added).

What is so striking about these arguments and the aspect of them that informs our analysis of democracy and imperialist wars, is how DPP advocates rarely turn their lens to focus critically on the quality or extent of democracy of the Western state using covert action. Instead they focus on or challenge only the democratic standing of the victimized state. For example, even as Weart maintains that "undemocratic" elements gained influence in the United States in such a way as to affect U.S. foreign policy toward certain democracies, these represent for him, at most, "a limited deviation from democratic principles" and one that is evident "on both sides" (p. 229). Russett (1993: 124) argues that in these cases democratic restraints "were strong enough to forestall open military action, but not strong enough to prevent a secret operation or to stop it belatedly." Weart does not seem to reflect on— or fully appreciate—his contention that "leaders who are already abnormally repressive" probably are not practicing democratic norms. Likewise, Russett does not seem to consider the possibility that states that cannot constrain their leaders from the arbitrary and secret use of force abroad are not exercising the requisite level of executive constraint expected from a democracy.[6]

Frankly, as Gilbert (1999) and others have noted, perhaps states that permit leaders to prosecute covert warfare against other (democratic) states are not really democracies.[7] Similarly, I maintain that perhaps states that have racism as a central element of their state's domestic and foreign policies are not really democracies. Such a view has received relatively short shrift among DPP advocates—especially where the focus is on Western states in the postwar era. But such rhetorical sleight of hand evident when democratic peace scholars confront the issues of imperialism and racism among democratic states is really not surprising given the extent to which DPP advocates wax eloquently on—and largely root their theoretical models in—the democratic pronouncements of theorists who clearly espoused white supremacism—especially Kant and Wilson, while remaining strangely silent on these authors' racist views and the implications of these views for the arguments they put forward. I maintain that democratic peace theorists interested in theoretical consistency would do better to reflect less on racist idealists such as Kant and Wilson and more on nonracist ones such as DuBois ([1903] 1961; [1947] 1987), who wrote laboriously on both the merits of democracy and the hypocrisy of its Euro-American form guided by a white supremacism that justified, in particular, the denial of the rights of citizens of African and Asian extraction, domestically, and the colonization and subjugation of Africans and Asians abroad. Martin Luther King ([1968] 1986) made a similar point repeatedly with respect to U.S. foreign policy during the Vietnam War, which he viewed as an imperialist extension of the country's racist domestic policies toward its black minority. This rather obvious relationship between a state's domestic and foreign policy—a centerpiece of classical liberalism—is too often minimized in the neoliberal preoccupation with the sanguine impact of democratic domestic politics on a state's foreign policy. But, when ignored, this relationship leaves the democratic peace thesis untethered to the reality that it seeks to explain: namely, how democracies that ostensibly recognize freedom as a basic human right pursue the subjugation of other people and the prosecution of war against them in order to effectuate their subjugation. The theoretical inconsistency evaporates once we appreciate that the "founding fathers" of the democratic peace advocated a Herrenvolk democracy. And following the logic of classical liberal theses of world politics, one would expect a Herrenvolk democracy to possess a Herrenvolk foreign policy. It is this type of white racist democracy that we observe in the West's imperialism. Therefore, we would expect that Western democracies are more likely to fight extrastate wars.

In addition, while most Western states are democratic today, there are many non-Western democracies as well, and most of those states have not been possessed of the dualism that has legitimized the subjugation of nonwhite, non-Western peoples while simultaneously promoting freedom as a basic human right. For such states there is very little of the imperialist spirit or the decisionmaking rationale to justify it. Therefore, for democratic states, in general, we would not expect heavy involvement in extrastate wars. Instead, we expect Western states to be more heavily involved in extrastate wars, while the obverse should obtain for non-Western states. Before analyzing the correlates of extrastate wars to determine if the patterns outlined above are consistent with the empirical evidence, in the next section I provide a more detailed description of extrastate wars and discuss why they have rarely been examined in DPP research.

Previous Research on the DPP
and Extrastate War

Extrastate War

Extrastate wars are defined by the Correlates of War (COW) project as armed conflicts between the military forces of sovereign states and nonstate political entities, such as colonies, suzerainties, and territorial possessions (Small and Singer, 1982).[8] That is, they are fought between the armed forces of recognized states and those of an adversary who "is not a member of the interstate system but is an independent nonmember of the system or a nonindependent national entity" (p. 81). In the past these have been primarily—though not exclusively—the West's colonial and imperial wars such as the French colonial war in Algeria, the British colonial war in Kenya, or Portugal's colonial wars in Mozambique, Angola, and Guinea-Bissau; but they also include such non-Western armed conflicts as China's intervention in Tibet, Ethiopia's intervention in Eritrea, or India's involvement in the First Kashmir and Hyderabad Wars.[9] Scholars have ignored systematically analyzing these wars for various reasons, not least of which is the relative inattention of quantitatively oriented Western scholars of world politics to systematically examine third world armed conflicts, in general. This marginalization of third world politics has been heightened under the present hegemony of neorealist analyses that often assume that world politics is synonymous with major power politics (e.g., Waltz, 1979).[10]

A less critical view of the alleged "empirical neglect" of extrastate wars by quantitative theorists focuses on the problems related to the operationalization and delineation of extrastate wars that may discourage scholars from including them in studies of international war, in general, and the DPP, in particular. For example, a major point of contention with respect to the extrastate war dataset is that Small and Singer (1982) do not include the battle deaths of the nonstate entities in these data. The result is that the extrastate war data are, as Vasquez (1993: 27) puts it, "woefully incomplete" for the nonstate entities. Small and Singer's (1982) rationale was that "while such deaths did not go unmourned, they often went uncounted or unrecorded"; therefore, they concluded that the figures related to the battle deaths of troops of nonstate entities were quite dubious. Concerns about the reliability of the battle death figures of the primarily non-European disputants in extrastate wars led Small and Singer (1982) to require that extrastate wars sustain 1,000 battle deaths *each* year in order to be included in their dataset, while interstate wars had only to attain a 1,000 battle death threshold over the entire course of the war in order to be included in the dataset.

Vasquez (1993: 27) opines that "the discrepancy in the quality of [the interstate war and extrastate war datasets] may be seen as part of the historical legacy of Western imperialism and racism that simply did not regard non-Western groups as civilized or as human beings equal to whites." Therefore, "it is not unfair to assume that such attitudes played some role in accounting for the fact that Western nations did not bother to record in any systematic way the fatalities sustained by nonnational groupings in imperial wars of conquest or pacification" (p. 27). Further, Vasquez is correct that "this historical legacy" compelled Small and Singer (1982: 56) to make "certain 'practical' data-collection decisions which resulted in the discrepancy in the two data sets." Nevertheless, it is clear that the COW coding rules "have the effect of making some people's deaths and wars not count, which is just the way the West viewed these conflicts in comparison to their own 'real' wars" (Vasquez, 1993: 27–28).

One may contend that Small and Singer's (1982) codings reflect an ideological bias; however, such a view ignores the fact that the inconsistency in the extrastate war data reflects more the biases in the recording of history and the compilation of governmental records than it does the ideological predisposition of the COW authors. Small and Singer were "faced with the fact that others, less objective than they . . . managed to shape and control the past so that part of the record is not easily reconstructed." Facing such constraints, "the only alternative would have been to make crude estimates, and they were unwilling to do this because it would have greatly reduced the scientific reliability of their data" (p. 28). Nonetheless, Small and Singer (1982)—while certainly conscious of their own coding rules—did not discourage the inclusion of extrastate wars in analyses of international war, although they conducted separate analyses of each type of war in their studies. In addition, although the decision not to include the battle deaths of nonstate entities has generated some contentious debate (Duvall, 1976), with respect to the analysis of the DPP, one is reminded that the inconsistencies in the coding rules of extrastate wars as compared to interstate wars has a greater impact on evaluations of the *duration* or *severity* of war instead of *involvement* in war, which is the focus of most DPP research.[11] Therefore, the extrastate war data are quite useful—and reliable—for analyses into the factors associated with a state's involvement in international war—the primary point of focus of research on the monadic DPP.

Nonetheless, it is understandable that one may be more confident of inferences drawn from the interstate war dataset than from the extrastate war dataset and that—depending on the research question—scholars should be careful to analyze these wars separately. However, the clearest reason for including these wars in our analyses is that the causes of extrastate wars may be dramatically different from the causes of interstate wars; therefore, generalizations about interstate war may not apply to extrastate wars and, by extension, to international wars conceived more broadly. Since most democratic peace researchers draw almost exclusively on interstate wars to inform their analyses, then the democratic peace may only apply to one type of international war.[12] It is not only the quantitative research on the democratic peace that has ignored extrastate wars; much of the data-based scholarship on international war, in general, has focused on interstate war as opposed to extrastate war. Further, drawing almost exclusively on interstate wars to inform their analyses of international war, democratic peace theorists may incorrectly assume that the absence of interstate war is synonymous with international peace when in fact it may only suggest the *decreased* likelihood of one type of international war (e.g., interstate war), which may coincide with an *increased* likelihood of a different type of international war (e.g., extrastate war).

Moreover, there appears to be an ethical inconsistency in the rationale by which democratic peace advocates laud the peacefulness of democracies, in general, and Western democracies, in particular, when by excluding extrastate wars from their analyses they are able to ignore the loathsome record of Western involvement in colonial and imperial wars. Incredibly, some "democratic peace" researchers accomplish this feat at the same time that they applaud the impact of peace-generating "norms" in inhibiting democratic states from the pursuit of bellicose foreign policies (e.g., Russett, 1993; Weart, 1998). If there are any consistent examples where such "norms" did not appear to inhibit Western democracies, it is in the lengthy and quite bloody record of the West's colonial and imperial wars (e.g., see Rodney, 1980; Hochschild, 1998). Therefore, a focus on extrastate wars is important not only for empirical reasons but for ethical reasons as well.

The DPP and Extrastate Wars

Beyond the early studies that included extrastate wars in their analysis of the DPP, two more recent studies of the democratic peace have not ignored extrastate wars. For example, Benoit's (1996: 645, n.12) study explicitly examines the monadic DPP, and although he does not offer any examination of extrastate wars, specifically, he insists that the inclusion of such wars in his analysis of the monadic DPP does not substantively affect his main finding that democratic states are more peaceful, in general, than nondemocracies. He finds that "democracies fought fewer wars *on average* than less-free regimes" from 1960 to 1980 (emphasis in original). However, as noted in Chapter 3, Benoit's study is not without problems, which seriously compromise the inferences about the monadic DPP that we can draw from it. For example, his findings are limited to a small sample of wars from 1960 to 1980, which ignores several wars involving democratic states since the end of World War II, which are included in the present analysis, such as the Korean War, the Sinai War, the Falklands/Malvinas War, the Lebanese War, and the Gulf War; therefore, it is likely that Benoit's findings are skewed by its limited temporal focus. In my estimation, Benoit's findings are probably heavily influenced by the negative relationship between democracy and war involvement during the period from 1973 to 1980 (as revealed in Chan's 1984 study), especially from 1976 to 1980 (as revealed in Rummel, 1983). In addition, his sensitivity tests with respect to the inclusion of extrastate wars in his analysis of the monadic DPP show that these wars do, in fact, affect—if only marginally—the significance of the relationship between democracy and war involvement (see his note 12). Therefore, it is not unrealistic to expect that the relationship between democracy and extrastate war involvement is either not as strong as that between democracy and interstate war or possibly even different in terms of direction (i.e., whether it is positive or negative). It makes sense, then, to explore the relationship between democracy and extrastate war involvement explicitly, in order to determine the extent to which a monadic DPP obtains.

In a later study, Gleditsch and Hegre (1997) included extrastate wars in their analysis of the DPP at the state, dyad, and system levels. They concluded, inter alia, that the inclusion of extrastate wars in their analysis of the DPP was problematic because it exaggerated the relative *war-proneness of democracies* "because nondemocratic opponents in colonial wars are not counted as separate actors" (p. 293). That is, since the state participants in extrastate wars are assumed to be predominantly democratic and regime data are not recorded for the nonstate participants, which are assumed to be predominantly nondemocratic, then the authors assume that findings regarding involvement in extrastate wars will be skewed against the DPP; however, this conclusion is flawed for several reasons. First, it largely disregards the involvement of nondemocratic states in extrastate wars such as China's intervention in Tibet, Ethiopia's intervention in Eritrea, and Iraq's attacks against its Kurds. In fact, Gleditsch and Hegre's (1997) perspective runs counter to Benoit's (1996) argument that his results from analyzing the DPP for extrastate wars "seem to be caused by the extrasystemic [extrastate] war states being highly *non-democratic*" (p. 645, emphasis added). Second, Gleditsch and Hegre (1997) seem to assume that because certain democratic states like Britain and France were heavily involved in extrastate wars that democracies, in general, are more likely to be involved in such conflicts; however, this is an empirical question and one that should not be assumed out of hand. Their logic in disregarding extrastate wars on these grounds is similar to the following: Since the majority of the imperial or colonial powers in the postwar era were democratic, and we know that imperial or colonial powers are more prone to be involved in extrastate wars, then one should not focus on extrastate wars when examining the war-proneness of democratic states. This is similar to the argument that since the majority of the major powers (three of five) in the postwar era were democratic, and we know that major powers are more prone to be involved in interstate wars, then one should not focus on interstate wars when examining the war-proneness of democratic states. The latter is clearly unacceptable, and by analogy, so is the former.

Third, the fact that extrastate war data is not coded for regime type for the nonstate entities involved in the conflict does not preclude the use of these data in examining monadic DPP because the latter does not focus on the "democraticness" of nonstate entities but only on that of sovereign states. Therefore, the absence of regime data for entities that clearly are not sovereign states is not necessarily problematic and does not diminish our ability to determine the war-proneness of democratic and nondemocratic *states* in the system.[13] In addition, the bias against the DPP, which is assumed to result from the inclusion of extrastate wars, is overstated since both democracies and nondemocracies had the opportunity to involve themselves in extrastate wars. Therefore, the inclusion of extrastate wars in analyses of the monadic DPP is not only permissible but crucial to our understanding of the relationship between democracy and international war at the state level.

In sum, recent assessments of the monadic DPP, for the most part, have failed to include extrastate wars in their analyses. Therefore, they were not only unable to determine the relationship between democracy and extrastate war, specifically, but also unable to determine the relationship between democracy and international war, in general, since extrastate wars are an important class of international war. I intend to circumvent these problems by analyzing the DPP against the record of extrastate wars, specifically, and international wars, in general, for the postwar era from 1946 to 1992—the period within which the "democratic peace" is presumably most evident. In the following section, I discuss the research design before conducting the empirical analysis.

Research Design

Outcome Variables: The Onset of Extrastate and International War

In this chapter I utilize the same basic research design as was used in Chapter 3 with a few modifications. There are two outcome variables: (1) extrastate war involvement, which is a dichotomous variable that is coded as "1" if the state becomes involved in an extrastate war in that year and "0" if it does not; and (2) international war, which is a dichotomous variable that is coded as "1" if the state becomes involved in either an extrastate war or an interstate war in that year and "0" if it does not. War data are from Singer and Small (1994).[14] The predictor and control variables are the same as those listed in Chapter 3, so they are not repeated here. Also, as in the previous chapter, a multivariate logistic regression model is estimated to evaluate the monadic level DPP (Menard, 1995). The basic model takes the following form: $\Pr(\textit{Extrastate War}_{i,t}) = 1 / (1 + e^{-Z_i})$. $\Pr(\textit{Extrastate War}_{i,t})$ is the probability that the outcome variable (the onset of extrastate war) equals 1; and Z_i is the sum of the product of the coefficient values (β_i) across all observations of the predictor variables ($X_{i,t}$), that is: $\beta_0 + \beta_1\textit{Democracy} + \beta_2\textit{Major power} + \beta_3\textit{Transition} + \beta_4\textit{Militarization} + \beta_5\textit{Development} + \beta_6\textit{Downturn} + \beta_7\textit{Civilization}_i \ldots n\text{--}1$.[15]

Findings

Before analyzing the impact of democracy on extrastate wars, I will examine the impact of democracy on international war in general in order to better contrast the results across the different types of armed conflict. Turning to the findings reported in the first column of Table 4.1 (Equation 1), which focus on international war as the outcome variable, I find that major power, poor, militarized, and Islamic states are more likely to be involved in international war. These results are consistent with previous research on state level factors in international war (see Geller and Singer, 1998) and also provide support for aspects of Huntington's (1996) thesis. Only the coefficients for *Transition*, *Downturns*, and *Western* are not significant. As in the case of interstate war, democracies are *more likely* to be involved in international war. These results contradict the monadic level DPP across an even broader range of warfare than that demonstrated by the findings in Chapter 3 while supporting and expanding on Small and Singer's (1976), Chan's (1984), and Weede's (1984) earlier findings that refuted the monadic DPP.

When I include the complete list of civilization variables (with African states as the baseline) in Equation 2, the greater war-proneness of democratic states is less evident. Although most of the significant variables in Equation 1 remain so in Equation 2, the inclusion of the remaining civilization variables reduces the significance of *Democracy*, although the coefficient remains positive. In addition, it's clear that *Islamic* states are not singularly bellicose but that *Hindu* (mainly India) and *Other* (mainly Israel) states are also more prone to become involved in war, which suggests that Huntington's (1996) assertion of the singular bellicosity of Islamic states is misplaced, at best. The findings with respect to the civilization variables in Equation 2 largely reflect the heightened degree of interstate war in South Asia and the Middle East since World War II.

In an attempt to determine the war-proneness of particular democracies, I also disaggregated the democracy variable by civilization membership, as was done in Chapter 3, and found that only the *Hindu* democracies (e.g., India) were significantly more likely to be involved in war. In sum, the findings from Equations 1–2 either refute or fail to substantiate the monadic DPP. It seems clear that, controlling for a host of political, economic, and cultural factors, democracies are not more

Table 4.1   Logistic Regression of Factors Associated with International War, 1946–1992

	Equation 1	Equation 2
Democracy	.033* (.018)	.01 (.02)
Major power	2.18*** (.29)	2.32*** (.33)
Development	−.53*** (.17)	−.41** (.19)
Militarization	1.36*** (.27)	1.31*** (.27)
Transition	−.04 (.68)	−.03 (.05)
Downturn	.15 (.25)	.07 (.25)
Buddhist	—	−.59 (.89)
Hindu	—	1.41* (.79)
Islamic	.86*** (.24)	1.09** (.56)
Japanese	—	−2.96 (9.69)
Latin American	—	−.31 (.69)
Orthodox	—	−1.27 (.97)
Other	—	1.30** (.65)
Sinic	—	.57 (.65)
Western	.02 (.35)	.25 (.66)
Constant	−1.44** (.59)	−1.76** (.86)
−2 log likelihood	913.57	892.25
N	4,727	4,727
X^2	93.57***	114.89***

Note: Standard errors are in parentheses; all p-values are estimated using two-tailed tests.
*p ≤ .10, **p ≤ .05 level, ***p ≤ .01 level

peaceful than nondemocracies, and there is some evidence that democracies are more likely to become involved in international war.

One might contend that the apparent refutation of the monadic level DPP results from my combining extrastate and interstate wars, which unfairly stacks the deck against the DPP as suggested by Gleditsch and Hegre (1997). If that's so, then analyzing international and extrastate wars separately should give us a more accurate picture of the relationship between democracy and war. Therefore, I reestimated Equation 1 from Table 4.1 using only extrastate war involvement as the outcome variable. If Gleditsch and Hegre (1997) are correct that the inclusion of extrastate wars biases the results against the DPP, then we would expect the findings to show that democratic states were *more likely* to be involved in extrastate wars since this would largely account for the positive relationship between democracy and international war evinced in Equations 1–2. However, the findings from Equation 3 in Table 4.2 clearly indicate that the more democratic regimes are, in fact, *less likely* to be involved in extrastate wars. That is, the findings provide evidence of a monadic level democratic peace with respect to extrastate wars. This finding challenges Gleditsch and Hegre's (1997) contention that the inclusion of extrastate wars in analyses of the DPP unduly biases the results against the DPP. What is evident is that since democracies are less likely to be involved in extrastate wars, including extrastate wars in analyses of the DPP can only increase the prospect that one will uncover support for the DPP. One is left with the conclusion that the reason the overall relationship between democracy and *international war* is positive is not because of heightened democratic state involvement in *extrastate wars* (which is not borne out empirically) but because individual democracies are more prone to fight *interstate* wars, as was demonstrated in Chapter 3.

Turning to the other relationships revealed by the empirical findings, it appears that while militarization and political transitions are less important in extrastate wars, economic downturns are positively and significantly associated with these wars. The latter finding provides greater support for Russett's (1990) more modest results and also provides some support for economic theses of imperialist wars, more generally. Given that I include data on imperial and colonial wars in the present analysis, Russett's arguments may be more salient in these extrastate conflicts. Also, while *Islamic* states are significantly involved in extrastate wars—as was the case with international wars—

Table 4.2   Logistic Regression of Factors Associated with Extrastate War, 1946–1992

	Equation 3	Equation 4
Democracy	−.11**	−.16**
	(.05)	(.07)
Major power	3.62***	4.78***
	(.64)	(1.12)
Development	−1.22***	−1.24***
	(.38)	(.41)
Militarization	.68	1.27*
	(.62)	(.70)
Transition	−.11	−.12
	(.09)	(.09)
Downturn	.91*	1.02**
	(.48)	(.51)
Buddhist	—	−7.05
		(25.11)
Hindu	—	−7.06
		(42.71)
Islamic	1.22*	.14
	(.66)	(.93)
Japanese	—	−1.89
		(70.99)
Latin American	—	−.23
		(1.29)
Orthodox	—	−8.69
		(29.87)
Other	—	.81
		(1.24)
Sinic	—	2.51
		(1.56)
Western	3.42***	2.04*
	(.82)	(1.16)
Constant	−6.96***	−4.99**
	(1.66)	(2.09)
−2 log likelihood	233.28	225.25
N	4,727	4,727
X^2	57.58***	65.62***

Note: Standard errors are in parentheses; all p-values are estimated using two-tailed tests.
*p ≤ .10, **p ≤ .05 level, ***p ≤ .01 level

Western statehood is even more strongly associated with involvement in extrastate wars.

The finding for the *Democracy* and *Western* variables support the earlier contention that while individual democracies are less prone to extrastate war involvement, *Western* states are more prone to experience them. These findings are consistent with what one would intuit from the experience of Western state involvement in imperialist and anticolonial wars in the Cold War era.

Equation 4 examines the monadic DPP for extrastate wars controlling for the full range of civilization membership as was done previously in Table 4.1 (Equation 2) with respect to international war. The results from Equation 4 are generally consistent with those of Equation 3 except that the coefficient for *Militarization* is significant. In addition, the findings from Equation 4 challenge Huntington's view that Islamic states are more war-prone; in the case of extrastate wars, Western states are much more bellicose than those of any other civilization. Disaggregating the democracies by civilization type, I found, not surprisingly, that the Western democracies, in particular, are the most bellicose with respect to extrastate war involvement.[16] This latter finding is particularly interesting in light of the fact that since democratic enlargement, which is aimed at expanding the community of democratic states, became a centerpiece of post–Cold War Western grand strategy, there has been a heightened degree of encouragement of a "democratic crusade" on the part of Western states in an effort to promote peace abroad (see Diamond, 1992; Layne, 1994).[17] In light of the imperatives of the democratic enlargement strategy, one should be particularly concerned about the (extrastate) war-proneness of Western states. In this respect, the findings from Equation 6 are quite disconcerting because unlike democratic states, in general, which have a reduced likelihood of extrastate war involvement, the Western democratic states—the prospective missionaries for "democratic peace"— have an increased likelihood of fighting extrastate wars.[18]

The findings reveal a hitch in the "democratic peace" with regard to extrastate wars insofar as democracies, in general, are *less war-prone* but Western states—including Western democracies—are *more war-prone*. While supporting the monadic DPP for extrastate wars, the findings suggest that Western democracies are poor candidates for spreading "democratic peace" since they are the most war-prone of all the democratic states. It follows that a democratic enlargement strategy led by the West may be the political equivalent of sending foxes to build better henhouses.

At this point, some may question the results insofar as they rely on a continuous operationalization of the regime variable when a dichotomous one may be more suitable; however, as noted previously, indicators of democracy in research on the DPP should be intervally scaled; nevertheless, I reestimated the basic equations using a dichotomous measure of democracy to test the sensitivity of the findings to a different specification of the primary predictor variable. The results of these analyses are reported in Equation 5 in Table 4.3.

Using the dichotomous specification of *Democracy*, I find a positive but nonsignificant relationship between coherent democracy and the likelihood of international wars (using coherent autocracies as a baseline and controlling for anocracies and the other variables in the original model). The nonsignificant finding raises concerns regarding whether it is the impact of interstate or extrastate wars—the two types of wars constituting international war—that is driving the relationship between democracy and international war into nonsignificance. Therefore, Equation 6 and Equation 7 are reestimations of Equation 5 using interstate and extrastate wars as the respective outcome variables. The findings from Equation 6 indicate that coherent democracies are significantly *more likely* to be involved in interstate wars—the class of wars most clearly associated with the DPP, which replicates the findings in Chapter 3.

By contrast the results from Equation 7 reveal that coherent democracies are significantly *less likely* to be involved in extrastate war (as are anocracies), which is consistent with Equations 3 and 4, which employ a continuous measure of regime type. Therefore, except in the case of international wars—where the coefficient for *Democracy* is positive but nonsignificant—the findings using the continuous specification of *Democracy* are largely borne out when using a dichotomous specification of *Democracy*. It appears that the combination of the positive and significant relationship between democracy and *interstate* war involvement and the negative and significant relationship between democracy and *extrastate* war involvement drives the overall relationship between democracy and international war involvement to nonsignificance.

In addition, I also conducted separate analyses excluding more contentious extrastate war cases (namely, the Philippine-Moro War,

Table 4.3   Logistic Regression of Factors Associated with International War, Using a Dichotomous Democracy Measure, 1946–1992

	Equation 5 (International War)	Equation 6 (Interstate War)	Equation 7 (Extrastate War)
Democracy	.49 (.31)	.89*** (.33)	−1.51** (.79)
Anocracy	.06 (.28)	.44 (.30)	−2.26** (1.07)
Major power	2.17*** (.29)	1.93*** (.35)	3.50*** (.64)
Development	−.52*** (.17)	−.32* (.19)	−1.40*** (.39)
Militarization	1.33*** (.27)	1.40*** (.30)	.85 (.61)
Transition	−.04 (.05)	−.03 (.06)	−.10 (.09)
Downturn	.16 (.25)	−.12 (.29)	.93** (.48)
Islamic	.84** (.24)	.86*** (.27)	1.23** (.66)
Western	.08 (.35)	−.64 (.40)	3.33*** (.83)
Constant	−1.71*** (.58)	−1.71*** (.63)	−5.79*** (1.51)
−2 log likelihood	914.58	722.41	229.95
N	4,727	4,727	4,727
X^2	92.56***	67.09***	60.91***

Note: Standard errors are in parentheses; all p-values are estimated using two-tailed tests.
*$p \le .10$, **$p \le .05$ level, ***$p \le .01$ level

1972–1980; the Kurdish Autonomy War, 1974–1975; and the Ogaden, 1976–1983, and Tigrean, 1978–1991, wars), and including the Namibian War (1975–1988), in order to determine the sensitivity of the relationships uncovered in the general findings. The results were consistent with those reported in Tables 4.1–4.3. All told, the findings support the monadic level DPP for extrastate wars; however, they reveal that the Western democracies, in particular, are especially prone to become involved in extrastate wars.

Discussion

The relationship between democracy and extrastate wars reflects the ambivalence of the DPP with respect to the likelihood of democratic imperialism. The findings reveal that democratic regimes are less prone to extrastate wars than nondemocratic regimes; however, Western states—including the Western democracies—are more likely to be involved in extrastate wars. One may argue that the greater probability of war involvement on the part of democratic states may reflect the greater adherence of democratic states to collective security requirements or their greater willingness to support democratic allies in ongoing wars; however, in the case of the extrastate wars involving Western states, it is clear that the Western states fighting in these wars were hardly the "victims" or "targets" in their predominantly imperial or colonial wars.

The finding that democracies, in general, are less likely to become involved in extrastate wars may provide some comfort for DPP advocates, but this finding must be tempered by the realization that the anti-colonial processes that generated many of the extrastate wars are largely by-products of a colonial era that is past. Therefore, the impact of democracy on international war today, and for the near future, will primarily be manifest in interstate wars and MIDs; in this type of international conflict, democracies are significantly more conflict-prone than nondemocracies.

One may counter that since extrastate wars are not exclusively colonial or anticolonial wars, then it is not clear that their era is completely past. In fact, extrastate wars are evident today in the conflicts in East Timor and Tibet. There are also several extrastate hot spots in Northern Ireland and the Basque region of Spain that may erupt in the new century within democratic states. The present conflict in the Middle East between Israel and the incipient but not fully established Palestinian state also continues to smolder. Moreover, some analysts argue that this type of war is likely to be even more prevalent in the post–Cold War era (e.g., Holsti, 1996; Huntington, 1996; Kaldor, 1999). Regardless, even given such developments, the greater war-proneness of Western democracies with respect to extrastate wars suggests that policies to prevent these wars should rely on the engagement of non-Western democracies, which are less prone to fight extrastate wars and, therefore, appear to be better suited as mediators of extrastate disputes.

Wedding the findings from the previous chapters with those report-ed here, it appears that by ignoring extrastate wars, scholars have failed to appreciate—as Vasquez (1993) warned—that the absence of *inter-state war* does not preclude the fighting of international wars. To be sure, the processes that give rise to interstate and extrastate wars seem to be very different. Clearly, the role of democracy in interstate and extrastate wars is different, with democracies more likely to fight the former and less likely to fight the latter. Nevertheless, either the appar-ent "democratic peace" in the case of extrastate wars is a by-product of a colonial era that is past, or, even if extrastate wars persist, the increased likelihood of Western democracies becoming involved in them does not inspire confidence in Western-led democratic enlarge-ment strategies as a means to ensure global peace and stability.

Conclusion

In this chapter, I examined the relationship between democracy and extrastate war through an explication of the role of imperialism in the democratic peace. The discussion of "liberal imperialism" led me to suspect that Western states should be more likely to pursue imperialist wars, while democracies, in general, should be less inclined to become involved in them. The findings revealed that democracies are indeed *less likely* to be involved in extrastate wars, but Western states are more likely to become involved in them. Interestingly, of all the democracies, I found that the Western democracies are *most likely* to be involved in extrastate wars. By including data on extrastate wars, I've also provid-ed a more inclusive test of the monadic DPP for international wars, in general. Controlling for a host of factors, I find that there is no signifi-cant relationship between democracy and international war, broadly conceived, which further contradicts the monadic DPP. The contrasting results of the impact of democracy on extrastate, interstate, and inter-national wars clearly indicate that democracy does not have a consis-tent impact—much less a consistent conflict-dampening impact—across the full range of international war.

The major research implications of the findings in this chapter are that scholars should include extrastate wars in their analyses of the DPP and not ignore them or assume that their correlates are identical to those of interstate wars. In addition, it is important to remember that if extrastate wars are not simply relics of a bygone colonial era, then scholarship on international war should delve into the causes of these wars in earnest in order to propose policies to reduce the likelihood of their recurrence. To be sure, it is highly likely that the number of nonstate political entities will increase in the upcoming years as communal groups become more successful at secession but not as effective in creating sovereign states. Nevertheless, international terrorist attacks such as occurred in the United States in September 2001 may result in full-scale war between targeted states and the host states of the terrorists, but these are more likely to result in interstate as opposed to extrastate wars. For example, the U.S.-led war in Afghanistan, which was initiated by a terrorist attack by a nonstate entity, may appear, for some, to be an extrastate war, but in actuality it is an interstate war (between the armed forces of the United States and its allies and those of the government of Afghanistan, the Taliban, and its allies), within an ongoing civil war (between the Taliban forces and those of the Northern Alliance). Similarly, conflicts emanating from efforts to counter narcoterrorism such as is ongoing in Colombia with the military and economic intervention of the Unites States are more likely to result in interstate rather than extrastate wars, but as in the previous case these are more likely to occur within the context of ongoing civil wars. With these types of situations in mind, there is ample reason to believe that the global reach of the Western democracies may encourage their continued high level of involvement in extrastate wars in the future as in the past.

As for policy implications, the findings suggest that the transformation of states in the present wave of democratization may decrease the likelihood that they become involved in extrastate wars while increasing the likelihood that they become involved in interstate war. Since democracy does not have a consistent effect on different types of international war, a policy such as democratic enlargement is likely to be ineffective at best and conflict-exacerbating at worst, since democracy reduces the likelihood of extrastate war but increases the likelihood of interstate war. All told, these findings seriously call into question foreign policy pursuits aimed at promoting democracy as a means of encouraging international peace.

Notes

1. For a critique of Oren's conclusions, see Maoz (1997: 182–191).

2. This view seems in marked contrast to Russett's more recent discussion of such matters (Russett and Starr, 2000: 111): "The transparency of democra-

cies, along with shared democratic norms and procedures, makes it nearly impossible for policymakers to dehumanize the people of another democracy through the manipulation of images of the other as the 'enemy.'"

3. Belgium registers +6 on the Polity III scale, which ranges from −10 to +10, for the relevant period in the nineteenth century while scoring between +6 and +10 for most of the twentieth century.

4. For an example of the egalitarian aspect of a traditional African society, see Thompson (1975: 63–64).

5. Russett (1993: 14) offers a straightforward rationale for his exclusion of "those 'colonial' wars fought for the acquisition of territory inhabited by 'primitive' people without recognized states, as practiced by nineteenth-century imperialism, or for the twentieth-century liberation of those people." He argues that since he is interested in "interstate" warfare, which requires that both entities are, in fact, states, these types of wars do not qualify for inclusion. He adds that "applying this definition may well display a Western cultural bias, but it is appropriate to the behavior of states which, in the period, also are defined as 'democratic' by the admittedly Western standards spelled out below." Beyond the obvious non sequitur Russett supplies as a justification (I'm sure a big problem was the availability of data for the nonstate entities, so it is understandable in that sense why he would not include analyses of these wars), he seems to have overlooked that in the same volume (chapter 5), he provides an analysis of the democratic peace in "nonindustrial societies"—not states, but "societies, each of which is a population that more or less contiguously inhabits a geographical area and speaks a language (or lingua franca) not normally understood by people in neighboring societies" (p. 99). With different definitions of warfare and democracy, he nonetheless proclaims the democratic peace vindicated with respect to this class of cases. In light of this, the rationale he provides for excluding extrastate wars, noted above, seems disingenuous. Moreover, his exclusion of extrastate wars implies that the behavior of democracies with respect to them is not inconsistent with the DPP. But this is an empirical question that Russett's research design cannot possibly address. Neither can any of the dyadic level studies that support the DPP mentioned previously. Interestingly, Small and Singer (1976), who both compiled the data on extrastate wars and also conducted the first longitudinal analysis of both monadic and dyadic versions of the DPP, did not exclude these wars from consideration in analyzing the conflict-proneness of democracies.

6. For a discussion of undemocratic policies in the United States during the Nixon regime, see Hersh (1983) and Summers (2000).

7. This is not meant as a knee-jerk reaction to the cases discussed above, but it actually emerges from the liberal theoretical underpinnings of the democratic peace thesis itself, which, as DPP advocates such as Kober (1994) have observed, maintains as a key element that democratic statehood is characterized by popular/civilian control of the military. The prosecution of covert wars circumvents the democratic process and in that way can be said to undermine democracy.

8. There is some inconsistency regarding the inclusion of "international-ized civil wars" in the extrastate war category. Although Small and Singer (1982: 52) list them as a "third type" of extrastate war, they include them only in the list of civil wars. Therefore, I do not include internationalized civil wars as extrastate wars in this study, and that seems to be consistent with the intent of the original COW authors (conversation with J. David Singer).

9. The list of extrastate wars (and the year they began) from the COW project for 1946–1992 include the following: Madagascan (1947); First Kashmir (1947); Malayan Rebellion (1948); Hyderabad (1948); Sino-Tibetan (1950); Kenya (1952); Algerian (1954); Cameroon (1955); Moroccan Independence (1953); Tibetan (1956); Kurdish (1961); Angola-Portugal (1961); Philippine-Moro (1972); Guinea/Bissau (1962); Mozambique (1964); Eritrean (1974); Kurdish Autonomy (1974); Tunisian Independence (1952); East Timor (1974); Western Sahara (1975); Ogaden (1976); and Tigrean (1978). For the complete list of extrastate and interstate wars see Singer and Small (1994).

10. Waltz (1979) argues, inter alia, that the behavior of the major powers as the oligarchic rulers of the system constitutes the core of international phe-nomena that scholars should focus on in explicating world politics.

11. Rummel's (1995) research is the exception in this regard.

12. In addition, since research on the success of democracies in interna-tional war did not include data on extrastate wars (e.g., Lake, 1992; Stam, 1996; Reiter and Stam, 1998a), one cannot state with confidence whether democracies are more likely to win their extrastate wars.

13. Nevertheless, one should not assume that all of the nonstate entities—especially during the imperial and colonial wars of the nineteenth and twenti-eth century—were not egalitarian.

14. There are forty-three international wars consisting of twenty-two interstate wars and twenty-one extrastate wars from 1946 to 1992.

15. Using the same diagnostics discussed in Chapter 3, I found the results robust with respect to autocorrelation.

16. I separately examined the bivariate relationships among the probabil-ity of extrastate war, *Democracy*, and *Western * Democracy*, which is the prod-uct of the two variables, *Western* and *Democracy*, respectively. The analyses revealed a nonsignificant relationship between *Democracy* and the probability of extrastate war but a positive and significant association between *Western * Democracy* and the probability of extrastate war. In order to determine the rel-ative war-proneness of Western democracies, I estimated an alternative model excluding *Democracy* and the nonsignificant civilization variables, which showed that the positive and significant relationship between *Western * Democracy* and the probability of extrastate war is robust.

17. While U.S. officials often championed democratic enlargement strat-egy while publicly shunning calls for a "democratic crusade" (e.g., Lake, 1993: 4), the interventionist imperative is implicit in the logic of the DPP because, as Layne (1994: 46) points out, if democracies are peaceful and nondemocracies

are not: "The conclusion is inescapable: the former will be truly secure only when the latter have been transformed into democracies, too."

18. Doubly troubling are Meernik's (1996: 391) findings that in the majority of cases, "regardless of the manner in which democratic change is measured, U.S. military interventions do not appear to lead to increased levels of democracy." Peceny (1999) maintains that only when military interventions are coupled with a clear commitment to democratic elections does U.S. military intervention lead to democratization in target states, but problems with his research design lead me to question his conclusions.

5

The Democratic Peace and Civil Wars

U

p to this point, we've examined the DPP with respect to international conflict; however, since 1945 most wars have occurred
within rather than *between* states, and most of these civil wars
have taken place in the former colonies of the imperial powers. As we
begin the twenty-first century, the violence in these postcolonial states is
among the most pressing problems in world politics, even as we experience an unprecedented period of peace among the former colonizers (i.e.,
the former colonial powers have not fought each other since World War
II). In this context, several theorists argue that there is a "democratic
peace" evident within this class of wars as well (e.g., Krain and Myers,
1997; Rummel, 1997). They maintain that the presence of democracy in
these states reduces their likelihood of experiencing civil war. In addition, analysts point out that postcolonial, or third world, states are the
most prone to civil war (Henderson and Singer, 2000). This perspective
draws heavily on the perception of the frailty of these states following
their independence due to institutional underdevelopment as a result of
colonization as well as the failure of postindependence political leadership to effectively integrate their societies into cohesive national entities.
Clearly, if the DPP is applicable to relations within states such that
democracy reduces the likelihood of civil wars, we should observe a
"domestic democratic peace" for the most civil war–prone states—the
postcolonial states of the third world. Previous work has not explicitly
tested the DPP for this specific group of states.

In this chapter, I examine the extent to which the DPP is evident
with respect to civil wars within postcolonial states. I begin with a gen-

eral discussion of the role of democracy in large-scale domestic conflict and outline previous findings on the DPP and civil wars. Since the discussion up to this point has centered on international phenomena, I provide a more detailed review of the theoretical arguments that attempt to explain the onset of civil war. Next, I present several propositions on the political, economic, and cultural factors that are most likely to give rise to civil wars. Following that, I evaluate the DPP on the likelihood of civil wars in postcolonial states in the postwar era. Finally, after presenting the findings, I discuss their implications for future research and policy.

The Democratic Peace and Civil War

A civil war is a sustained, violent conflict between the military forces of a state and insurgent forces composed mainly of citizens (or residents) of the state (Henderson, 1999b). Although there is a dearth of large-N, longitudinal, data-based studies of civil wars—as compared to those that focus on international wars—there have been many attempts to determine the correlates of the broader category of domestic political conflict, which is a rather diverse amalgam of civil strife ranging from protests, strikes, riots, plots, assassinations, coups d'état, to civil war. But civil war is distinct from other forms of domestic conflict in terms of objectives, the degree of coordination required for its successful prosecution, and its more protracted nature and level of destructiveness.[1] Gurr (1970) pointed out that the distinctiveness of civil war suggests that scholars should focus on it as a separate form of domestic conflict.[2] His concerns are understandable in light of the consistent findings that the correlates of different types of domestic conflict vary (Gurr, 1970; Gurr and Duvall, 1973; Hardy, 1979; Boswell and Dixon, 1990). For example, the presence of a democratic regime is associated with an increased likelihood of protests but a decreased likelihood of rebellions (Gurr and Lichbach, 1979). Similarly, while economic development reduces the likelihood of major domestic conflicts such as civil wars, it appears to increase the likelihood of lesser forms of domestic conflict such as protests, demonstrations, and strikes (Gurr and Duvall, 1973; Eichenberg et al., 1984).

The most straightforward applications of the democratic peace thesis to civil wars include Krain and Myers's (1997) study, which uncovered a negative relationship between democracy and civil war. Krain and Myers argued that their findings indicated that the DPP was applicable to intrastate wars as well as interstate wars. Similarly, Rummel's (1997) study uncovered evidence that democracy reduces "intense violence" within states, leading him to conclude that the DPP was applicable to the domestic sphere, as well. In fact, a review of the literature reveals that of the few large-N, longitudinal, data-based studies that focus specifically on civil wars, most of these argue in favor of the conflict-dampening impact of democracy, which is consistent with a domestic variant of the DPP. The theoretical argument for the domestic version of the DPP appears to be much more straightforward than those proffered as explanations of the international variant. For the most part, the domestic DPP claims that democracies are resistant to civil wars because they provide legitimate channels for dispute resolution that are absent from nondemocracies.

Just as evidence in favor of a domestic democratic peace was being uncovered, new findings indicated that the relationship between regime type and intrastate war was more complex than first understood. For example, several scholars argued that the conflict-dampening impact of democracy was not linear (e.g., Goemans, 1997; Hegre et al., 1997; Henderson and Singer, 2000). They agreed that democracies were less likely to experience civil wars because of their provision of legitimate channels to funnel dissent, but they also observed that due to their efficient use of political repression to stifle dissent, autocracies should also be less likely to experience civil war. The result was that an "autocratic peace" was just as likely as a "democratic peace." Hegre et al. (1997) and Henderson and Singer (2000) went further to assert that the most likely candidates for civil war were those states with intermediate regime types, "semidemocracies," or states that were neither full-fledged democracies nor full-fledged autocracies.[3] The semidemocracy thesis maintains that the relationship between democracy and civil war is negative and curvilinear, approximating an inverted U shape with both autocracies and democracies relatively less prone to civil war and semidemocracies the most prone to civil war.

The theoretical argument as to why semidemocracies are more prone to civil war rests on the assumption that they do not provide effective channels for the nonviolent resolution of dissent, while leaders of these states are not checked by institutional and popular constraints such as are found in full-fledged democratic regimes. Semidemocratic states also rarely possess the more expansive repressive machinery that full-fledged autocracies have at their disposal to deter insurgency. As for dissidents in semidemocracies, the demands that they make on the state are rarely effectively addressed through the limited (and often resource-strained) governmental channels, while at the same time they do not have to fear an overarching repressive state apparatus, which is usually absent. In this context, neither the potential for resolving conflict peacefully nor the threat of repression is sufficient to prevent insurgency. Prior to the establishment of full-fledged democracy (or without the repressive machinery of a full-fledged autocracy), semidemocratic states are beset by demands from dissidents who have both the opportunity and willingness to pursue insurgency.

Various examples throughout the postcolonial world bear out the relationship between intermediate levels of democracy and domestic conflict. For example, incidents of civil violence in India, according to Ganguly (1996: 144), "have been exacerbated in part by the success of India's democratic institutions." Increased access to education, technology, media, and grassroots political power by previously disenfranchised groups such as Muslims and "untouchables" has improved their relative standard of living. However, these successes have generated a backlash from segments of the Hindu community, most notably the right-wing Bharatiya Janata Party, which prior to coming to power accused the former government of "pampering" Muslims. Further, "despite the fact that 80 percent of India's population remains Hindu, zealous activists portrayed Hindus as fast becoming an endangered minority" (p. 146). In fact, "they painted an image of India buffeted in a sea of Muslim nations stretching from Algeria to Indonesia" (p. 146). The rise of insurgent violence in Kashmir since 1989 is tied to this "paradox of Indian democracy" (p. 151).

Africa seems to evince a "paradox of democracy" that might be even more problematic than that in South Asia. Clearly, Africa's civil wars have been among the world's worst, with those in Angola, Ethiopia, Mozambique, Rwanda, Somalia, Sudan, and Uganda each resulting in between 500,000 and 1,000,000 total casualties through battlefield losses or deaths from war-related famine and disease (Stedman, 1996: 237). Mazrui (1988: 181–186) observes that Africa's semidemocratic regimes often fall prey to insurgency. For example, Uganda's nascent democracy was terminated by the civil war in the summer of 1966; Nigeria's Third Republic was overturned by the civil violence of 1984; Burundi's civil war was precipitated by the assassination of its first democratically elected president; Angola's civil war was rekindled following the refusal of the insurgent UNITA forces to accept the outcome of internationally observed elections; and the recent civil war in Congo-Brazzaville began shortly after the country's first democratically elected president took office.

In order to test the applicability of the DPP to civil wars, it is important to contrast the linear DPP assumption with the nonlinear "semidemocracy" thesis. Although these arguments are not mutually exclusive, they point to very different dynamics in the relationship between democracy and large-scale conflict. For example, the linear DPP thesis recommends a clear policy for the prevention of civil war in postcolonial states: the promotion of democracy. On the other hand, the nonlinear semidemocracy thesis suggests that increased levels of democracy may actually lead to increased violence in postcolonial states. It also recognizes the awful truth that autocratic rule can reduce the likelihood of civil war through effective repression of dissent. Moreover, it counsels caution in the case of democratization and implies that efforts to promote democracy should ensure that the process result in the institutionalization of a full-fledged democracy, which is less likely to experience civil war, rather than a semidemocracy, which is most likely to experience civil war.

In this chapter, I'll examine the degree to which the DPP is applicable to civil wars by analyzing both theses to determine which one better captures the actual relationship between democracy and civil war in the postcolonial world. I utilize a research design that is a bit different from those used in the previous chapters that focused on international conflict. I also control for several variables that have not been used in the previous analyses. Including these political, economic, and cultural variables as controls will allow us to better capture the actual relationship between democracy and civil war and hopefully avoid spurious inferences. In the next section, I discuss several of these variables and their potential relationship to civil war before testing the main thesis of this chapter.

Research Design

Definition of Civil War

I use the COW project's operational definition of civil war as sustained military combat, primarily internal, resulting in at least 1,000 battle deaths per year, pitting central government forces against an insurgent force capable of effective resistance, determined by the latter's ability to inflict upon the government forces at least 5 percent of the fatalities that the insurgents sustain (Small and Singer, 1982: 210–220). The COW definition is useful in that it focuses on the three dimensions of civil war that are most clearly characteristic of this phenomenon: internality, types of participants, and effective resistance (pp. 210–218). It has been used in quantitative analyses of the phenomenon (Mason and Fett, 1996; Regan, 1996; Goemans, 1997; Collier, 1998; Collier and Hoeffler, 1998) as well as several case studies of civil war (e.g., Licklider, 1993).

Outcome Variable: The Onset of Civil War

I examine the DPP across cases of postcolonial civil wars from 1946 to 1992 beginning with the communist insurgency in China in 1946 and ending with the civil war in Angola in 1992. Following COW criteria, there have been fifty-three civil wars in this spatial-temporal domain. The unit of analysis is the state-year, which is the annual observation for each of the ninety postcolonial states in the dataset.[4] The outcome variable is the onset of civil war (*Civil war*) and is coded as "1" if a civil war began during the year and "0" if it did not; war data are from Singer and Small (1994).

Predictor Variables

The primary predictor variable, *Democracy*, is measured as the difference between the democracy and autocracy scores of the state, using the codings from the Polity III dataset (Jaggers and Gurr, 1996), and assumes values from -10 (most autocratic) to $+10$ (most democratic). This is identical to the monadic level variable used to estimate the DPP in Chapters 3 and 4.

Control Variables: Political, Economic, and Cultural Factors

It is also important to control for the various political, economic, and cultural factors that have been found to significantly affect the war-proneness of states in order to limit the likelihood of drawing spurious inferences from simple bivariate results. Moreover, since these controls have been shown to affect the likelihood of civil war, we need to deter-

mine the extent to which they vitiate the relationship between democracy and war, which is the central focus of our study. These variables
will serve as the control variables in the analysis of the domestic DPP.

Semidemocracy. Beginning with political factors, in order to test the
proposition that semidemocracies are more prone to civil wars, I
include a dichotomous variable, *Semidemocracy*, which equals 1 for
those cases where *Democracy* ranges from 0 to +5 and otherwise
equals 0. That is, the range of *Semidemocracy* is bounded by the non-
negative values of the difference between the state's democracy and
autocracy scores and a level below that of a "coherent democracy" on
the Polity III scale.

Economic development. Turning to economic factors, analysts have long
observed that a postcolonial state's level of economic development is a
strong predictor of its probability of experiencing civil war (Mullins,
1987; Findlay, 1996; Collier and Hoeffler, 1998). This relationship
reflects the commonly held view that the economic well-being of the
state is the primary responsibility of the political leadership. A populace
facing economic penury is likely to hold the sitting political regime
responsible for their hardship. The fragility of the postcolonial state's
economic system is often translated into instability for its political system as economically marginalized citizens provide fodder for insurgency. While more developed states have resources that can be distrib-
uted to disaffected groups to maintain their support of the status quo,
resource-strained postcolonial states often divert their limited revenue
into military spending, which has the dual impact of truncating economic development while also providing resources to the militarized
elements in the society that are often quite eager to usurp political
authority.

The conflict-dampening impact of economic development is evident throughout the postcolonial world. For example, Findlay (1996:
187) observes that in Southeast Asia, economic growth and effective
governance have led to a decline since the 1970s in internal armed conflict in Malaysia, Singapore, and Thailand while poor economic
growth, inter alia, in the Philippines and Burma has allowed their internal conflicts to persist. Further, he insists that targeted policies of
"shared growth" enabled governments to establish their legitimacy and
win public support by ensuring that economic development would benefit all major groups (p. 185), thereby reducing the likelihood of insur-

gencies. Although Huntington (1968) posited that the likelihood of stability and modernization was quite low in the developing world, several Southeast Asian countries have become more stable "while experiencing what may be the fastest rate of modernization in history" (Findlay, 1996: 185). Similarly, economic development in African states such as Botswana, as well as in several of the oil-rich states of the Middle East, have contributed to their greater stability. Empirical studies largely support the view that economic development provides a prophylactic against insurgency (Weede, 1981; Eichenberg et al., 1984; Muller and Weede, 1990; Hegre et al., 1997); therefore I expect that the greater a state's level of economic development, the lower its likelihood of civil war. *Development* is measured as the log of the ratio of the state's energy consumption to its total population.

Military spending. A state's level of military spending is an additional economic factor that is associated with the likelihood of civil war. Although high rates of military spending might appear to reflect a state's concern with its external security environment, most of the military spending in postcolonial states is not aimed at external enemies but at internal ones (real or imagined). In these "quasi-states" (Jackson, 1990), elites often suffer from an "insecurity dilemma" (Job, 1992) where they are more concerned with potential usurpation from disaffected elements within their society than with fears of external aggression. Leaders in these quasi-states hardly fear external aggression since international law (or major power or regional patronage) protects the sovereignty (i.e., juridical statehood) of their states. This is reflected in the fact that postcolonial states have experienced fewer than 20 percent of all interstate wars from 1946 to 1992, while experiencing well over 60 percent of all civil wars during that era. In such a context, elites often privilege their militaries in budgeting decisions (Gyimah-Brempong, 1989, 1992), but this may have a negative impact on investment and growth (Deger, 1986; Lebovic and Ishaq, 1987). Further, the opportunity costs associated with increased military spending often crowd out social welfare, health, and education expenditures that might benefit the civilian population. Although the literature on the "guns versus butter" argument is varied and often contradictory (see Chan, 1985, 1995), Heo's (1998) empirical analysis of data from eighty countries largely corroborates Frederickson and Looney's (1983: 637) findings that the opportunity costs of military spending are most evident in resource-constrained countries such as those found throughout the postcolonial world. It appears, then, that the social dislocations wrought from the privileging of the military—beyond the economic downturns associated with it—are likely to heighten domestic discontent and provide a breeding ground for insurgency. Therefore, I expect that the greater a state's level of military spending, the greater the likelihood of civil war. The military spending variable, *Milspending*, is measured as the log of the ratio of a state's military expenditures (in constant, 1990 U.S. dollars) to its total population. Data for both economic variables are from the COW Material Capabilities dataset (Singer and Small, 1995).

Cultural polarization. Beyond economic factors, Posen (1993: 328) insists that in situations where ethnic groups cannot rely on the central government to provide protection, a security dilemma writ small at the ethnic-group level emerges, from which "interethnic civil wars" are likely to result. This thesis received support from Kaufmann (1996) but was challenged by Mason and Fett's (1996: 561–562) finding of "no relationship between the ethnic basis of the conflict and likelihood of a settlement" in their analysis of fifty-seven civil wars from 1945 to 1992 and by Regan's (1996: 351) finding that "ethnic conflicts" are *more likely* to be resolved than "ideological" conflicts. Nevertheless, Findlay (1996: 175) suggests that many Southeast Asian conflicts (e.g., in Burma, Cambodia, and Vietnam) are driven by ethnoreligious factors, while Bronson (1996: 207–212) is less persuaded that ethnoreligious differences are at the heart of the conflicts in the Middle East and North Africa, such as those in Algeria, Yemen, Lebanon, or the West Bank or those involving Kurdish populations in Iran and Iraq. Sub-Saharan Africa has served as a veritable laboratory for the analysis of interethnic conflicts due largely to the dominant view that the culturally diverse African states are the most likely candidates for "ethno-political conflicts" (Gurr, 1994); nevertheless, there are competing findings on the relationship between cultural factors and civil wars in this region as well (see Barrows, 1976; Schlichte, 1994; Fearon and Laitin, 1996; Collier, 1998; Collier and Hoeffler, 1998).[5]

Collier (1998) and Collier and Hoeffler (1998) aver that the most likely candidates for civil war are those states that evince a polarization of their culture groups, where two relatively equal but distinct cultural groups account for most of a state's population.[6] Their basic contention is that coordinating insurgency is facilitated where rebels are bound by a common identity distinct from that of their adversaries, and common culture—especially common language—is assumed to provide a basis for such self-identification. Since heterogeneous societies are more likely to be fractionalized, they offer little prospect for successful insurgency, and culturally homogeneous states lack cultural fissures and thus face few if any cultural challengers. Therefore, I examine the extent to which cultural polarization of a state increases the likelihood of civil war. Cultural polarization, *Polar*, is a dummy variable that reflects the extent to which the distribution of a state's culture groups approximates a 50-50 split. Polarized states are those in which the sum of the squared percentage shares of the two largest cultural groups is at least 50 percent of the total population, with group B (the second largest group) having no less than half the population of group A (the largest group), and group C (the third largest group) having no more than half the population share of group B. Following these coding rules, states with distributions such as 50-50, 40-40-20, or 45-45-10 are polarized, while states with distributions such as 70-30 or 40-35-25-5 are not. Polarized states are coded "1" and those that are not are coded "0." The polarization measures are estimated using data for each state's language groups from the COW cultural composition dataset (Singer, 1995).[7]

Ethnopolitical conflict. In addition, since Gurr (1994) suggests that the presence of certain types of "politicized ethnic groups" or "ethno-political groups" is associated with domestic conflict, a useful measure of the extent to which cultural factors are associated with civil wars should focus on the impact of these groups on the likelihood of insurgency. Therefore, I examine the extent to which the presence of ethnopolitical groups increases the likelihood of civil war. In their study of "minorities at risk," Gurr and Harff (1994: 190) define ethnopolitical groups as "ethnic groups that have organized to promote their common interests," and it is these groups that engage in "ethno-political conflict." There are four types of ethnopolitical groups; among them, ethnonationalists and communal contenders are most often associated with conflict (the other two groups are "ethnoclasses" and "indigenous peoples"). Gurr (1994: 355, 360) contends that "of the 233 politicized communal groups included in the Minorities at Risk study, eighty-one pursued ethnonational objectives; their conflicts were on average more intense than those in which other issues were manifest and increased markedly in numbers and magnitude from the 1950s to the 1980s." Cultural contenders were also involved in a high degree of ethnopolitical conflict, according to Gurr (1994: 354–355). Therefore, our second cultural variable, *Ethnopolitical*, is a dummy variable that is coded "1" for those postcolonial states that contain either ethnonationalists or communal contenders in the 1990s as reflected in the Minorities at Risk dataset, and is coded "0" for states that do not.

Region. I also construct three dummy variables *(Africa, Asia,* and *Middle East)* to designate the location of the postcolonial states in our study so that we can account for the impact of region on the likelihood of civil war.

Data Analysis

A multivariate logistic regression model is estimated to evaluate the propositions. The logistic regression model takes the following form: $Pr(Civil\ War_{i,t}) = 1 / (1+ e^{-Z_i})$ where $Pr(Civil\ War_{i,t})$ is the probability that the outcome variable (the onset of civil war) equals 1; and Z_i is the sum of the product of the coefficient values (β_i) across all observations of the predictor variables $(X_{i,t})$, that is: $\alpha + \beta_1 Democracy + \beta_2 Semidemocracy + \beta_3 Development + \beta_4 Milspending + \beta_5 Polar + \beta_6 Ethnopolitical + \beta_7 Asia + \beta_8\ Middle\ East.$[8]

Findings

The results from the application of the DPP to postcolonial civil wars are reported in Table 5.1.[9] The findings indicate that there is a positive and barely significant relationship between democracy and the probability of civil war, but this result may be due to specification error reflecting the attempt to capture a nonlinear process using a linear specification. I test this supposition by using a quadratic specification of the democracy variable, which requires that I add the square of the democracy variable to the model. If the semidemocracy thesis holds, I would expect an inverted U relationship between democracy and civil war, and this would be represented by a positive coefficient for the democracy variable and a negative coefficient for the squared democracy variable. This is exactly what is found in Equation 2; therefore, I can be more confident that the quadratic specification is the correct one. At this point, I can explicitly test the semidemocracy thesis using *Semidemocracy* instead of the two democracy variables, which provides us with a more parsimonious test of the thesis. The findings for this model (Equation 3) reveal that *Semidemocracy* is significantly associated with an increased likelihood of civil war, which is consistent with recent studies on the impact of regime type on civil war, as noted earlier. Of the semidemocracies, Indonesia was the most war-prone, having been the only semidemocratic state to experience three civil wars (in 1950, 1953, and 1956). It appears that there is not a straight-forward linear democratic peace. In addition, I estimated a revised model that included separate democracy and autocracy variables and found that their coefficient values were both negatively though not sig-nificantly associated with the probability of civil war (while the rela-tionship among the other variables and civil war likelihood was con-sistent with those reported in Table 5.1). We're reminded of the rather

Table 5.1   Logistic Regression of Factors Associated with Civil War, 1946–1992

	Equation 1	Equation 2	Equation 3
Democracy	.04*	.02	.01
	(.03)	(.03)	(.03)
Democracy^2	—	−.02***	—
		(.01)	
Semidemocracy	—	—	1.33***
			(.43)
Development	−1.46***	−1.34***	−1.47***
	(.33)	(.33)	(.33)
Milspending	.48**	.47*	.55**
	(.25)	(.25)	(.25)
Ethnopolitical	.45	.53	.36
	(.32)	(.33)	(.32)
Polar	—	—	—
Asia	.98***	1.01***	.96***
	(.37)	(.37)	(.37)
Middle East	1.03**	.96**	.96**
	(.45)	(.44)	(.44)
Constant	−6.20***	−5.29***	−6.50***
	(.63)	(.68)	(.63)
−2 log likelihood	423.50	411.78	414.22
N	2,317	2,317	2,317
X^2	28.16***	39.88***	37.45***

Note: Standard errors are in parentheses; *p ≤ .10, **p ≤ .05 level, ***p ≤ .01 level

disquieting observation, noted above, that autocracies—as well as democracies—deter insurgency; however, one should be careful in drawing even tentative conclusions from the latter findings because neither autocracy nor the democracy coefficient was significant. Nevertheless, it seems clear that democracy is not effective protection against civil wars in postcolonial states.

In addition, the findings indicate that increased development is associated with a decreased likelihood of civil war, which is consistent with findings from recent analyses of civil war (Goemans, 1997; Hegre et al., 1997; Collier, 1998; Collier and Hoeffler, 1998). The results indicate that the conflict-dampening impact of development, which may be barely evident in all states, is markedly evident in postcolonial states. In fact, this is corroborated by Auvinen (1997: Annex 2, p. 193), whose results from a logit regression using the COW civil war data indicate a significant negative relationship between economic development and the likelihood of civil war for the seventy less-developed countries in his study.[10]

The results also indicate that *Milspending* is significantly associated with an increased likelihood of civil war, which challenges the view that by privileging the military in their budgetary decisions, political elites stave off potential insurgency (e.g., Gyimah-Brempong, 1992). Although the budgetary prophylactic may obtain in certain instances, it appears that bloated militaries do not provide effective checks against insurgency. In fact, the trade-offs in domestic spending from hyperspending on the military might hasten internal conflict. Moreover, the military itself, propped up by the diversion of resources from state leaders, may move on its previous patrons. To be sure, the history of military-inspired insurgencies in the postcolonial world suggests that political leaders cannot buy the military but can only rent it.

I do not find support for the conflict-inducing impact of cultural polarization (in fact the variable is so highly nonsignificant that it is dropped from the model and the subsequent equations are estimated without it), nor is there a significant relationship between the presence of a mobilized ethnopolitical group and the probability of civil war. It appears that the relationship between ethnopolitical factors and civil war is actually quite tenuous. In order to determine the robustness of the relationship between *Ethnopolitical* and *Civil war*, I disaggregated the temporal domain and examined the relationship between the two variables for the period from 1960 to the present, 1970 to the present, 1980 to the present, and 1990 to the present; yet, there was no significant relationship between the presence of an ethnopolitical group and the likelihood of civil war. Separate analyses on each respective region also fail to uncover any significant relationship between the two variables. I conclude that the impact of ethnopolitical variables on civil wars is vitiated by other factors, most likely regime type.

This viewpoint is largely driven by Gurr's (1994) and Gurr and Harff's (1994) perspective that an important conflict-dampening factor in ethnopolitical disputes is the ability (or willingness) of the political system to provide a nondiscriminatory political environment and one in which institutions of government can effectively redress the legitimate claims of aggrieved ethnopolitical groups. While democracies may prevent "ethnopolitical conflict" through the establishment of a nondiscriminatory environment and autocracies may prevent "ethnopolitical insurgency" through brutal repression, semidemocracies—for reasons discussed earlier—are usually not able to pursue either approach. Therefore, I expect that the impact of ethnopolitical mobilization on the onset of civil war is likely to be mitigated by political factors such as regime type; moreover, the likelihood of insurgency should largely be a function of the presence of semidemocracy rather than the presence of ethnopolitical groups. In fact, this is what we find. For example, in the simple bivariate case, the relationship between *Ethnopolitical* and *Civil war* is positive and significant. However, when I compute the partial correlation between *Ethnopolitical* and *Civil war*, controlling for *Semidemocracy*, the relationship is no longer significant. On the other hand, when I compute the partial correlation between *Semidemocracy* and *Civil war*, controlling for *Ethnopolitical*, I find that the relationship remains positive and highly significant (as it is in the bivariate case). These relationships indicate that *Semidemocracy* washes out the impact of *Ethnopolitical* on *Civil war*.

In addition, the vitiating impact of regime type on ethnopolitical factors is not simply the result of an interaction effect whereby the combination of both variables is actually the precipitant to civil war. When we include an interaction variable, which takes the value of the product of *Ethnopolitical* and *Semidemocracy,* in the original equation in Table 5.1, the coefficient value for *Ethnopolitical* is not significant while the coefficient value of *Semidemocracy* remains significant (the interaction variable is not significant). It follows that it is not the interaction of ethnopolitical and regime factors that increases the probability of civil war but rather the independent impact of semidemocracy—whether there is an ethnopolitical conflict or not. In short, the presence of semidemocracy vitiates the relationship between ethnopolitical factors and civil war. To be sure, one should not infer from this finding that a policy aimed at reducing the likelihood of postcolonial civil war should not focus on the protection of the rights of ethnopolitical groups (see Gurr and Harff, 1994; Singer, 1996; Henderson, 1999b), only that one should not assume that "ethnopolitical conflict," in and of itself, is a harbinger of civil war.[11]

The results also reveal a positive and significant association between the regional variable, *Asia*, and the probability of civil war. This finding suggests that Asian states are more likely to experience civil war as compared to Middle Eastern and African states. It largely reflects the fact that Asia has experienced more civil wars (n = 23) than Africa (n = 19) and the Middle East (n = 11), although Africa has more state-years (n = 1, 343) than either Asia (n = 911) or the Middle East (n = 696). It follows that Asia's ratio of civil wars per state-year is higher (.025) than that of either the Middle East (.016) or Africa (.014).

Discussion

In sum, the findings challenge the domestic democratic peace for postcolonial states. Instead, I find that states with a modicum of democracy are the most prone to civil war. The finding that postcolonial civil wars are largely driven by the extent of democracy is consistent with the thesis that tensions related to the challenges of state building and nation building constitute the "taproot of insurgency" in postcolonial states (see Cohen et al., 1981; Henderson, 1999b). For example, European states had many decades—for some, centuries—to develop effective institutions of governance and a domestic environment in which citizens swore fealty to a central government. Moreover, among European states, nation building followed state building; therefore, European elites were able to address and resolve problems associated with each sequentially. Not only have postcolonial states had a much shorter time in which to build effective state structures and cohesive national identities, but they have usually needed to accomplish both simultaneously. One result is that postcolonial political elites face a "state-strength dilemma" wherein "the attempt to create strong states creates the resistance that will further weaken [it]," largely because the heterogeneous groups within these societies are not possessed of an overarching national identity that recognizes the legitimacy of the central government (Holsti 1996: 128). Nevertheless, even as leaders of postcolonial states risk the disintegration of their societies, they have disincentives to providing institutional and infrastructural development out of fear that political development might lead to the political mobilization of disparate groups and the construction of rival power centers that might threaten their incumbency (Job, 1992). Many of these elites, unable or unwilling (or both) to garner legitimacy from a disaffected, generally poor, heterogeneous, and often disgruntled citizenry, turn to government sponsored repression in order to ensure the security of their regime while devoting resources to the military to stave off insurgency. The result for many postcolonial states is often the very insurgency that the governing elites' policies were meant to deter.[12]

A counterargument to the domestic DPP derives from Huntington's (1968) contention that political decay and instability occur when popular mobilization outpaces political institutionalization. Therefore, one may posit that it is not regime type, per se, that is associated with civil war but the degree of institutionalization with more institutionalized states less prone to civil war and less institutionalized states more prone to civil war. One would need to control for the degree of institutionalization in the state in order to determine the accuracy of these assumptions. Benson and Kugler (1998) undertake such an analysis, and despite several limitations of their study (e.g., they do not address the role of semidemocracy, and their observations are limited to twenty-six states for the period 1985 to 1989, without any African cases), their findings lend greater support to the role of regime type rather than institutionalization in internal conflicts.

It is also important to remember that Hegre et al. (1997: 25) find that "regime change clearly cannot serve as an explanation for the higher level of civil war in semidemocracies"; instead, they insist that "there is something about semidemocracies which makes them more prone to violent domestic conflict, even when they have had time to stabilize from the regime change."[13] Since the findings also implicated militarization and underdevelopment as precipitants of civil war, it follows that postcolonial states require a more expansive and multifaceted conflict-prevention strategy that focuses on these issues instead of a singular—arguably myopic—strategy centering only on democracy as a precursor to domestic peace. Such a comprehensive approach is necessary because too often "remedies" intended to alleviate problems related to one class of factors (e.g., economic development) often exacerbate difficulties related to other factors (e.g., political stability). For example, states that attempt to develop economically while navigating the maelstrom of semidemocracy are often compelled to appeal to international organizations for assistance. However, Auvinen's (1996, 395) analysis of seventy less-developed states from 1981 to 1989 implicates the IMF's high-conditionality structural adjustment programs in generating political protest even in more developed and democratic third world states. In fact, semidemocratic regimes appear to suffer greater instability *with* these programs than *without* them (pp. 392–393, see figure 2). It is this type of cross-relationship that keeps many postcolonial states severely hampered from ending their immiseration and the domestic conflict that it often spawns. Ironically, the challenge to demilitarize and develop is made even more difficult with the end of the Cold War because postcolonial states continue to be hamstrung by huge debts and poor economies (especially in sub-Saharan Africa) while development aid floods into Eastern Europe and away from the South (Ihonvbere, 1998: 11–12). For example, even with the well-publicized efforts to address the economic penury of much of the postcolonial world over the past twenty years, "the North-South gap widened dramatically in the decade after 1982. . . . Between 1985 and 1992, Southern nations paid some $280 billion more in debt service to Northern creditors than they received in new private loans and government aid" (Broad and Cavanagh, 1998: 19). Moreover, "in 1960 developing countries' gross domestic product (GDP) per capita was 18% of the industrial nations; in 1990, at 17%, the gap was almost unchanged." From 1980 to 1991, GNP per capita "increased only by an average of 1% in the South (and in sub-Saharan African, it declined by 1.2), while it increased 2.3% in the North—suggesting a widening gap" (Broad and Landi, 1996: 8). The further widening of the gap between North and South has come to reflect not only the disparate economic fortunes of these two regions but their disparate politico-military fates as "zones of peace" and "zones of war," respectively (Singer and Wildavsky, 1993).

Conclusion

In this chapter, I have attempted to ascertain the extent to which the DPP is applicable to civil wars in the postcolonial world. The results refute the DPP for civil wars; instead, they corroborate previous findings that semidemocracy is associated with an increased likelihood of civil war. I also find that greater economic development reduces the probability of civil war in postcolonial states, while militarized post-colonial states are more likely to experience civil war, as are Asian—more than Middle Eastern and African—states. The primary implica-tion of the findings is that democracy does not appear to reduce the likelihood of postcolonial civil war even if it is fully implemented; instead, partial democracies, or "semidemocracies," are the most civil war–prone states. Coupled with the findings from Chapter 4, these results suggest that democratic enlargement as a strategy for peace is not likely to work for those states that need it most (i.e., postcolonial states). This does not mandate an abandonment of democracy, but it does suggest that efforts at democratization should be guided by the realization that it is often a conflict-riven process that exacerbates inequalities and encourages disaffected people to pursue insurgency or even carry out bellicose foreign policy (e.g., see Gelpi, 1997; Snyder, 2000). It is important to remember that even if full-fledged democracy were to engender peace within postcolonial states—which is not indi-cated by the findings reported here—it would also likely generate con-flict internationally, since, as shown in Chapter 3, democracies are more prone than nondemocracies to initiate and become involved in interstate wars and militarized disputes. The promise of egalitarianism, which is the true appeal of democracy, seems to involve a Hobson's choice for citizens of postcolonial states: *equality* with an increased likelihood of *domestic instability* or *inequality* with a decreased likeli-hood of *international stability*. Such tragic choices rarely appear on the radar screen of democratic peace theorists who seem to assume that democracy immunizes states from domestic and international conflict. Such a view minimizes or ignores the troubling dilemmas facing the billions of third world people who have yet to experience the "end of history" or the "triumph of Kantian peace."

Notes

1. It may be less obvious to some but a civil war is also distinct from an internal war, which may or may not involve fighting between government and insurgent forces (e.g., it may involve conflict between groups within a state, not necessarily the armed forces of the government, such as occurred between rival warlords in Somalia).

2. This position is consistent with Gurr's (1970: 334) admonition that scholars distinguish among (1) relatively spontaneous and unstructured con-flict (i.e., turmoil); (2) small-scale political violence (e.g., conspiracy); and (3)

large-scale organized violence aimed at overthrowing a regime (i.e., civil war). According to Gurr (1970: 334), there are three justifications for separately analyzing these phenomena: (1) theoretical arguments that they have generally distinguishable causes; (2) their substantially different effect on political systems; and (3) empirical evidence indicates that they tend to occur separately.

3. Other studies substantiate the relationship between semidemocracy and domestic conflict. For example, Boswell and Dixon (1993) find support for the semidemocracy thesis in their study, which focuses on the magnitude of deaths from political violence as an outcome variable. Auvinen's (1996, 1997) findings support the semidemocracy thesis for both political protest and political conflict; however, Auvinen does not include coefficients on the relationship between regime type and internal war in his findings (p. 193; also see p. 188). Regan and Henderson (in press) also find a relationship among semidemocracy, threats, and political repression.

4. The cases include the following ninety states: Afghanistan, Algeria, Angola, Bahrain, Bangladesh, Benin, Bhutan, Botswana, Burkina Faso, Burundi, Cambodia, Cameroon, Cape Verde, Central African Republic, Chad, China, Comoros, Congo, Democratic Republic of Vietnam, Djibouti, Egypt, Equatorial Guinea, Ethiopia, Fiji, Gabon, Gambia, Ghana, Guinea, Guinea-Bissau, India, Indonesia, Iraq, Israel, Ivory Coast, Jordan, Kazakhstan, Kenya, Kuwait, Laos, Liberia, Lebanon, Lesotho, Libya, Madagascar, Malaysia, Malawi, Maldives, Mali, Mauritania, Mauritius, Mongolia, Morocco, Mozambique, Myanmar (Burma), Nepal, Niger, Nigeria, Oman, Pakistan, Papua New Guinea, People's Republic of Korea, Philippines, Qatar, Republic of Korea, Republic of Vietnam, Rwanda, Sao Tome and Principe, Saudi Arabia, Senegal, Seychelles, Sierra Leone, Singapore, Somalia, South Africa, Sri Lanka, Sudan, Swaziland, Syria, Taiwan, Tanzania, Togo, Tunisia, Uganda, United Arab Emirates, Yemen Arab Republic, Yemen's People's Republic, Yemen (United), Zaire, Zambia, and Zimbabwe. I include Ethiopia, Liberia, and South Africa, which were never actually colonized in the traditional sense, but a case can be made that their development and civil-military relations were constrained by processes quite similar to those operative throughout the postcolonial world. I also wanted to include the Central Asian states of the former USSR (which also were not "colonies" in the traditional sense), but data were only available for Kazakhstan, which is included. Sensitivity tests do not indicate that the exclusion of these states has any significant impact on the findings.

5. There is also disagreement on the role of cultural factors in other forms of domestic conflict such as coups d'état within Africa (see Henderson, 1998b).

6. Interestingly, Auvinen (1997) found that "ethnic dominance" increased the extent of political conflict for developing states from 1981 to 1989, while Hegre et al. (1997: 20–24) uncovered no significant relationship between ethnic heterogeneity and civil war.

7. Cases where a state's homogeneity score was greater than 110 percent of its total population in the COW material capabilities dataset were deleted.

For a discussion of problems and blind spots in the dataset, see Henderson (1997; 1998a: 471–473).

8. I do not include each regional variable in the equation because that would create a linear combination and preclude estimation; therefore, I exclude *Africa* so that it can be used as the baseline with which to determine the impact of the other regional variables.

9. In order to ensure that the findings were not skewed by missing data, which is more of a problem in analyses of postcolonial states, I reestimated entries for seventeen, mostly African, cases of civil war by using the values of the variable for the prior or subsequent year closest to the missing observation, and the findings reported in Table 5.1 rely on these estimates. Employing Beck et al.'s (1998) autocorrelation diagnostic, I find that the results are robust.

10. I also reestimated the original model to include the annual percentage rate of change of the *Development* variable in order to determine whether "growth" rather than "development" had the strongest conflict-dampening impact, as suggested by Boswell and Dixon (1990) and Schock (1996). I found that the direction of the coefficients for the variables in the model were consistent with those reported in Table 5.1; however, while the "growth" variable was negatively though not significantly associated with the probability of civil war ($\beta = -.13$; p = .73), the impact of *Development* remained negative and highly significant ($\beta = -1.31$; p < .01). It appears that development more than growth provides the stronger prophylactic against civil war onset, which is generally consistent with Hardy's (1979) and Goemans's (1997) findings.

11. I also reestimated the original model using annual lags on the *Semidemocracy*, *Development*, *Milspending*, and *Ethnopolitical* variables in order to check the temporal order of the associations among the predictors and the outcome variable. I found that the direction of the relationships was consistent with the original results. The only difference between the findings was that the coefficient for *Milspending*, while positive, was not significant below the .10 level. On the whole, the impact of the predictors appears to be temporally prior to the outcome.

12. Though I recognize that international factors play an important role in these conflicts, it appears that factors internal to the state, such as the level of democracy, greatly affect the likelihood of civil war. To be sure, when one considers the plethora of postcolonial civil wars, one is immediately confronted by the bloody record of Soviet and American efforts to establish, maintain, and expand their spheres of influence throughout postcolonial regions. While foreign intrigue often plays a major role in the *expansion* and *escalation* of postcolonial civil wars, it is much less obvious that international factors are strongly associated with the *onset* of these wars, which is the focus of this chapter (see Luard, 1972, 1989; MacFarlane, 1991: 135; Ayoob, 1995: 189; Holsti, 1996).

13. In additional analyses I found, controlling for semidemocracy, no significant relationship between regime transition—coded as the difference in a state's annual regime score of either one or more, two or more, or five or more

units on the Polity III scale, respectively—and the probability of civil war. I also used Ward and Gleditsch's (1998: 37, table 3) research design that examines changes over a ten-year period and found that the direction of the coefficients for current regime score, direction of regime change, regime change, and variance of regime change variables are identical; however, none of the variables are significant when controlling for semidemocracy ($\beta = 1.13$, p < .05).

6

An Alternative Explanation of the Postwar "Democratic Peace"

The argument and the statistical evidence up to this point largely refute the DPP for international and civil wars; however, one might still, understandably, be struck by the absence of warfare between democracies in the postwar era. Although this apparent "democratic peace" is not significantly different from what we'd expect to occur randomly (given the controls utilized in the statistical analyses), for some, the absence of warfare between democracies—whether it is statistically significant or not—demands an explanation because it is substantively interesting. In this chapter, I'll address this perspective, which asks the question, If not a democratic peace, then what accounts for the absence of warfare between democracies in the postwar era? To my mind, the assumption that political regime type is responsible for the absence of war between democratic states draws attention away from more consistent though admittedly less elegant explanations of the phenomenon. I contend that a combination of factors including bipolarity, nuclear deterrence, alliance aggregation, and trade links contributed to the formation of an international security regime among the major-power democracies and their minor power democratic allies. It was this international regime—more than joint democracy—that allowed for postwar joint democratic stability. This view is supported by the empirical evidence in the preceding chapters, and it reflects the confluence of events in the postwar era that marked it not only as an era of a putatively "democratic peace" but as one characterized as a "long peace," as well (Gaddis, 1987). A focus on international regimes explains the postwar stability among the superpowers and the democratic states in the system. Such an approach reflects an appreciation of the myriad factors that affect foreign policy while eschewing single-factor explanations like the democratic peace thesis, whose attractiveness—and major shortcoming—is its simplicity.

The chapter proceeds in several sections. Initially, I outline several factors that emerged in the post–World War II era that contributed to the reduction of conflict among democracies. Next, I explain the emergence of an international regime that reduced interstate conflict. After a brief discussion of how this regime emerged, I show how the interplay of bipolarity, nuclear deterrence, alliance aggregation, and trade interdependence increased the general stability of the postwar system and helped to reduce major-power conflict and interstate violence between democratic states. Following that, I delineate the factors that give rise to international security regimes and show how such a regime laid the groundwork for the postwar stability among democratic states. Finally, I conclude with a brief recapitulation of the main argument.

The Roots of the Alternative Theoretical Argument on the Democratic Peace

The argument that the postwar stability among democratic states resulted mainly from the impact of an international regime borrows heavily from the neoidealist approach to world politics (see Henderson, 1999a). Neoidealism is a recent variant of the idealist paradigm, which is the classical liberal perspective of world politics. Whereas idealists posit that cooperation among states should emerge from an underlying harmony of interests among peoples and states that compels them to pursue democracy, collective security, and commercial ties, neoidealists eschew this rationale and propose different mechanisms to account for the emergence of cooperation among states. For them, the motivation for international cooperation derives primarily from the interests of state actors viewed as egoistic and rational expected utility maximizers. Eschewing the "utopic" aspects of classical idealism, neoidealists rely on functionalist arguments rooted in Axelrod's (1984) explication of cooperation among egoists and Keohane's (1984) emphasis on the role of market failure in generating interstate cooperation. The basic neoidealist argument is that state (and nonstate) actors pursue cooperation in order to deal effectively with market failure in important issue areas, and they construct international regimes in order to secure gains through interstate cooperation. Interstate cooperation ensues from a reduction in transaction costs, decreased uncertainty, and the formation of institutions to reward cooperation and punish noncooperation with the rules and norms of the international regime. This cooperative behavior results, in part, from homogenization of interstate behavior through a process similar to that proposed by Waltz (1979: 73–77), whereby the impact of international anarchy, sovereignty, and self-help serves to regularize the behavior of states throughout the system. There is some disagreement on whether regimes require a hegemon for their establishment and maintenance. Gilpin's (1981) analysis is consistent with neorealist assessments in general, which view hegemony as necessary for the establishment of regimes, but others challenge this view and contend that regimes can persist "after hegemony" (Keohane, 1984; also see Young, 1989).

The importance of international regimes is that they affect the coordination of international behavior in ways that comport with expectations from rational actor models. The focus on decisionmakers as egoistic rational actors distinguishes the neoidealist version of *homo politicus* from the classical idealist variant (in fact, it largely appropriates the realist version). The result is that just as neorealists reject Morgenthau's emphasis on the role of human nature in foreign policy— substituting the impact of system structure on world politics—neoidealists reject the Wilsonian reliance on shared norms and altruism as motivation for international cooperation.

It is commonly assumed that democratic peace findings are consistent with neoidealist approaches to international security, but this is incorrect. For example, Bremer (1992: 388) points out that his findings, which support the democratic peace thesis, "suggest that a deeper examination of the idealist position might bring us closer to understanding the conditions that foster peace" and that "perhaps it's time to seriously entertain neoidealism." Neoidealists argue that, ceteris paribus, the coaction of states (of varying political regime types, economic systems, cultural composition, military capabilities, etc.)—beset by problems of market failure—leads to the construction of international regimes to facilitate agreements, institutionalize rules, and provide norms for interstate interaction in some issue areas. In this way, norms emerge from international regimes and thus are *extrinsic* to states and are not incumbent on political regime type. This is a core tenet of neoidealism. Both the normative and the institutional versions of the democratic peace thesis, however, are at odds with the neoidealist perspective insofar as they suggest that norms and institutional constraints that proscribe the use of force between democracies are *intrinsic* to states. These two views are not consistent.

Neoidealist explanations of the absence of warfare between democracies in the postwar era draw our attention to developments in world politics particular to that period that may have given rise to interstate cooperation in security affairs. Two are immediately apparent because they were unprecedented: global bipolarity and the presence of nuclear weapons.[1] As will be shown below, both appear to have significantly contributed to the development of an international security regime among democracies. Neoidealists assert that international security regimes are the primary instruments for the maintenance of interstate stability. To my mind, the postwar stability among democratic dyads suggests that during this era democracies might have been able to construct an international security regime that reduced the level of conflict among them. This is not to argue that the mere absence of war demonstrates the presence of a security regime or vice versa, because the absence of war may not result from purposive policies but might emerge from a random process or mere coincidence.

Like international regimes in general, an international security regime is an institutionalized set of principles, norms, rules, and decisionmaking procedures (Keohane, 1984); however, it is focused on security issues. If a security regime had emerged among democracies, these states would have had to overcome relative gains problems that allegedly inhere in security issues and make cooperation difficult if not impossible (Grieco, 1988). Realists remind us that even though absolute gains may accrue from cooperation, if such cooperation enables one state to gain relative to another, then one must consider that relative advantages might be used to increase the capability of the gaining state, which may then use these increased capabilities against the losing state. States will forgo cooperation, the argument goes, if they conclude that the benefits of absolute gains are offset by the danger of relative losses. Thus realists insist that states must be concerned with relative—more than absolute—gains that might accrue from cooperation (Grieco, 1988). Relative gains problems, it is argued, are more severe in security issues because of the nature of security itself. In the realist view, security is primarily a function of a state's relative capability, which provides the basis for a state's protection of its sovereignty and largely determines a state's rank in the international hierarchy. State leaders have great difficulty in assessing another state's capabili-

ties (or its leader's intentions), and the security dilemma makes it difficult to attain (or accurately know) the requisite capability level that will
ensure a state's security. Since relative gains or losses in the security
sphere have major implications for state survival, realists insist that
interstate cooperation in this realm (beyond flexible alliance making) is
unlikely.

Scholars have effectively challenged the neorealist relative gains
argument and have showed that relative gains problems emerge only in
special circumstances while they have only negligible effects on the
likelihood of interstate cooperation in situations involving many actors
with opportunities to link issues (Snidal, 1991ab). Werner (1997: 291)
argues that "even if there is no central authority and violence is an
effective and efficient tool of state policy such that security fears pre-
dominate, states do not necessarily maximize relative gains and that
cooperation is far more possible than neorealists claim." In fact, she has
demonstrated that security concerns, themselves, may provide the basis
for cooperative relations. These conclusions reinforce Powell's (1991)
assertion that a permissive environment for the use of force does not
necessarily follow from the assumption of anarchy but depends on the
decreased cost of the use of force and the increased fear of interstate
aggression. Only where the costs of the use of force are low are relative gains markedly salient and likely to preclude cooperation; however, where the costs of the use of force are high, cooperation is indeed
likely, even absent a central authority.

Among the various challenges to neorealist relative gains arguments, Matthews's (1996) analysis has important implications for a
neoidealist explanation of the "democratic peace." He points out that
the debilitating impact of relative gains on interstate security cooperation is overcome in issue areas where the defense is dominant and the
cumulation effects of cooperation are low. Where such conditions
obtain, leaders do not fear that relative gains in one bargaining round
can be used to increase the likelihood of gains in the next round
(Powell, 1991). That is, since the defense is dominant and unilateral
action is possible, states do not fear preemption or surprise attack.
Utilizing this perspective, Matthews (1996) explains how nuclear
weapons agreements (an issue area where the defense is dominant and
cumulation effects are low), such as the Nonproliferation Treaty (NPT),
the Strategic Arms Limitation Treaty (SALT), and the Intermediate
Nuclear Forces Treaty (INF) as well as agreements on antiballistic missile (ABM) deployment, were successfully concluded during the Cold

War while conventional weapons agreements (an issue area where the offense is dominant and cumulation effects are high), such as the Mutual and Balanced Force Reduction (MBFR), were not. Recognition of the role of cumulation effects in fostering interstate cooperation in security affairs provides neoidealists a means to circumvent relative gains problems in security issues and suggests the basis for the emergence of international security regimes in world politics.

Further, if certain types of nuclear weapons agreements are not circumscribed by relative gains problems, as argued by Matthews, then nuclear-armed states—primarily the major powers—might be more inclined to cooperate in important nuclear weapons issues such as non-proliferation and strategic arms limitation. Since the major powers were polarized into rival camps we would not expect them to be cooperative in general, which is why superpower competition colored the postwar canvass. Nonetheless, during the postwar period of "dual hegemony" (Gaddis, 1992), one by-product of *interbloc* competition was the creation of certain *intrabloc* relationships that helped provide stability within each bloc. Not only was there a tightening of the links among bloc members and their respective superpower hegemon, but trade ties lubricated the links among bloc members, particularly those in the Western bloc where most major-power (and conflict-prone) democratic states were situated. Building on the reduced salience of relative gains problems in important security issues in the postwar context, democratic major powers and their democratic allies appear to have been motivated to create an international security regime through alliance networks. Let's consider these points more fully.

Alliances and International Regimes

In the postwar period, the two alliance systems, the North Atlantic Treaty Organization (NATO) and the Warsaw Pact, became the principal alignment mechanisms for the major powers that were largely bifurcated across ideological lines. Realists, drawing on the experience of the classical multipolar balance of power system in Europe, insist that ideological issues should not inform alliance making; however, in the bipolar Cold War era, factors other than relative capability became salient because minor powers could not effectively tilt the military balance (though they could potentially draw their superpower allies into their disputes and instigate major-power crises and war). Ideology

largely reflective of the worldview of the hegemon—an advanced capitalist society intent on promoting, inter alia, global trade in order to
maintain its power position—appeared to be salient, in the realist view,
because it served the hegemon's military interests. For realists, this ideology was actually superstructure to the more capability driven base.
For neoidealists, the ascendancy of ideology primarily reflected the
free-trade imperatives born of the capitalist global economy in opposition to those emanating from the socialist camp.

Consistent with the neoidealist argument, Simon and Gartzke
(1996: 633) maintain that "the superpower-led alliances of the cold war
period were more ideological in nature than alliances have been
throughout the past 180 years." In this environment, the prospect of
nuclear annihilation provided an absolute-loss threshold that states
dared not traverse. From the promulgation of NSC-68 in 1950 to the
successful management of the Cuban Missile Crisis of 1962, the superpowers came to appreciate that the possession of nuclear weapons by
both of them made their use suicidal since a first strike by either of
them would result in a devastating counterstrike against the initiator.
Early in the Cold War, the dominant perspective in strategic circles had
been to view nuclear weapons simply as bigger bombs. Following publication of Brodie's (1946) work, the broader implications of the
"absolute weapon" were such that deterrence more than victory, and
success in crises more than wars, became primary objectives of superpower military strategy.[2] A nuclear taboo slowly emerged that restrict-
ed war to the conventional level while mutual assured destruction
(MAD) provided for superpower stability wrought from a delicate "balance of terror" (Wohlstetter, 1959).

The nuclear taboo provided a security threshold for all states in the
system, and their refusal to violate it reflected a greater concern with
the potential absolute losses (i.e., nuclear conflagration) of "going
nuclear" than with relative gains born of short-term military victory
that might have resulted from the use of nuclear weapons. In this way,
the threat of nuclear holocaust in a context where defense was dominant alleviated relative gains problems among bloc members as they
became more concerned with the potential for absolute loss (nuclear
annihilation) that might result from interbloc instability but that also
might emerge from *intrabloc* disruptions that could drag the superpowers into interbloc conflict. Specifically, the superpowers were
intent on reducing the likelihood of (1) *interbloc* conflict that might
precipitate superpower war, and (2) *intrabloc* conflict that might waste

resources of alliance members and thereby reduce interbloc war-fighting capabilities by weakening allies and leaving them vulnerable to insurgency. One implication of the limitations on the use of nuclear weapons was the increased significance of conventional (and increasingly, special-operations) forces as leaders sought to develop a "flexible response" capability for international crises. Bipolarity and the nuclear standoff further heightened the utility of conventional forces as the superpowers responded to, intervened in, or initiated militarized disputes below the nuclear level. Such use of force allowed the superpowers to solidify their respective blocs and to defend the perimeters of their respective spheres of influence.

In short, the nuclear standoff provided interbloc stability through effective nuclear deterrence. In a study of militarized disputes, Small and Singer (1979: 77) point out, "the fact that the 20 major versus major confrontations since V-J Day have gone to neither conventional nor nuclear war . . . strongly suggests that the nuclear deterrent, as clumsy and fragile as it is, seems to exercise an inhibiting effect."[3] In addition, bipolarity increased the salience of *intrabloc* stability through its impact on postwar alliance-aggregation, specifically, the emergence of the two major alliances, NATO and the Warsaw Pact. Although alliances are more often associated with wars (Levy, 1981), especially large wars (Siverson and King, 1979), enduring alliances—those that are more long term—evince more benign effects (Ostrom and Hoole, 1978; Wayman, 1990). Therefore, while alliances are positively associated with war involvement in the short term, they are negatively associated with war involvement in the long term.[4] Postwar bipolarity and the nuclear standoff gave rise to long-term alliances that were more peaceful, thus reducing the likelihood of conflict among allied dyads.

Moreover, since democracies were more likely to be allied in the postwar era, low levels of intra-alliance conflict may have resulted in low levels of joint democratic conflict, which is consistent with the findings in Chapter 2. Siverson and Emmons (1991: 295) found that from 1946 to 1965, "democracies allied with each other at almost 80% more than the rate they would have by chance." During this period there were 129 exclusively democratic alliances out of 367 alliances that included at least one democracy (35.2 percent) as compared to the interwar period, 1919–1939, when there were only 10 out of 87 (10.3 percent) such alliances. In addition, Siverson and Emmons found that "democratic major powers formed considerably greater numbers of alliances with democratic minor powers," at a rate more than 300 percent higher than what would be expected (p. 302). At the same time, democratic major powers evinced "no particular proclivity to enter into alliances with nondemocratic minor powers," which, for Siverson and Emmons, reflects the tendency of democratic major powers to "protect the weaker democracies" (p. 302). In addition, democratic minor powers were far less likely to ally with nondemocratic minor powers.

A fear of destabilizing the Western Alliance through internecine conflict might also have motivated the democratic states to limit violence among themselves. In addition, the fear of sanctions from the United States, which furnished collective goods—especially security and access to trade—provided additional incentive for intrabloc stability. For example, this was evident in the U.S. response to the British, French, and Israeli invasion of Egypt in 1956 in an attempt to overthrow Nasser and wrestle control of the Suez Canal. Eisenhower did not countenance what he perceived as the unilateral policies of the troika, and he "used the UN General Assembly to call for a truce and then cut off oil exports from the Americas until Britain, France, and Israel complied" by withdrawing their forces, which was accomplished by the end of the year (McCormick, 1989: 124). In the Cold War context, "nations allied with the same superpower effectively lose the decision-latitude to make wars against the other allies of the same superpower" (Weede, 1992: 378).

Evidence of intrabloc stability is provided by Weede's (1983) study, which found that formal allies of superpowers did not fight wars from 1962 to 1980. Ray (1993: 429) noted that "no two formal allies of states with nuclear weapons and not allied to each other fought wars against each other from 1945 to 1986." The implication for democratic pairs of states was that since most of the democracies—especially those that were more conflict-prone (i.e., major powers and contiguous states)—were clustered, then their joint alliance membership more than their regime type probably accounted for their reduced conflict levels in the postwar era.[5] This view is partly consistent with Gowa (1999), but she proposes it for the prewar era and not the postwar era, which she suggests is marked by a democratic peace. Moreover, since the Western Allies were dominated by the global hegemon, the United States, it stands to reason that its presence would increase the conflict-dampening impact of intrabloc stability for its alliance members to a greater extent than would be evident in the rival Warsaw Pact alliance. Therefore, while superpower alliance-aggregation would tend to dampen both jointly democratic and jointly nondemocratic conflict, the effect on the former would be more evident than that on the latter. One reckons that were the global hegemon in the socialist camp, then we would be considering the "socialistic peace."

Observers might point out that the alleged intervening role of alliances in the democratic peace is gainsaid by the various multivariate analyses demonstrating that the presence of alliances does not vitiate the impact of joint democracy on peace (e.g., Bremer, 1992; Maoz and Russett, 1992; Oneal and Russett, 1997; Oneal and Ray, 1997); however, these findings are refuted by those in Chapter 2, which indicate that, controlling for political distance, alliance membership, more than joint democracy, contributed to peace in the postwar era. Nonetheless, the observation that democracies often ally with each other does not suggest that they ally because they are democracies. In fact, by joining an alliance, a nondemocracy may be encouraged to become more democratic. One need only reflect on the process of alliance-aggregation in the early years of NATO to appreciate these effects. Clearly, the establishment of NATO was driven by the leadership of the democratic states of the Atlantic Alliance, primarily the United States and Great Britain, and its preamble states that it is "founded on the principles of democracy, individual liberty and the rule of law." Interestingly, it appears that alliance membership for several NATO states preceded—and more than likely helped to make possible—their subsequent democracy. For example, Portugal was an original signatory of the NATO Treaty in 1949, but it did not become democratic until 1976. Stuart (1989: 78) notes that although attempts were made to assuage "Western consciences" by suggesting that participation in a "democratically oriented alliance system might have a reformatory effect on the Portuguese regime over time," nonetheless, the autocratic Salazar regime made public pronouncements that it would resist such "meddling" in Portugal's affairs. Only following the revolution of 1974 did Portugal move toward its present democratic form of government. In addition, Greece joined NATO in 1952 when it also was clearly not democratic. According to Polity III data, Greece did not become a democracy until 1975. Turkey, which like Greece joined the alliance in 1952, was democratic in that year (regime score of 10); however, for the years 1953 to 1959 it descended into anocracy (regime score of 4) and has fluctuated regime types over the years prior to settling into its present democratic form of government. It follows that alliance membership may have induced both the democratization of these states and the concomitant reductions in the likelihood of their experiencing joint democratic conflict.

In fact, Simon and Gartzke (1996: 633) find "a strong tendency for regimes of most types to prefer alliances with dissimilar regimes" while maintaining that "it may be the case that regimes of similar type prefer each other as alliance partners for primary or major alliances in bipolar systems only"—such as occurred in the post–World War II era (p. 633). Nonetheless, the neoidealist argument put forward here does not rely simply on the mitigating impact of alliances on interstate conflict, per se, but centers on the interdependent impact of alliance-aggregation and trade on the development of an international security regime that reduced joint democratic conflict. This security regime emerged in a context of global bipolarity and the superpower nuclear standoff, both of which provided the impetus for reductions in postwar interstate conflict among the major powers, in general, while the interplay of alliance-aggregation and intra-alliance trade (as will be shown later) provided the lubricant for the emergence of the regime, which in turn reduced interdemocratic conflict, specifically. So, importantly, it was a combination of alliance-aggregation and trade interdependence that provided the proximate cause for the rise of an international security regime among democracies. In the next section, I discuss the manner by which the alliance-trade relationships emerged and helped reduce joint democratic conflict in the postwar era.

Trade and the Rise of International Regimes

One is reminded that bipolarity and the superpower standoff not only inspired a nuclear arms race but also encouraged alliance-aggregation, which served to increase trade links among bloc members as the interests of the superpowers (especially those of the United States) came to guide global and intrabloc trade. Gowa (1994: 3) reminds us that, without exception, NATO members became signatories of GATT (the liberal international trade regime, now the World Trade Organization, or WTO), and Warsaw Pact members joined COMECON. Empirical evidence demonstrates a consistent negative relationship between trade and interstate conflict at the dyadic (Polachek, 1980) and system (Mansfield, 1994) levels. Since trade "follows the flag" (Pollins, 1989ab), one can assume that state decisionmakers' utility function with regard to trade includes not only the potential economic benefits that might accrue from commerce but also the extent to which the foreign policy interests of partners are convergent with one's own. This is consistent with Gowa's

(1994) view that there are security externalities of trade since the returns of trade can potentially be used to increase the military capabilities of states. She maintains that potential trading partners recognize such externalities and coordinate their trade accordingly. One result is that free trade is more likely *within* rather than *across* alliances. Gowa (1994) and Gowa and Mansfield (1993) demonstrate that in bipolar systems there is an increased likelihood of *intra-alliance* trade and a decreased likelihood of *inter-alliance* trade.[6] Further, in bipolar (more than multipolar) systems, alliances have a greater impact on trade and an increased likelihood of evolving into free-trade coalitions.

Considering the consistent negative relationship between trade and conflict, and the increased impact of alliances on trade in bipolar systems, one can argue that bilateral trade links among alliance partners within the largely democratic Western bloc exerted a dampening effect on intrabloc, thus joint democratic, conflict. It follows that common trade links—largely born of alliance membership and system structure—contributed to reductions in joint democratic conflict. If such relationships actually obtained, one would expect that, inter alia, controlling for trade interdependence would wash out the impact of joint democracy on interstate conflict in the postwar era. In fact, this is exactly what was demonstrated in Chapter 2. It appears that in the postwar era major-power democratic allies coordinated their trade ties in order to realize security externalities and in so doing reduced the levels of conflict among their states while providing the basis for an international security regime. Further, the system's bipolar structure provided a supportive context for the formation of a free-trade coalition among democratic allies while U.S. hegemony provided a resin for the cooperative linkages among the major-power democracies and their minor-power democratic allies. The convergence of these factors reduced conflict levels among democracies by encouraging the creation of an international security regime among these states. An appreciation of the factors that give rise to security regimes will allow us to more clearly discern the manner in which democracies constructed their own international security regime in the postwar period.

The Rise of an International Security Regime

Since Deutsch et al.'s (1957) discussion of pluralistic and amalgamated security communities, research on the etiology of international security regimes has been relatively sparse largely due to regime theorists' conceding much of the security realm to neorealists in the past few decades (e.g., Keohane, 1984). Scholars differ on whether security regimes exist(ed) in the post–World War II era. For example, Jervis (1983) maintains that while the Concert of Europe was a regime, MAD and superpower arms agreements in the postwar era did not constitute security regimes because superpower agreements and precedents were neither "unambiguous or binding." Further, these postwar agreements, for him, simply reflected the "narrow and quite short-run self-inter-est[s]" of the major powers, and these interests—more than regimes—"can account for most of the restraints" on the superpowers in this era (p. 187). Nye (1987) agrees that there is an absence of an overall super-power security regime in the postwar era; however, he recognizes regimes in "subissues" related to nuclear weapons, including the destructive power of nuclear weapons, control problems, proliferation, arms race stability, and deterrent force structure. Smith (1987) takes the view that the postwar era witnessed the emergence of a security regime in nonproliferation (in a manner inconsistent with hegemonic stability or functionalist perspectives), while Tate (1990) and Brzoska (1992) differ on whether the NPT was a regime.

Although this literature is interesting (though inconclusive), it deals mainly with the existence of a security regime between super-powers. However, the argument presented here does not rely on the existence of a security regime between the superpowers but only the presence of a security regime among the democratic major powers con-centrated in the Atlantic alliance and other multilateral and bilateral relationships among democracies. What is necessary to reconcile the postwar absence of international war between democratic states with the theoretical argument presented here is evidence that a security regime existed among democracies that constrained violence between them. A case could be made that a security regime is an independent variable in the democratic peace process if alliance membership (and resultant trade links) actually preceded democracy within some of the major democracies (as noted above); therefore, we might suggest that the security regime is not simply epiphenomenal of joint democracy. I use Jervis's (1983) index of the factors that give rise to security regimes in order to support the view that the conditions that give rise to securi-ty regimes obtained for the postwar democracies.

Jervis (1983) suggested the following criteria for security regime formation: (1) the major powers want to establish a regime (i.e., a regulated issue area); (2) the actors perceive that others share their security interests; (3) major powers eschew expansion as a security option; (4) war is perceived as costly; and (5) "offensive and defensive weapons and policies are distinguishable but the former are cheaper and more effective than the latter, or they cannot be distinguished but it is easier to defend than attack" (p. 178). Even a cursory review of the historical record reveals that Jervis's criteria are satisfied for the postwar major-power democracies and their democratic allies and trading partners.

First, the United States and its democratic major-power allies were intent on creating a security sphere as a result of the exigencies of the Cold War that began with the pronouncement of the Truman Doctrine. Since power alone did not define the adversarial relationship between the superpowers (they had been formal allies in World War II), ideology, especially the espousal of capitalism (and later the presence of democracy for membership in NATO), became an important determinant of alliance membership and a causeway to the realization of economic gains that would accrue to allies (Simon and Gartzke, 1996: 633). Second, the democratic major powers appear to have desired a regime because it was clear that following World War II, U.S. power was unmatched, and the United States appeared to be the only state that could provide the collective goods of free trade and security for the capitalist democracies—and arguably the global system as a whole. The Marshall Plan and the World Bank laid the basis for the reconstruction of the Western European states lying prostrate after the war. Also, unlike in the interwar period, the United States aggressively pursued both an activist foreign policy in Europe and international economic leadership evident in its dominance of the major postwar international governmental organizations (IGOs): the UN and the Bretton Woods institutions. Third, the Western bloc sought to check perceived Soviet expansionism and rationalized its own foreign adventures through the policy of containment. Actually, both superpowers sought to solidify their respective spheres of influence more than expand them. U.S. foreign policy, in particular, was largely one of developing the capacity of former and potential trading partners in Western Europe and East Asia. Fourth, major-power war was clearly viewed as costly (especially following the Korean War), and superpower war was proscribed (though this did not preclude proxy wars). Fifth, the spread of nuclear weapons ushered in a period of unsurpassed defense dominance in military strategy even though many nuclear weapons systems had both offensive and defensive applications. In sum, using Jervis's criteria, it appears that conditions facilitating the emergence of a democratic security regime were present in the postwar era.

While Jervis's criteria allow us to determine whether the conditions were ripe for the formation of a security regime among democratic states, Gowa's (1994) and Gowa and Mansfield's (1993) research explains the process behind its emergence. Specifically, Gowa (1994: 45) asserts that "countries can use their ability to affect their terms of trade to correct the market failure produced by trade in an anarchic system." Her research on security externalities of trade establishes a clear connection between market failure (the fulcrum on which neoidealist arguments on interstate cooperation rests) and contextual factors such as bipolarity, alliances, and trade links in the development of security regimes. Since the extent to which allies trade with each other depends largely on the risk of exit (which is lower in bipolar systems), then free trade is more likely to emerge in bipolar systems because the security externalities of free trade agreements are likely to remain internalized in alliances under bipolarity (pp. 41, 53). Enforcement problems in international regimes are also reduced in agreements among allies because incentives to defect (rooted in political and economic interests) are limited. All told, just as international regimes, in general, form in response to market failure, security regimes have a similar etiology and are more likely to form from intra-alliance trade relationships in bipolar systems where cumulation effects are low (Gowa and Mansfield, 1993; Gowa, 1994; Matthews, 1996). Again, this etiology of regime formation dovetails with neoidealist arguments that specify that the emergence of an international regime is not dependent on the regime type of the state. What I assert here—building on Gowa's arguments—is that international security regimes are rather a function of the alliance and trade ties under conditions of bipolarity as states seek to confront problems of market failure in the global anarchy.

During the Cold War era, it appears that allied democratic states realized security externalities of trade—that are more pronounced under bipolarity—while intrabloc stability provided by "dual hegemony" and nuclear deterrence led to the creation of a security regime among the vast majority of democratic states, resulting in the absence of war between them. Following this logic, the "democratic peace" emerged from an international security regime molded largely from the interplay of unit (i.e., state response to market failure), dyadic (i.e., alliance ties and trade links), and system (i.e., bipolarity) level variables rather than simply from shared political regime type. The alliance-trade links that reinforced the international security regime among democratic states were less evident among the nondemocratic states. Though the impact of bipolarity and alliance-aggregation are similar for nondemocratic states, as explained earlier, nondemocracies did not demonstrate the affinity to ally and develop free-trade links.

The conflict-dampening impact of the security regime on the foreign policy of democratic dyads resulted largely from the fact that free-trade links appear to have been more pronounced among democratic allies than among their nondemocratic contemporaries. This is hardly surprising considering that the global hegemon happened to be situated in the democratic bloc. Intrinsically, the states' regime type probably mattered less than the fact that the global system was dominated by this particular hegemon that operated in a bipolar environment and encouraged a particular pattern of alliance-aggregation and intrabloc trade. It is important to remember that the emergence of a security regime among democracies of the global scope suggested by democratic peace arguments rests primarily on the activity of the major-power democracies—chief among them, the United States, the global hegemon. Clearly, such an international regime can have global scope and impact even if every individual democracy is not tied to it through intra-alliance trade links. Instead, less powerful democracies often become linked to the international regime informally through the acceptance of the basic rules, norms, procedures, and institutions of the regime. This is evocative of Kant's argument with regard to the impact of a "federation of free republics" on the behavior of states outside of the federation, about which Huntley (1996: 56) observes, "Once initiated, the federation's benefits to its members create competitive pressures on nonmembers to reform themselves sufficiently to join as well." This is consistent with Krasner's (1983b: 361) analysis of the feedback relationship among international regimes, basic causal variables, and foreign policy behavior and outcomes in that "once principles, norms, rules, and decisionmaking procedures [regimes] are entrenched they may alter the egoistic interests and power configurations that led to their creation in the first place." The centerpiece of this arrangement—less a Kantian federation and more an international security regime—was underwritten by forces beyond political regime type. This process is evocative of that which Deutsch et al. (1957) described with respect to security communities. Democracy may have been associated with the creation of a security regime in an idiosyncratic way, given the role of the Western democracies led by the United States in its institutionalization; nevertheless, the expansion and maintenance of this regime (and its conflict-dampening attributes) are rooted, to a greater extent, in the interplay of bipolarity, alliance-aggregation, and security externalities of trade. One result of this international regime was to reduce the likelihood of conflict between democratic states in the postwar era.

Conclusion

The Cold War era witnessed the convergence of several conflict-dampening factors that resulted in the "democratic peace," including bipolarity, which is negatively correlated with large wars (Wayman, 1984); nuclear deterrence, which decreased the likelihood of great-power war (Small and Singer, 1976); enduring alliances, which are negatively correlated with war (Ostrom and Hoole, 1978; Wayman, 1990); heightened alliance-aggregation among democracies, which reduced conflict (Siverson and Emmons, 1991; Simon and Gartzke, 1996); increased trade among allies (Gowa, 1994), which is negatively correlated with interstate war (Polachek, 1980; Mansfield, 1994); "dual-hegemony" among superpowers (Gaddis, 1992), which decreased conflict within their respective blocs (Weede, 1983); and the emergence of an international security regime (Jervis, 1983), which ultimately reduced conflict among democratic states. Gaddis (1992) is correct that the stability of the postwar era is overdetermined; yet an analysis of the role of international security regimes provides a more compelling explanation of the "democratic peace," especially given that there is no significant relationship between joint democracy and peace in the postwar era.

Nevertheless—and evocative of Mearsheimer (1990)—policymakers must consider the following question: If the absence of wars among democracies is best understood as the result of an international security regime born largely of Cold War exigencies, then how can we be sure the irenic structures that emerged from the Cold War will persist now that it has ended? Well, even if the factors that gave rise to the international security regime were primarily a function of the Cold War (which is not wholly accurate), it is evident, as Keohane (1984) and others point out, that regimes can persist even after the circumstances that brought them into existence have passed. Therefore, it is not necessary to wax nostalgically about a Cold War "stability" that must inevitably desist with the era's passing. Further, it is important to remember that while the democratic major powers limited intra-alliance violence among their fellow democracies and held their allies in check in order to maintain the balance of power during the Cold War, they also supported or participated in the slaughter of millions in the wars endemic throughout the periphery. Therefore, although the Cold War may have been marked by a "long peace" for the major powers, states in the periphery suffered a long trauma often exacerbated by major-power intervention. This is hardly an era to recall nostalgically, at least not for the majority of the world's people, who reside in the postcolonial states.

All told, the line of argument presented here reinforces the view that factors beyond regime type led to the relative absence of interstate war between democracies. Further, it suggests the need to appreciate the multifaceted aspects of foreign policy that often converge to provide the trajectories of international interaction that we observe in world politics. By focusing on the effect of international security regimes on conflict reduction, we are likely to depend less on either Cold War–oriented realpolitik or the spread of democracy as facilitators of peace in the post–Cold War era, and more on the establishment of international institutions to more effectively foster interstate cooperation. While democracy as a political system has many virtues, international stability—much less international peace—depends on something beyond the proliferation of democratic states, which are among the most war-prone states, to bring it about. To be sure, leaders should be concerned about the development of democracy in states throughout the globe as a matter of humanitarian interest; however, the assumption that Russia's or China's democratization, for example, will encourage those states to become more peaceful is gainsaid by the findings in the previous chapters. Further, this chapter suggests that leaders concerned with the peacefulness of Russia and China, in particular, should give greater consideration to including them in the prominent international institutions—namely, NATO and the WTO—that provided the core of the international security regime that allowed for "democratic peace" in the Cold War era. To be sure, stability in the post–Cold War era is not likely to rely simply on the replication of processes operative during the Cold War. Although the present era has witnessed the end of the nuclear standoff and the proxy wars stimulated by the superpower rivalry, it has also presented new challenges unseen in the previous era that to some degree emerge from the transformation of that era. These new challenges, some of which I'll discuss in Chapter 7, make it all the more imperative that states orient their foreign policy away from monocausal models such as the democratic peace, which grossly oversimplify the complexity of the processes that encourage peace and embrace more multifaceted and multidimensional strategies to help us navigate the often forbidding terrain of world politics.

Notes

1. Although Hopf (1991) suggests that there was a period of bipolarity between the Hapsburg and Ottoman Empires from 1521 to 1559, clearly, his focus is regional and not global, and most scholars agree that global bipolarity emerged only after World War II (see Waltz, 1979; Gaddis, 1992).

2. While early strategic thought was marked by prudent analyses such as Brodie (1946), a rival school emerged around theorists such as Wohlstetter (1959) and Kahn (1960), who argued for war-fighting, war-winning, and war-surviving approaches to nuclear strategy.

3. For an opposing viewpoint see Vasquez (1991).

4. There is a slight disagreement between Ostrom and Hoole (1978) and Wayman (1990) on the timing of the reversal of the positive relationship between alliance membership and war. The former point out that the dampening effect occurs after only four years while the latter suggests that it occurs between six and seven years, and after ten years.

5. This conclusion is not gainsaid by Bueno de Mesquita's (1981) statistical findings that allied states are more likely to fight each other because controlling for contiguity washes out this relationship (Bremer, 1992; Maoz and Russett, 1992).

6. In contrast, Liberman (1996) maintains that multipolar systems are more likely to reduce relative gains problems in trade and encourage cooperation among rivals in a manner evocative of Deutsch and Singer's (1964) classic argument with regard to the impact of "interaction opportunities."

7

The Democratic Peace: A Great Illusion?

n this chapter, I summarize the main findings of the study and briefly discuss their research and policy implications. The main finding resulting from the statistical analyses is that democracy is not significantly associated with a decreased likelihood of international wars, militarized disputes, or civil wars in postcolonial states. There does not appear to be a dyadic democratic peace or a monadic one. To the extent that a democratic peace obtains, it does for extrastate wars, which are more than likely relics of a bygone era; nevertheless, even for these wars, while democracies in general are less likely to become involved in them, Western states—especially Western democracies—are more likely to fight them. These findings result from analyses using straightforward research designs, similar data, and identical statistical techniques as those found in research supporting the DPP. They suggest that politico-economic factors in the postwar era greatly contributed to the phenomenon that is erroneously labeled the "democratic peace." Further, they imply that foreign policy strategies aimed at increasing the likelihood of peace in the future by spreading democracy are likely to be ineffective, at best, or conflict exacerbating, at worst.

Each of the analytical chapters examined the DPP at different levels of aggregation or for different types of armed conflict. In the sections that follow, I'll briefly recap the findings from each of these analyses before summing up the main contribution of this study.

Are Democracies Less Likely to
Fight Each Other?

The replication and extension of Oneal and Russett (1997), which is one of the most important studies on the DPP, showed that democracies are not significantly less likely to fight each other. The results demonstrate that Oneal and Russett's (1997) findings in support of the DPP are not robust and that joint democracy does not reduce the probability of international conflict for pairs of states during the postwar era. Simple and straightforward modifications of Oneal and Russett's (1997) research design generated these dramatically contradictory results. Specifically, by teasing out the separate impact of democracy and political distance (or political dissimilarity) and by not coding cases of ongoing disputes as new cases of conflict, it became clear that there is no significant relationship between joint democracy and the likelihood of international war or militarized interstate dispute (MID) for states during the postwar era. These findings suggest that the post–Cold War strategy of "democratic enlargement," which is aimed at ensuring peace by enlarging the community of democratic states, is quite a thin reed on which to rest a state's foreign policy—much less the hope for international peace.

Are Democracies More Peaceful
than Nondemocracies with
Respect to Interstate Wars?

The results indicate that democracies are *more* war-prone than non-democracies (whether democracy is coded dichotomously or continuously) and that democracies are *more likely* to initiate interstate wars. The findings are obtained from analyses that control for a host of political, economic, and cultural factors that have been implicated in the onset of interstate war, and focus explicitly on state level factors instead of simply inferring state level processes from dyadic level observations as was done in earlier studies (e.g., Oneal and Russett, 1997; Oneal and Ray, 1997). The results imply that democratic enlargement is more likely to increase the probability of war for states since democracies are more likely to become involved in—and to initiate—interstate wars.

Are Democracies More Peaceful than Nondemocracies with Respect to Extrastate Wars?

Controlling for several factors implicated in the onset of international war, I find that democracies are *less likely* to become involved in extrastate wars, but Western states are *more likely* to become involved in them. Interestingly, I find that of all the democracies, the Western democracies are *most likely* to become involved in extrastate wars. In addition, I find no significant relationship between democracy and international war (viewed as the sum of interstate and extrastate wars). Although the finding that democracies, in general, are less likely to fight extrastate wars may provide some support for DPP claims, this finding should be tempered by the realization that the anticolonial processes that generated many of the extrastate wars are by-products of a colonial era clearly past. Therefore, the impact of democracy on international war today, and in the near future, will primarily be manifest in interstate wars and MIDs. In this type of international conflict democracies are significantly more conflict-prone than nondemocracies. The results suggest that since democracy does not have a consistent effect on different types of international war, a policy such as democratic enlargement is likely to be ineffective at best and conflict-exacerbating at worst, since democracy reduces the likelihood of certain types of international war but increases the likelihood of others.

Are Democracies in the Postcolonial World Less Likely to Experience Civil Wars?

The results fail to support the democratic peace for civil wars in postcolonial states since democracy is not significantly associated with a decreased probability of intrastate war in postcolonial states. Instead, the results corroborate previous findings that semidemocracy is associated with an increased likelihood of civil war. Therefore, although coherent democracy does not appear to reduce the likelihood of postcolonial civil wars, partial democracy exacerbates the tensions that result in civil war. Given the findings from Chapter 6, these results suggest that democratic enlargement as a strategy for peace is not likely to succeed for those states that need it most—the postcolonial, or third world, states. Further, even if full-fledged democracy were to engender peace within these states—which is not indicated by the findings reported here—it would likely generate conflict, internationally, since democracies are more prone to initiate and become involved in inter-state wars and militarized disputes. As noted earlier, the promise of egalitarianism, which is the true appeal of democracy, seems to involve a Hobson's choice for citizens of postcolonial states: *equality* with an increased likelihood of *domestic instability* or *inequality* with a decreased likelihood of *international stability*.

If Not Democracy, Then What?

The results from the data analyses, which contradict the DPP for most large-scale international and domestic conflicts, beg the question, "If not democracy, then what factor(s) accounted for the absence of war between democratic states in the postwar era?" I maintain that the "peace" among democracies during the Cold War was overdetermined. The second half of the twentieth century witnessed the convergence of several conflict-dampening factors across different levels of aggrega-tion: bipolarity, which is negatively correlated with large wars; nuclear deterrence, which decreased the likelihood of great-power war; endur-ing alliances, which are negatively correlated with war; heightened alliance-aggregation among democracies, which reduced their conflict levels; increased trade among allies, which is negatively correlated with interstate war; "dual-hegemony" among superpowers, which decreased conflict within the respective blocs; and the emergence of an international security regime, which ultimately facilitated the reduction in conflict levels between democratic states.

As noted, it is clear that while democracy as a political system has many virtues, international stability, much less international peace, is not likely to emerge from the proliferation of democratic states. This is not to say that we shouldn't be concerned about the development of democracy in states throughout the globe as a matter of humanitarian interest. Instead, the findings remind us that even the promotion of what most would agree is a positive good (i.e., democratic government) may result in unexpected and undesired outcomes. The relationship between democracy and peace is prismatic, in that sense. The findings have par-ticular relevance for the democratization of the two nondemocratic major powers, Russia and China, since they challenge the popular assumption that these states will become more peaceful as they become more democratic. Similarly they cast doubt on the prospects for peace among postcolonial states in the present wave of democratization.

To be sure, the behavior and interaction of leaders are not limited to the patterns revealed in the statistical analyses, which, at best, can only tell us how the variables of interest such as democracy and war have been associated with each other in the past. Leaders may learn lessons from history so as not to repeat past mistakes. In addition, international contexts may change and encourage different relationships among the variables of interest. Further, there are myriad factors that affect decisions to go to war, and we cannot hope to account for all of them. Neither can we perfectly anticipate those that may affect the decisions of leaders in the future. So forecasts from statistical analyses should be approached with caution. However, one can meaningfully conjecture from the evidence on the likelihood of certain developments in the future given what we have observed of similar processes in the past. Since the theoretical argument presented in this study suggests that the peace among democratic states in the Cold War era resulted less from democracy, as such, than from factors associated with the creation of an international security regime, it is reasonable to examine the likelihood that these conflict-dampening factors will persist in the post–Cold War era.

At the risk of appearing even more pessimistic than I have already, I maintain that it is not clear that the factors that exerted a conflict-dampening impact on states in the Cold War era will have a consistent irenic impact in the post–Cold War era. For example, although the focus on the role of international security regimes in promoting stability in the Cold War casts a favorable light on the role of international institutions in global peace, the extent to which such a regime will continue to exhibit such an impact on international relations rests to a large degree on its ability to perform similar functions in the unipolar post–Cold War era. But a key element in the maintenance of this regime was the bipolar structure of the system, which encouraged not only the creation of superpower alliances, but, as Gowa (1994: 120) observed, "less dispersion of market power than had prevailed earlier. As a consequence, it made the evolution of political-military alliances into free-trade coalitions more likely." This dynamic, which eventually resulted in an international regime that limited warfare among democracies, was largely rooted in the interplay between two key institutions, NATO and the WTO. But these institutions have become more fluid in the post–Cold War era, and it's not clear whether their impact will be consistent across the two eras. This is most evident in the case of NATO.

With the end of the Cold War there was an emergent view that NATO had outlived its purpose and that the international relations of the states of the two Cold War blocs would no longer be marked by the unilateral pursuit of their respective bloc's interests but by a commitment to multilateral initiatives. This perspective gained increasing support as a result of the behavior of the United States and the former Soviet Union during the Gulf War. In the first major military engagement of the post–Cold War era, the United States amassed an effective and unlikely coalition of over thirty states ranging from staunch allies such as Britain to staunch adversaries such as Syria to dislodge Iraq's military forces from Kuwait. The Gulf War witnessed a U.S.-led coalition receiving the tacit endorsement of the former Soviet Union, Saudi Arabia allowing Western states to stage troops on its territory, and Israel—which had initiated a surprise attack on Iraq's incipient nuclear weapons building facilities a decade earlier—refraining from retaliating against Iraq even as Saddam Hussein's forces rained SCUD missiles down upon it. U.S. President George H. Bush feverishly rallied international support for what would become known as Operation Desert Storm, in order to ensure that it took on a multilateral character. This was accomplished primarily through consultation with the UN. The result was Resolution 660, which demanded Iraq's withdrawal from Kuwait; Resolution 661, which imposed a trade embargo on Iraq; and, finally, Resolution 678, which authorized member states to use "all necessary means" to evict Iraq from Kuwait.

What was no less impressive (and quite controversial at the time) was that after expelling Iraqi forces from Kuwait the U.S.-led UN coalition forces exercised restraint by not occupying Baghdad and in this way acted in strict accordance with the UN resolutions under which the forces operated. The prosecution of the Gulf War was hailed by many as a harbinger of the multilateralism that would mark the post–Cold War era. President's Bush consultation with UN representatives helped both to legitimize in the eyes of many—especially those in the Arab world—the expulsion of Iraq from Kuwait and to strengthen the post–Cold War visage of the UN. But if observers thought that U.S. policies in the Gulf War would provide a blueprint for its post–Cold War military engagements, their conclusions were shown to be premature at best.

What disabused many analysts of the view that international organizations such as the UN had increased in salience with respect to major-power international security issues occurred less than a decade later, when U.S. President Clinton chose to bypass the UN regarding his plan to have NATO air forces strike the Federal Republic of Yugoslavia in response to the government's attacks on its own citizens in the region of Kosovo. Although NATO air strikes had been used briefly and selectively against Serb positions around Sarajevo in the previous conflict in Yugoslavia regarding the fate of Bosnia-Herzegovina, NATO bombing in this round of Balkan violence began in March 1999 and lasted seventy-eight days with NATO aircraft flying more than 37,000 sorties against Yugoslavia. Clinton argued that the cessation of attacks against Kosovar Albanians by the Serbian-dominated Yugoslavian armed forces constituted a "moral imperative" for the United States and NATO. Interestingly this "moral imperative" did not extend to atrocities committed by U.S. allies in the region, such as those committed by Turkey against its Kurdish populations. Moreover, this seems to be more of a case of "selective moral outrage" given the Clinton administration's refusal to intervene to prevent the Rwandan genocide and its guidance to diplomats and staff to avoid using the term *genocide* in discussions of the slaughter that would result in 500,000–800,000 deaths. The highest estimate of the number of people killed in Kosovo does not represent a tenth of the lowest estimate of victims in Rwanda.

U.S. decisionmaking was more likely motivated by the fear that the conflict in Kosovo would spill over into neighboring states such as Macedonia (which it eventually did) and possibly threaten stability among NATO allies themselves (especially Greece). As Kegley and Raymond (2002: 228) point out, "If NATO acted without a UN Security Council resolution specifically authorizing the use of force against Yugoslavia, it would violate the UN Charter. Article 2(4) prohibits 'the threat or use of force against the territorial integrity or political independence of any state,' except in self-defense (Article 51) or when authorized by the Security Council (Chapter VII)." None of these exceptions applied in Kosovo. As the administration put forth its own propositions to justify its actions, it became clear that in matters of U.S. military interests, multilateralism represented by appeals to the UN was not imperative. Further, the U.S. prosecution of the war in Kosovo through NATO as opposed to the UN seems to indicate that the lone superpower is not as committed to international organizations and multilateralism as may have been inferred from its behavior leading up to the Gulf War.

The use of NATO air strikes in Kosovo is all the more telling since NATO, as an alliance, did not fire a shot in anger against any Warsaw Pact member's armed forces during the Cold War even in cases of clear Soviet aggression in Hungary in 1956, Czechoslovakia in 1968, and Afghanistan in 1979. Some analysts aver that through its actions in Kosovo, NATO, "which was founded in 1949 as a collective defense alliance to deter an attack on Western Europe by the Soviet Union, inaugurated its new Strategic Concept that expanded NATO security concerns to crisis management operations outside of its original scope" (Kegley and Raymond, 2002: 230). NATO's use of force in Kosovo also inaugurates a new phase in the post–Cold War era, one in which the overwhelming hegemony of the United States allows it to bypass the UN, leaving major international institutions to play second fiddle to power politics. This case shows that the lone superpower is no more committed to international institutions in what it construes as important security issues than what was evident among the superpowers during the Cold War. It also reminds us of NATO's changing role in the post–Cold War era, which calls into question the extent to which NATO will be able to provide the bedrock for a security regime. This conclusion is not gainsaid by the recent NATO actions in the U.S.-Afghan War since the September 2001 attacks on the United States (a NATO member) allowed NATO to invoke its self-defense clause for the first time in its history. The U.S.-led "war on terrorism" is likely to lose its multilateral cast as the "antiterrorism" coalition disintegrates around the divergent interests of its individual members such as occurred with the Gulf War coalition. Beyond these recent ventures, what are likely to be more common are more single-minded U.S. military initiatives such as those in Colombia ostensibly aimed at countering narcoterrorism but in actuality placing U.S. troops within a bitter and ongoing civil war and casting them in a role strikingly similar to that of U.S. "advisers" in Vietnam in the early 1960s with little hope for the establishment—by military force—of stability or democracy in Colombia, much less peace.

For democratic peace advocates, it may seem obvious that now more than ever NATO can provide the basis for international security among democracies because of its ability to democratize member states and thereby increase the likelihood of peaceful relations among them. This impact, the argument suggests, will be even more apparent as

NATO pursues its present policy of enlargement, which brought three new states into the alliance in 1999—Poland, Hungary, and the Czech Republic—and led nine other states to petition for membership (Albania, Bulgaria, Estonia, Latvia, Lithuania, Macedonia, Romania, Slovakia, and Slovenia). Even if one accepts against the evidence presented here that democracies are more peaceful than nondemocracies, it is evident, as Reiter (2001) acknowledges, that NATO has not "spread democracy" in the post–Cold War era because the new members of NATO had embarked on a course of democratization before and quite apart from their solicitation for entry into the organization. Moreover, NATO enlargement has done little to assuage the suspicions of Russian leaders who fear Western encroachment and the potential threat of a renewed arms race driven by the U.S. desire to develop antiballistic missile technology and President George W. Bush's desire to scuttle the ABM Treaty. Further, it is yet to be seen if NATO assertiveness in the Balkans can be balanced with its democratization mission in an environment where both of these orientations—especially the latter—are increasingly seen as the domain of the dominant regional organization, the European Union, which has been much more committed to spreading democracy and is much less likely to alienate Russia (see Reiter, 2001). In fact, NATO is viewed more today as an impediment to the development of an effective European security system.

Although it is premature to determine whether NATO's actions in Afghanistan will generate democracy in that country, few analysts of the region think that is likely given that prominent members of the U.S.-backed Northern Alliance had egregious records of human rights abuses before they were toppled by the even more brutal Taliban regime. Further, the selective support for repressive regimes such as was evident in the Gulf War in the case of Kuwait and Saudi Arabia (whose domestic policies are nearly as repressive as those of the Taliban), and in the Afghan War with respect to Pakistan (which had previously been accused by Western intelligence agencies of supporting terrorism) will further undermine the view of NATO as an instrument of democratization. Moreover, the war in Afghanistan has exacerbated the decades long India-Pakistan dispute resulting in renewed conflict between those nuclear-armed rivals. With further military and nonmilitary actions threatened in other states that are viewed as supporters of terrorism, the U.S.-led coalition is likely to fracture around the divergent interests of its members. The internal conflicts will not simply reflect the rift between Western and Islamic members of the coalition amid charges that the United States promptly responds militarily to terrorism committed by those who associate themselves with Islam but often supports or is silent in the face of state-sponsored terrorism committed by its ally Israel, against Palestinian Muslims in the Occupied Territories, or by its NATO ally Turkey, against its predominantly Muslim Kurdish population. These charges have largely been ignored by the West and, in the face of jingoistic support for military retaliation against the attacks on the United States, are likely to continue to fall on deaf ears until the embers of the destruction of September 11, 2001, have died out. But with the discussion of subsequent military forays in the "war on terrorism" turning to targets such as Somalia, the Phillipines, Yemen, Iraq, Iran, and possibly others, disputes are likely to emerge from within the NATO alliance itself, as the members begin to resist the subordination of their own foreign policy interests and their conception of the appropriate direction for NATO to those of the United States, especially given the absence of an overarching threat that would galvanize the alliance, such as was evident during the Cold War, and emerging controversy over which states are legitimate targets of "antiterrorist" strikes. Clearly, even the presence of such a threat during the Cold War did not prevent France from withdrawing from NATO's military command structure in 1966. Given the increasing economic power of the EU, it is only a matter of time before it flexes its muscles in the security sphere. In such a context, the multilateralism of NATO that played such a key role in the creation of the international security regime among democracies during the Cold War is likely to decline in the post–Cold War era. With that, the incentives of its members to recreate or sustain the multilateral support necessary for the maintenance of the Cold War era security regime and the "democratic peace" that it spawned will be significantly reduced.

But it is not only NATO that faces changes and challenges in the post–Cold War environment. The other major institution of the Cold War's "democratic peace," the WTO, is also affected by the changed context of international relations. The most obvious difference is the change from a bipolar to a unipolar system, which is a seminal transformation since the global system has never been unipolar. Although, as argued in Chapter 6, the linkage between alliance membership and trade interdependence gave rise to—and in large part sustained—the international regime among democracies in the bipolar Cold War era, it is not at all clear that this type of relationship will persist in a unipolar system—although the ascent of China to the WTO seems propitious on its face. Some might contend that in a unipolar system, it is more likely that international regimes will be created to allow the hegemon to coordinate international relations in the key areas of security and trade. But, in fact, it is hard to imagine that international trade will follow the patterns manifest during the Cold War era when trade "followed the flag." Without the Cold War to provide the ideological glue binding allies and trading partners, it is likely that some trade patterns will assume different trajectories and that new trading partnerships will develop while others come to an end.[1] Further, though trade interdependence is likely to continue to reduce the probability of armed conflict, in the post–Cold War era one would expect a greater influence of regionally based trade associations such as the European Union (EU), NAFTA, Mercosur, APEC, and to some extent the SADC.[2] As these associations become more institutionalized, they may emerge as regionally based regimes (the EU has already progressed beyond this stage). The resultant regionally based regimes might then come into conflict with the hegemon's more globally based ones, such as the WTO. Since security externalities of trade persist, and market failure is an enduring concern, the issue is not so much whether international regimes will emerge, but rather whose interests they will reflect. The post–Cold War era is likely to witness increasing tensions between regionalism and unipolarity, which have the potential to fracture the hegemon's existing trading regime and undermine the stability it has helped to provide. In sum, there are potential challenges to the ability of those institutions that helped generate peace among democracies in the Cold War era to perform similarly in the post–Cold War era.

Conclusion

We began this investigation of the "democratic peace" by reflecting on the relevance of Angell's (1910) and Bloch's (1899) conclusions on the changed nature of warfare in the industrial age and the lessons it portended for future large-scale conflict among the major powers. Both agreed that given the level of destructiveness of weaponry at the time and the immense value of the profits from trade that would be lost as a result of sustained combat, major-power war would become obsolete if political and military elites of the major powers recognized the inherently Pyrrhic nature of the enterprise. Such arguments rely on the changing international environment to encourage adaptive behavior on the part of state leaders navigating the maelstrom of international relations. But often, as in the case of World War I, leaders fail to heed the lessons enunciated by those who recognize such transformations.

Democratic peace scholars, in many ways, are of a similar lot. But instead of acknowledging a transformation in the nature of warfare, per se, they substitute for it an argument on the difference in international context for certain types of states in the system—democracies, which they argue operate largely outside the Clausewitzian security environment, at least in their relations with other democracies. Democratic peace advocates insist that once leaders recognize the pacific benefits of democratic government, they will come to appreciate that the expansion of democracy throughout the global system is among the most— if not is *the* most—effective means of ensuring peace. The findings in this book contribute to disabusing scholars of the notion that democracies are more peaceful with each other, that they are more peaceful than nondemocracies, or that they are more peaceful with respect to civil wars in postcolonial states. However, the findings do not challenge the appropriateness of "democracy" as a form of government or an ideal to be pursued among and within nations. Instead, they challenge the democratic peace proposition, which, in its most prominent form, suggests that democracy generates peaceful international relations. As such, they challenge—as did Guetzkow (1950) more than a half-century ago—the appropriateness of monocausal "theories" of foreign policy that emphasize a single factor (or two) to explain complex phenomena such as war. The major theoretical implication of this study is that stability, much less peace, in the post–Cold War era—just as in the Cold War era—will not be provided by democratic enlargement. Instead it will require, as a first order, complex, multifaceted, multilateral foreign policies and flexible domestic policies that recognize and are responsive to the challenges of a dynamic international political economy. The findings also remind us of the need to examine factors across various levels of aggregation: system (the persistence of regimes), dyad (trade interdependence), unit (semidemocracy), and individual (perceptions of racial or cultural difference) in formulating our theoretical arguments. They also suggest the need to move beyond statistical tests of the DPP, focusing instead on detailed case studies of the foreign policies of democratic states in order to make causal arguments about the relationship between democracy and war (see Henderson, 1999a: 212).

Finally, it is important to remember that Bloch correctly assessed the awesome destructiveness of future major-power war. The bloody records of the world wars bear this out, but of course the major-power elites did not attend to his thesis. The much-maligned Angell was also correct that the view that military conquest—not warfare in general—would be an effective means of pursuing a state's economic interests in a highly interdependent world was, in fact, a "great illusion." The statistical findings and theoretical argument of this study indicate that international stability—much less international peace—does not result from the proliferation of democracies, which are among the most war-prone states. Therefore, the democratic peace is hardly an empirical law; in fact, it appears to be a "great illusion."

Notes

1. Huntington (1996) argues that culture as articulated through major civilizations has replaced ideology as the hub around which world politics spins in the post–Cold War era. For an empirical assessment of Huntington's theoretical arguments, see Russett et al. (2000) and Henderson and Tucker (2001).

2. While trade clearly has a conflict-dampening role in international relations, I maintain that it accomplishes this apart from any impact it has on promoting democracy—since democracy increases the likelihood of interstate conflict for a state. It is also important to remember that free trade does not necessarily encourage democracy as the examples of authoritarian free traders such as Singapore and Malaysia attest. Likewise, it is not at all evident that China's increased trade is having a liberalizing effect on that country's political institutions. For example, Kaplan (2001: 27) observes, "The rapid expansion of China's trade ties to the outside world over the past decade has coincided with a worsening of political repression at home." It is yet to be seen whether China's recent ascent to membership in the WTO significantly affects its liberalization or its conflict propensity.

Appendix

Estimation of DPP Using General Estimating Equation (GEE) and Robust Standard Errors

	Equation A (Replication of Oneal and Russett, 1997)	Equation B (Drop Ongoing Dispute Years)	Equation C (Add Political Dissimilarity)	Equation D (Drop Ongoing Dispute Years, Add Political Dissimilarity)
Democracy$_{LO}$	−.05*** (.01)	−.03* (.016)	−.003*** (.001)	−.01 (.02)
Economic growth$_{LO}$	−.02** (.01)	−.03** (.013)	−.02** (.01)	−.04*** (.01)
Allies	−.82*** (.22)	−.65*** (.21)	−.77*** (.21)	−.52*** (.20)
Contiguity	1.24*** (.23)	1.66*** (.21)	1.31*** (.23)	1.78*** (.22)
Capability ratio	−.003*** (.001)	−.002*** (.001)	−.003*** (.001)	−.002*** (.001)
Trade ratio$_{LO}$	−40.64** (20.52)	−41.23** (23.02)	−43.26** (21.17)	−42.36* (23.55)
Political dissimilarity	—	—	.02 (.01)	.04*** (.01)
Constant	−3.26*** (.18)	−3.97*** (.17)	−3.44*** (.22)	−4.33*** (.22)
Deviance	6,957.57	4,974.48	6,931.83	4,940.70
N	20,985	20,985	20,985	20,985
X^2	78.20***	110.77***	81.21***	112.00***

Note: Robust standard errors are in parentheses; all p-values are estimated using two-tailed tests.

*p ≤ .10, **p ≤ .05 level, ***p ≤ .01 level

References

Acharya, Amitav. 1992. "Regionalism and Regime Security in the Third World: Comparing the Origins of the ASEAN and the GCC," in Brian Job, ed., *The Insecurity Dilemma*. Boulder, CO: Lynne Rienner, pp. 143–164.

Angell, Norman. 1910. *The Great Illusion: A Study of the Relation of Military Power in Nations to Their Economic and Social Advantage*. New York: Putnam.

Auvinen, Juha. 1996. "IMF Intervention and Political Protest in the Third World: A Conventional Wisdom Refined," *Third World Quarterly* 17, 3: 377–400.

———. 1997. "Political Conflict in Less Developed Countries, 1981–89," *Journal of Peace Research* 34, 2: 177–195.

Axelrod, Robert. 1984. *The Evolution of Cooperation*. New York: Basic Books.

Ayoob, Mohammed. 1995. *The Third World Security Predicament*. Boulder, CO: Lynne Rienner.

Babst, Dean. 1964. "Elective Governments—A Force for Peace," *The Wisconsin Sociologist* 3, 1: 9–14.

———. 1972. "A Force for Peace," *Industrial Research* (April): 55–58.

Barbieri, Katherine. 1996. "Economic Interdependence: A Path to Peace or a Source of Interstate Conflict," *Journal of Peace Research* 33 (February): 29–49.

Barrows, Walter. 1976. "Ethnic Diversity and Political Instability in Black Africa," *Comparative Political Studies* 9, 2: 139–170.

Beck, Nathaniel, Jonathon Katz, and Richard Tucker. 1998. "Taking Time Seriously in Binary Time-Series-Cross-Section Analysis," *American Journal of Political Science* 42, 4: 1260–1288.

Bennett, D. Scott, and Allan Stam. 1998. "The Declining Advantages of Democracy: A Combined Model of War Outcomes and Duration," *Journal of Conflict Resolution* 42, 3 (June): 344–366.

———. 2000. "Research Design and Estimator Choices in the Analysis of Interstate Dyads: When Decisions Matter," *Journal of Conflict Resolution* 42, 3 (October): 653–685.

Benoit, Kenneth. 1996. "Democracies Really Are More Pacific (in General): Reexamining Regime Type and War Involvement," *Journal of Conflict Resolution* 40, 4 (December): 636–658.

Benson, Michelle, and Jacek Kugler. 1998. "Power Parity, Democracy, and the Severity of Internal Violence," *Journal of Conflict Resolution* 42, 2: 196–209.

Blainey, Geoffrey. 1988. *The Causes of War,* 3rd ed. New York: Free Press.

Bloch, Ivan. 1899. *The Future of War*. New York: Doubleday and McClure.

Boswell, Terry, and William Dixon. 1990. "Dependency and Rebellion: A Cross-National Analysis," *American Sociological Review* 55, 4: 540–559.

———. 1993. "Marx's Theory of Rebellion: A Cross-National Analysis of Class Exploitation, Economic Development, and Violent Revolt," *American Sociological Review* 58, 5: 681–702.

Bremer, Stuart. 1992. "Dangerous Dyads: Conditions Affecting the Likelihood of Interstate War, 1816–1965," *Journal of Conflict Resolution* 36: 309–341.

———. 1993. "Democracy and Militarized Interstate Conflict, 1816–1965," *International Interactions* 18, 3: 231–250.

Broad, Robin, and John Cavanagh. 1998. "Don't Neglect the Impoverished South," in Robert Griffiths, ed., *Annual Editions: Developing World 98/99*. Guilford, CT: McGraw-Hill, pp. 18–25.

Broad, Robin, and Christina Landi. 1996. "Whither the North-South Gap," *Third World Quarterly* 17, 1: 7–17.

Brodie, Bernard. 1946. *The Absolute Weapon*. New York: Basic Books.

Bronson, Rachel. 1996. "Cycles of Conflict in the Middle East and North Africa," in Michael Brown, ed., *The International Dimensions of Internal Conflict*. Cambridge, MA: MIT Press, pp. 205–234.

Brush, Stephen. 1996. "Dynamics of Theory Change in the Social Sciences: Relative Deprivation and Collective Violence," *Journal of Conflict Resolution* 40, 4: 523–545.

Brzoska, Michael. 1992. "Is the Nuclear Non-Proliferation System a Regime? A Comment on Trevor Morris Tate," *Journal of Peace Research* 29 (May): 215–220.

Bueno de Mesquita, Bruce. 1981. *The War Trap*. New Haven: Yale University Press.

Bueno de Mesquita, Bruce, and David Lalman. 1990. "Domestic Opposition and Foreign War," *American Political Science Review* 84, 3 (September): 747–766.

————. 1992. *War and Reason: Domestic and International Imperatives*. New Haven, CT: Yale University Press.

Bueno de Mesquita, Bruce, James Morrow, Randolph Siverson, and Alastair Smith. 1999. "An Institutional Explanation of the Democratic Peace," *American Political Science Review* 93, 4 (December): 791–807.

Bueno de Mesquita, Bruce, Randolph Siverson, and Gary Woller. 1992. "War and the Fate of Regimes: A Comparative Analysis," *American Political Science Review* 86, 3 (September): 747–766.

Busch, Marc. 2000. "Democracy, Consultation, and the Paneling of Disputes Under GATT," *Journal of Conflict Resolution* 44, 4 (August): 425–446.

Chan, Steve. 1984. "Mirror, Mirror on the Wall . . . Are the Freer Countries More Pacific?" *Journal of Conflict Resolution* 28 (December): 617–649.

————. 1985. "The Impact of Defense Spending on Economic Performance: A Survey of Evidence and Problems," *Orbis* 29, 2: 403–434.

————. 1995. "Grasping the Peace Dividend: Some Propositions on the Conversion of Swords into Plowshares," *Mershon International Studies Review* 39, 1: 53–95.

Clinton, William. 1996. *A National Security Strategy of Engagement and Enlargement*. Washington, DC: U.S. Government Printing Office.

Cohen, Raymond. 1994. "Pacific Unions: A Reappraisal of the Theory That Democracies Do Not Fight One Another," *Review of International Studies* 20 (August): 207–224.

Cohen, Youssef, Brian Brown, and A. F. K. Organski. 1981. "The Paradoxical Nature of State Making: The Violent Creation of Order," *American Political Science Review* 75, 4: 901–910.

Collier, Paul. 1998. "The Political Economy of Ethnicity," Working Paper Series 98-8, Centre for the Study of African Economies, Oxford, UK (April).

Collier, Paul, and Anke Hoeffler. 1998. "On Economic Causes of Civil War," *Oxford Economic Papers* 50 (October): 563–573.

Crescenzi, Mark, and Andrew Enterline. 1999. "Ripples from the Waves? A Systemic, Time-Series Analysis of Democracy, Democratization, and Interstate War," *Journal of Peace Research* 36, 1 (January): 75–94.

Davies, James. 1962. "Toward a Theory of Revolution," *American Sociological Review* 27, 1: 5–19.

Davis, David, and Will Moore. 1997. "Ethnicity Matters: Transnational Ethnic Alliances and Foreign Policy Behavior," *International Studies Quarterly* 41: 171–184.

Deger, Saadet. 1986. *Military Expenditure in Third World Countries*. London: Routledge and Kegan Paul.

Deutsch, Karl, Sidney Burrell, Robert Kahn, Maurice Lee, Martin Lichterman, Raymond Lindgren, Francis Loewenheim, and Richard Van Wagenen. 1957. *Political Community and the North Atlantic Area*. Princeton: Princeton University Press.

Deutsch, Karl, and J. David Singer. 1964. "Multipolar Power Systems and International Stability," *World Politics* 16 (April): 390–406.

Diamond, Larry. 1992. "Promoting Democracy," *Foreign Policy* 87 (Summer): 25–46.

Dixon, William. 1993. "Democracy and the Peaceful Settlement of International Conflict," *Journal of Conflict Resolution* 37, 1: 42–68.

———. 1994. "Democracy and the Management of International Conflict," *American Political Science Review* 88, 1: 14–32.

Dower, John. 1986. *War Without Mercy: Race and Power in the Pacific War.* New York: Pantheon.

Doyle, Michael. 1983a. "Kant, Liberal Legacies, and Foreign Affairs, Part 1," *Philosophy and Public Affairs* 12, 3: 205–235.

———. 1983b. "Kant, Liberal Legacies, and Foreign Affairs, Part 2," *Philosophy and Public Affairs* 12, 4: 323–353.

———. 1986. "Liberalism and World Politics," *American Political Science Review* 80 (Summer): 1151–1170.

———. 1997. *Ways of War and Peace.* New York: W. W. Norton.

DuBois, W. E. B. 1961 [1903]. *The Souls of Black Folk.* Greenwich, CT: Fawcett.

———. 1987 [1947]. *The World and Africa.* New York: International Publishers.

Duvall, Raymond. 1976. "An Appraisal of the Methodological and Statistical Procedures of the Correlates of War Project," in Francis Hoole and Dina Zinnes, eds., *Quantitative International Politics: An Appraisal.* New York: Praeger, pp. 67–98.

East, Maurice, and Philip M. Gregg. 1967. "Factors Influencing Cooperation and Conflict in the International System," *International Studies Quarterly* 11, 3 (September): 244–269.

East, Maurice, and Charles K. Hermann. 1974. "Do Nation-Types Account for Foreign Policy Behavior?" in James N. Rosenau, ed., *Comparing Foreign Policies.* New York: Wiley, pp. 269–303.

Eichenberg, Richard, Brigitta Widmaier, and Ulrich Widmaier. 1984. "Projecting Domestic Conflict Using Cross-Section Data: A Project Report," in J. David Singer and Richard Stoll, eds., *Quantitative Indicators in World Politics.* New York: Praeger, pp. 11–33.

Elman, Miriam. 1997. "Unpacking Democracy: Presidentialism, Parliamentarism, and the Democratic Peace Theory." Paper presented to the American Political Science Association, August, Washington, DC.

Enterline, Andrew. 1996. "Correspondence: Driving While Democratizing," *International Security* 20, 4 (December): 183–196.

Eyerman, Joe, and Robert Hart. 1996. "An Empirical Test of the Audience Cost Proposition: Democracy Speaks Louder than Words," *Journal of Conflict Resolution* 40, 4: 597–616.

Farber, Henry, and Joanne Gowa. 1995. "Polities and Peace," *International Security* 20 (Fall): 123–146.

————. 1997. "Common Interests or Common Polities? Reinterpreting the Democratic Peace," *Journal of Politics* 59 (May): 393–417.

Fearon, James. 1994. "Domestic Political Audiences and the Escalation of International Disputes," *American Political Science Review* 88 (September): 577–592.

Fearon, James, and David Laitin. 1996. "Explaining Interethnic Cooperation," *American Political Science Review* 90, 4: 715–735.

Findlay, Trevor. 1996. "Turning the Corner in Southeast Asia," in Michael Brown, ed., *The International Dimensions of Internal Conflict*. Cambridge, MA: MIT Press, pp. 173–204.

Finel, Bernard, and Kristin Lord. 2000. "The Surprising Logic of Transparency," in Bernard Finel and Kristin Lord, eds., *Power and Conflict in the Age of Transparency*. New York: Palgrave, pp. 137–179.

Forsythe, David. 1992. "Democracy, War, and Covert Action," *Journal of Peace Research* 29, 4: 385–395.

Frederickson, Peter, and Robert Looney. 1983. "Defense Expenditures and Economic Growth in Developing Countries," *Armed Forces and Society* 9, 4: 633–645.

Friedrich, Robert. 1982. "In Defense of Multiplicative Terms in Multiple Regression Equations," *American Journal of Political Science* 26, 4 (November): 797–833.

Gaddis, John. 1987. *The Long Peace: Inquiries into the History of the Cold War*. New York: Oxford University Press.

————. 1992. *The United States and the End of the Cold War*. New York: Oxford University Press.

Ganguly, Sumit. 1996. "Conflict and Crisis in South and Southwest Asia," in Michael Brown, ed., *The International Dimensions of Internal Conflict*. Cambridge, MA: MIT Press, pp. 141–172.

Gartzke, Erik. 1998. "Kant We All Just Get Along? Opportunity, Willingness, and the Origins of the Democratic Peace," *American Journal of Political Science* 42: 1–27.

————. 2000. "Preferences and the Democratic Peace," *International Studies Quarterly* 44, 2: 191–210.

Gates, Scott, Torbjorn Knutsen, and Jonathon Moses. 1996. "Democracy and Peace: A More Skeptical View," *Journal of Peace Research* 33 (February): 1–11.

Geller, Daniel. 1985. *Domestic Factors in Foreign Policy*. Cambridge, MA: Schenkman.

Geller, Daniel, and J. David Singer. 1998. *Nations at War*. Cambridge, UK: Cambridge University Press.

Gelpi, Christopher. 1997. "Democratic Diversions: Government Structure and the Externalization of Domestic Conflict," *Journal of Conflict Resolution* 41: 255–282.

Gelpi, Christopher, and Joseph Grieco. 2000. "Democracy, Crisis Escalation, and the Survival of Political Leaders, 1918–1992." Unpublished manuscript, Duke University.

Gilbert, Alain. 1999. *Must Global Politics Constrain Democracy? Great Power Realism, Democratic Peace, and Democratic Internationalism.* Princeton: Princeton University Press.

Gilpin, Robert. 1981. *War and Change in World Politics.* Cambridge: Cambridge University Press.

Gleditsch, Kristian S., and Michael D. Ward. 1997. "Double Take: A Reexamination of Democracy and Autocracy in Modern Polities," *Journal of Conflict Resolution* 41: 361-383.

Gleditsch, Nils Petter. 1995a. "Geography, Democracy, and Peace," *International Interactions* 20: 297–323.

————. 1995b. "Democracy and the Future of European Peace," *European Journal of International Relations* 1, 4: 539–571.

Gleditsch, Nils, and Havard Hegre. 1997. "Peace and Democracy: Three Levels of Analysis," *Journal of Conflict Resolution* 41 (April): 283–310.

Gochman, Charles. 1980. "Status, Capabilities, and Major Power Conflict," in J. David Singer, ed., *The Correlates of War II: Testing Some Realpolitik Models.* New York: Free Press, pp. 83–123.

————. 1996. "Correspondence: Democracy and Peace," *International Security* 21, 3: 177–186.

Goemans, Hein. 1997. "The Democratic Peace and Civil War." Paper presented to the Annual Conference of the American Political Science Association, August, Washington, DC.

Gowa, Joanne. 1994. *Allies, Adversaries, and International Trade.* Princeton: Princeton University Press.

————. 1999. *Ballots and Bullets.* Princeton: Princeton University Press.

Gowa, Joanne, and Edward D. Mansfield. 1993. "Power Politics and International Trade," *American Political Science Review* 87 (June): 408–420.

Gregg, Phillip, and A. Banks. 1965. "Dimensions of Political Systems: Factor Analysis of 'A Cross-Polity Survey,'" *American Political Science Review* 59: 602–614.

Grieco, Joseph. 1988. "Anarchy and the Limits of Cooperation: A Realist Critique of the Newest Liberal Institutionalism," *International Organization* 42 (Summer): 485–507.

Guetzkow, Harold. 1950. "Long Range Research in International Relations," *The American Perspective* 4 (Fall): 421–440.

Gurr, Ted. 1968. "A Causal Model of Civil Strife: A Comparative Analysis Using New Indices," *American Political Science Review* 62, 4: 1104–1124.

————. 1970. *Why Men Rebel.* Princeton: Princeton University Press.

————. 1980. "On the Outcomes of Violent Conflict," in Ted Gurr, ed., *Handbook of Political Conflict.* New York: Free Press, pp. 238–294.

———. 1994. "Peoples Against States: Ethnopolitical Conflict and the Changing World System," *International Studies Quarterly* 38 (September): 347–377.

Gurr, Ted, ed. 1993. *Minorities at Risk: A Global View of Ethnopolitical Conflict*. Washington, DC: U.S. Institute of Peace.

Gurr, Ted, and Raymond Duvall. 1973. "Civil Conflict in the 1960s: A Reciprocal Theoretical System with Parameter Estimates," *Comparative Political Studies* 6, 2: 135–169.

Gurr, Ted, and Barbara Harff. 1994. *Ethnic Conflict in World Politics*. Boulder, CO: Westview.

Gurr, Ted, and Mark Lichbach. 1979. "Forecasting Domestic Political Conflict," in J. David Singer and Michael Wallace, eds., *To Augur Well: Early Warning Indicators in World Politics*. Beverly Hills, CA: Sage, pp. 153–193.

Gurr, Ted, and Will Moore. 1998. "Ethnopolitical Rebellion: A Cross-Sectional Analysis for the 1980s with Risk Assessments for the 1990s," *American Journal of Political Science* 41, 4: 1079–1103.

Gyimah-Brempong, Kwabena. 1989. "Defense Spending and Economic Growth in Sub-Saharan Africa: An Econometric Investigation," *Journal of Peace Research* 26, 1: 79–90.

———. 1992. "Do African Governments Favor Defense in Budgeting?" *Journal of Peace Research* 29, 2: 191–206.

Haas, Ernst. 1958. *The Uniting of Europe*. Stanford, CA: Stanford University Press.

Haas, Michael. 1965. "Societal Approaches to the Study of War," *Journal of Peace Research* 2, 4: 307–323.

Hardy, Melissa. 1979. "Economic Growth, Distributional Inequality, and Political Conflict in Industrial Societies," *Journal of Political and Military Sociology* 7 (Fall): 209–227.

Hegre, Havard, Tanja Ellingsen, Nils Petter Gleditsch, and Scott Gates. 1997. "Towards a Democratic Civil Peace? Democracy, Democratization, and Civil War 1816–1992." Paper presented to the Annual Conference of the Peace Science Society (International), November, Indianapolis, IN.

Henderson, Errol. 1995. *Afrocentrism and World Politics: Towards a New Paradigm*. Westport, CT: Praeger.

———. 1997. "Culture or Contiguity: Ethnic Conflict, the Similarity of States, and the Onset of Interstate War, 1820–1989," *Journal of Conflict Resolution* 41, 5: 649–668.

———. 1998a. "The Democratic Peace Through the Lens of Culture, 1820–1989," *International Studies Quarterly* 42, 3: 461–484.

———. 1998b. "The Impact of Culture on African Coups d'Etat, 1960–1997," *World Affairs* 161, 1: 10–21.

———. 1999a. "Neoidealism and the Democratic Peace," *Journal of Peace Research* 36, 2: 203–231.

————. 1999b. "Civil Wars," in Lawrence Kurtz, ed., *The Encyclopedia of Violence, Peace and Conflict.* San Diego, CA: Academic Press, pp. 279–287.

————. 2000. "When States Implode: The Correlates of Africa's Civil Wars, 1950–92," *Studies in Comparative International Development* 35, 2: 28–47.

————. 2001. "Through a Glass Darkly: Afrocentrism, War, and World Politics," *New Political Science* 23, 2: 203–223.

Henderson, Errol, and J. David Singer. 2000. "Civil War in the Postcolonial World, 1946–92," *Journal of Peace Research* 37, 3: 275–299.

————. In press. "New Wars and Rumors of New Wars," *International Interactions.*

Henderson, Errol, and Richard Tucker. 2001. "Clear and Present Strangers: The Clash of Civilizations and International Conflict," *International Studies Quarterly* 45: 317–338.

Heo, Uk. 1998. "Modeling the Defense-Growth Relationship Around the Globe," *Journal of Conflict Resolution* 42, 5: 637–657.

Hersh, Seymour. 1983. *The Price of Power: Kissinger in the Nixon White House.* New York: Simon and Schuster.

Hewitt, Joseph, and Jonathan Wilkenfeld. 1996. "Democracies in International Crisis," *International Interactions* 22: 123–142.

Hibbs, Douglas. 1973. *Mass Political Violence.* New York: Wiley.

Hochschild, Adam. 1998. *King Leopold's Ghost.* New York: Mariner Books.

Holsti, Kalevi. 1996. *The State, War, and the State of War.* Cambridge: Cambridge University Press.

————. 1997. "International Theory and Domestic War in the Third World: The Limits of Relevance." Paper presented to the Annual Conference of the International Studies Association, March, Toronto, Canada.

Holsti, Ole, Robert C. North, and Richard Brody. 1968. "Perception and Action in the 1914 Crisis," in J. David Singer, ed., *Quantitative International Politics.* New York: Free Press, pp. 132–158.

Hopf, Ted. 1991. "Polarity, the Offense-Defense Balance, and War," *American Political Science Review* 85 (September): 475–493.

Horowitz, Donald. 1985. *Ethnic Groups in Conflict.* Berkeley, CA: University of California Press.

Hunt, Michael. 1987. *Ideology and U.S. Foreign Policy.* New Haven, CT: Yale University Press.

Huntington, Samuel. 1968. *Political Order in Changing Societies.* New Haven, CT: Yale University Press.

————. 1996. *The Clash of Civilizations and the Remaking of World Order.* New York: Simon and Schuster.

Huntley, Wade. 1996. "Kant's Third Image: Systemic Sources of the Liberal Peace," *International Studies Quarterly* 40 (March): 45–76.

Huth, Paul. 1996. *Standing Your Ground: Territorial Disputes and International Conflict.* Ann Arbor, MI: University of Michigan Press.

Ihonvbere, Julius. 1998. "The Third World and the New World Order in the 1990s," in Robert Griffiths, ed., *Annual Editions: Developing World 98/99*. Guilford, CT: McGraw-Hill, pp. 8–17.

Jackman, Robert. 1978. "The Predictability of Coups d'Etat: A Model with African Data," *American Political Science Review* 72, 4: 1262–1275.

Jackson, Robert. 1990. *Quasi-States: Sovereignty, International Relations and the Third World*. Cambridge: Cambridge University Press.

Jaggers, Keith, and Ted Gurr. 1995. "Tracking Democracy's Third Wave with the Polity III Data," *Journal of Peace Research* 32, 4: 469–482.

———. 1996. Polity III Data. Available online at http://wizard.ucr.edu/~wm/polity/polity.html [accessed May 1996].

James, Patrick, and Glenn Mitchell. 1995. "Targets of Covert Pressure: The Hidden Victims of the Democratic Peace," *International Interactions* 21, 1: 85–107.

James, Patrick, Eric Solberg, and Murray Wolfson. 1999. "An Identified Systemic Test of the Democracy-Peace Nexus," *Defence and Peace Economics* 10, 1: 1–37.

Jenkins, J. Craig, and Augustine Kposowa. 1990. "Explaining Military Coups d'Etat: Black Africa, 1957–1984," *American Sociological Review* 55, 6: 861–875.

———. 1993. "The Structural Sources of Military Coups in Postcolonial Africa, 1957–1984," *American Journal of Sociology* 99, 1: 126–163.

Jervis, Robert. 1976. *Perception and Misperception in International Politics*. Princeton: Princeton University Press.

———. 1983. "Security Regimes," in Stephen D. Krasner, ed., *International Regimes*. Ithaca, NY: Cornell University Press, pp. 173–194.

Job, Brian, ed. 1992. *The Insecurity Dilemma*. Boulder, CO: Lynne Rienner.

Johnson, Thomas, Robert Slater, and Patrick McGowan. 1984. "Explaining African Military Coups d'Etat, 1960–1982," *American Political Science Review* 78, 3: 622–640.

Kahn, Herman. 1960. *On Thermonuclear War*. Princeton: Princeton University Press.

Kaldor, Mary. 1999. *New and Old Wars*. Stanford, CA: Stanford University Press.

Kant, Immanuel. 1991 [1795]. *Kant's Political Writings*, 2nd ed. Hans Reiss, ed. H. B. Nisbet, trans. Cambridge: Cambridge University Press.

———. 1994 [1795]. "Perpetual Peace," in Richard Betts, ed., *Conflict After the Cold War: Arguments on Causes of War and Peace*. Boston, MA: Allyn and Bacon, pp. 128–135.

Kaplan, Lawrence. 2001. "Why Trade Won't Bring Democracy to China," *The New Republic* 4, 512, and 4, 513 (July 9 and 16): 23–27.

Karnow, Stanley. 1989. *In Our Own Image: American Empire in the Philippines*. New York: Random House.

Kaufmann, Chaim. 1996. "Possible and Impossible Solutions to Ethnic Civil Wars," *International Security* 20 (Spring): 136–175.

Kegley, Charles. 1993. "The Neoidealist Moment in International Studies? Realist Myths and the New International Realities," *International Studies Quarterly* 37 (June): 131–146.

———. 1995. "The Neoliberal Challenge to Realist Theories of World Politics: An Introduction," in Charles W. Kegley, Jr., ed., *Controversies in International Relations Theory: Realism and the Neoliberal Challenge.* New York: St. Martin's, pp. 1–24.

Kegley, Charles, and Gregory Raymond. 2002. *From War to Peace: Fateful Decisions in International Politics.* New York: Bedford/St. Martin's.

Kemp, Anita. 1977. "A Path Analytic Model of International Violence," *International Interactions* 4: 53–85.

Keohane, Robert. 1984. *After Hegemony.* Princeton: Princeton University Press.

Keohane, Robert, ed. 1986. *Neorealism and Its Critics.* New York: Columbia University Press.

Keohane, Robert, and Joseph Nye. 1977. *Power and Interdependence.* Boston, MA: Little, Brown.

Khong, Yuen. 1992. *Analogies at War: Korea, Munich, Dien Bien Phu, and the Vietnam Decisions of 1965.* Princeton: Princeton University Press.

King, Martin L. 1986 [1968]. "Remaining Awake Through a Great Revolution," in James Washington, ed., *A Testament of Hope: The Essential Writings and Speeches of Martin Luther King.* San Francisco: HarperCollins, pp. 268–278.

Kober, Stanley. 1994. "Idealpolitik," in Richard K. Betts, ed., *Conflict After the Cold War: Arguments on Causes of War and Peace.* New York: Macmillan, pp. 250–262.

Kposowa, Augustine, and J. Craig Jenkins. 1992. "The Political Origins of African Military Coups: Ethnic Competition, Military Centrality, and the Struggle over the Postcolonial State," *International Studies Quarterly* 36 (September): 271–292.

Krain, Matthew, and Marissa Myers. 1997. "Democracy and Civil War: A Note on the Democratic Peace Proposition," *International Interactions* 23, 1: 109–118.

Krasner, Stephen. 1983a. "Structural Causes and Regime Consequences: Regimes as Intervening Variables," in Stephen D. Krasner, ed., *International Regimes.* Ithaca, NY: Cornell University Press, pp. 1–21.

———. 1983b. "Regimes and the Limits of Realism: Regimes as Autonomous Variables," in Stephen D. Krasner, ed., *International Regimes.* Ithaca, NY: Cornell University Press, pp. 355–368.

Lake, Anthony. 1993. "From Containment to Enlargement." Presentation to the School of Advanced International Studies, Johns Hopkins University, September 21. Washington, DC: Office of the Press Secretary, the White House.

Lake, David. 1992. "Powerful Pacifists: Democratic States and War," *American Political Science Review* 86 (March): 24–37.

Layne, Christopher. 1994. "Kant or Cant: The Myth of the Democratic Peace," *International Security* 19 (Fall): 5–49.

Lebovic, James, and Ashfag Ishaq. 1987. "Military Burden, Security Needs, and Economic Growth in the Middle East," *Journal of Conflict Resolution* 31, 1: 106–138.

Leeds, Brett, and David Davis. 1999. "Beneath the Surface: Regime Type and International Interaction, 1953–78," *Journal of Peace Research* 36, 1 (January): 5–21.

Leifer, Michael. 1989. *ASEAN and the Security of South-East Asia.* London: Routledge.

Lemke, Douglas, and William Reed. 1996. "Regime Type and Status Quo Evaluations: Power Transition Theory and the Democratic Peace, *International Interactions* 22, 2: 143–164.

Leng, Russell. 1983. "When Will They Ever Learn? Coercive Bargaining in Recurrent Crises," *Journal of Conflict Resolution* 27: 379–419.

Levy, Jack. 1981. "Alliance Formation and War Behavior: An Analysis of the Great Powers, 1495–1975," *Journal of Conflict Resolution* 25 (December): 581–613.

———. 1983. "Misperception and the Causes of War," *World Politics* 36: 76–99.

———. 1989. "Domestic Politics and War," in Robert Rotberg and Theodore Rabb, eds., *The Origin and Prevention of Major Wars.* Cambridge: Cambridge University Press, pp. 79–99.

Liberman, Peter. 1996. "Trading with the Enemy: Security and Relative Economic Gains," *International Security* 23 (Summer): 147–175.

Lichbach, Mark. 1987. "Deterrence or Escalation? The Puzzle of Aggregate Studies of Repression and Dissent," *Journal of Conflict Resolution* 31, 2: 266–297.

———. 1995. *The Rebel's Dilemma.* Ann Arbor, MI: University of Michigan Press.

Licklider, Roy, ed. 1993. *Stopping the Killing: How Civil Wars End.* New York: New York University Press.

Lindstrom, Ronny, and Will Moore. 1995. "Deprived, Rational or Both? 'Why Minorities Rebel' Revisited," *Journal of Political and Military Sociology* 23 (Winter): 167–190.

Luard, Evan. 1972. *The International Regulation of Civil Wars.* New York: New York University Press.

———. 1989. *The Blunted Sword.* New York: New Amsterdam Books.

Lunde, Tormund. 1991. "Modernization and Political Instability: Coups d'Etat in Africa 1955–85," *Acta Sociologica* 34, 1: 13–32.

MacFarlane, Neil. 1991. "The Impact of Superpower Collaboration in the Third World," in Thomas Weiss and Meryl Kessler, eds., *Third World Security in the Post–Cold War Era.* Boulder, CO: Lynne Rienner, pp. 125–145.

Macfie, A. L. 1938. "The Outbreak of War and the Trade Cycle," *Economic History* 3: 89–97.

Mansfield, Edward. 1994. *Power, Trade, and War*. Princeton: Princeton University Press.

Mansfield, Edward, and Jack Snyder. 1995. "Democratization and the Danger of War," *International Security* 20 (Summer): 5–38.

Maoz, Ze'ev. 1997. "The Controversy over the Democratic Peace: Rearguard Action or Cracks in the Wall?" *International Security* 22 (Summer): 162–198.

———. 2000. "The Democratic Peace Puzzle: Connecting National, Dyadic, and Systemic Levels-of-Analysis in the Study of Democracy and War." Revised version of paper prepared for Conference on "War in a Changing World," November 5–6, 1996, Tel-Aviv University.

Maoz, Ze'ev, and Nasrin Abdolali. 1989. "Regime Types and International Conflict, 1816–1976," *Journal of Conflict Resolution* 33 (March): 3–35.

Maoz, Zeev, and Bruce Russett. 1992. "Alliance, Contiguity, Wealth, and Political Stability: Is the Lack of Conflict Among Democracies a Statistical Artifact?" *International Interactions* 17, 3: 245–267.

———. 1993. "Normative and Structural Causes of Democratic Peace, 1946–1986," *American Political Science Review* 87 (September): 624–638.

Mason, T. David, and Patrick Fett. 1996. "How Civil Wars End: A Rational Choice Approach," *Journal of Conflict Resolution* 40, 4: 546–568.

Matthews, John. 1996. "Current Gains and Future Outcomes," *International Security* 21 (Summer): 112–146.

Mazrui, Ali. 1988. *The Africans: A Triple Heritage*. Boston: Little, Brown and Co.

———. 1990. *Cultural Forces in World Politics*. London: James Currey.

McAdam, Doug, John McCarthy, and Mayer Zald, eds. 1996. *Comparative Perspectives on Social Movements*. New York: Cambridge University Press.

McCormick, Thomas. 1989. *America's Half-Century, United States Foreign Policy in the Cold War*. Baltimore, MD: Johns Hopkins University Press.

McLaughlin, Sara, Scott Gates, Havard Hegre, Ranveig Gissinger, and Nils Petter Gleditsch. 1998. "Timing the Changes in Political Structures: A New Polity Database," *Journal of Conflict Resolution* 42, 2: 231–242.

McLaughlin-Mitchell, Sara, Scott Gates, and Havard Hegre. 1999. "Evolution in Democracy-War Dynamics," *Journal of Conflict Resolution* 43, 6 (December): 771–792.

Mearsheimer, John. 1990. "Back to the Future: Instability in Europe After the Cold War," *International Security* 15, 1: 5–56.

Meernik, James. 1996. "United States Military Intervention and the Promotion of Democracy," *Journal of Peace Research* 33, 4: 391–402.

Menard, Scott. 1995. *Applied Logistic Regression Analysis*. Beverly Hills, CA: Sage.

Midlarsky, Manus. 1975. *On War*. New York: Free Press.

Mitrany, David. 1943. *A Working Peace System*. London: Royal Institute of International Affairs.

Moore, Will. 1998. "Dissent and Repression: Substitution, Context and Timing," *American Journal of Political Science* 42, 3: 851–873.

Morgan, T. Clifton, and Sally Campbell. 1991. "Domestic Structure, Decisional Constraints and War," *Journal of Conflict Resolution* 35 (June): 187–211.

Morgan, T. Clifton, and Valerie Schwebach. 1992. "Take Two Democracies and Call Me in the Morning: A Prescription for Peace?" *International Interactions* 17, 4: 305–320.

Morrow, James. 1997. "When Do 'Relative Gains' Impede Trade?" *Journal of Conflict Resolution* 41 (February): 12–37.

Mousseau, Michael. 1997. "Democracy and Militarized Interstate Collaboration," *Journal of Peace Research* 34: 73–87.

———. 1998. "Democracy and Compromise in Militarized Interstate Conflicts," *Journal of Conflict Resolution* 42, 2 (April): 210–230.

———. 2000. "Market Prosperity, Democratic Consolidation, and Democratic Peace," *Journal of Conflict Resolution* 44, 4 (August): 472–507.

Muller, Edward, and Erich Weede. 1990. "Cross-National Variation in Political Violence: A Rational Actor Approach," *Journal of Conflict Resolution* 34, 4: 624–651.

Mullins, A. F. 1987. *Born Arming: Development and Military Power in New States*. Palo Alto, CA: Stanford University Press.

Nkrumah, Kwame. 1965. *Neo-Colonialism: The Last Stage of Imperialism*. London: Panaf.

Nye, Joseph. 1987. "Nuclear Learning and U.S.-Soviet Security Regimes," *International Organization* 41 (Summer): 371–402.

Organski, A.F.K., and Jacek Kugler. 1980. *The War Ledger*. Chicago: University of Chicago Press.

Oneal, John, Frances H. Oneal, Ze'ev Maoz, and Bruce Russett. 1996. "Liberal Peace: Interdependence, Democracy, and International Conflict," *Journal of Peace Research* 33 (February): 11–28.

Oneal, John, and James Lee Ray. 1997. "New Tests of Democratic Peace: Controlling for Economic Interdependence, 1950–1985," *Political Research Quarterly* 50, 4 (December): 751–775.

Oneal, John R., and Bruce Russett. 1997. "The Classical Liberals Were Right: Democracy, Interdependence, and Conflict, 1950–1985," *International Studies Quarterly* 41 (June): 267–293.

———. 1998. "The Kantian Peace: Assessing the Pacific Benefits of Democracy, Interdependence, and International Organizations, 1885–1992." Paper presented to the American Political Science Association, September 4, Boston, MA.

———. 1999a. "Assessing the Liberal Peace with Alternative Specifications: Trade Still Reduces Conflict," *Journal of Peace Research* 36: 423–442.

————. 1999b. "The Kantian Peace: The Pacific Benefits of Democracy, Interdependence, and International Organizations, 1885–1992," *World Politics* 52: 1–37.

————. 1999c. "Is the Liberal Peace an Artifact of Cold War Interest? Assessing Recent Critiques," *International Interactions* 25, 3: 213–241.

————. 2000. "Why 'An Identified Systemic Analysis of the Democracy-Peace Nexus' Does Not Persuade," *Defence and Peace Economics* 11, 2: 1–18.

Oren, Ido. 1995. "The Subjectivity of the 'Democratic' Peace: Changing U.S. Perceptions of Imperial Germany," *International Security* 20 (Fall): 147–184.

Organski, A. F. K. 1965. *Stages of Political Development*. New York: Knopf.

Ostrom, Charles, and Francis Hoole. 1978. "Alliances and War Revisited: A Research Note," *International Studies Quarterly* 22 (June): 215–236.

Owen, John. 1994. "How Liberalism Produces Democratic Peace," *International Security* 19 (Fall): 87–125.

Peceny, Mark. 1999. "Forcing Them to Be Free," *Political Research Quarterly* 52, 3 (September): 549–582.

Polachek, Solomon. 1980. "Conflict and Trade," *Journal of Conflict Resolution* 24 (March): 55–78.

————. 1997. "Why Democracies Cooperate More and Fight Less: The Relationship Between International Trade and Cooperation," *Review of International Economics* 5, 3 (August): 295–309.

Pollins, Brian. 1989a. "Does Trade Still Follow the Flag?" *American Political Science Review* 83 (June): 465–480.

————. 1989b. "Conflict, Cooperation, and Commerce: The Effects of International Political Interactions on Bilateral Trade Flows," *American Journal of Political Science* 33: 737–761.

Posen, Barry. 1993. "The Security Dilemma and Ethnic Conflict," in Michael Brown, ed., *Ethnic Conflict and International Security*. Princeton: Princeton University Press, pp. 103–124.

Powell, Robert. 1991. "Absolute and Relative Gains in International Relations Theory," *American Political Science Review* 85 (December): 1303–1320.

Ray, James. 1974. "Status Inconsistency and War Involvement Among European States, 1816–1970." Ph.D. dissertation, University of Michigan, Ann Arbor.

————. 1989. "The Abolition of Slavery and the End of International War," *International Organization* 43 (Summer): 405–439.

————. 1993. "Wars Between Democracies: Rare or Nonexistent?" *International Interactions* 18, 3: 251–276.

————. 1995. *Democracy and International Conflict*. Columbia, SC: University of South Carolina Press.

————. 1997. "On the Level(s): Does Democracy Correlate with Peace?" Paper presented at the Norman Thomas Lectures on Scientific Knowledge of War, March 14–16, Vanderbilt University.

Regan, Patrick. 1996. "Conditions of Successful Third-Party Intervention in Intrastate Conflicts," *Journal of Conflict Resolution* 40, 2: 336–359.

Regan, Patrick, and Errol Henderson. In press. "Democracy, Threats, and Political Repression in Developing Countries: Are Democracies Internally Less Violent?" *Third World Quarterly.*

Reiter, Dan. 2001. "Why NATO Enlargement Does Not Spread Democracy," *International Security* 25, 4 (Spring): 41–67.

Reiter, Dan, and Allan Stam. 1998a. "Democracy and Battlefield Military Effectiveness," *Journal of Conflict Resolution* 42, 3 (June): 259–277.

————. 1998b. "A Structural-Consent Model of Domestic Politics and International Conflict." Paper presented to the American Political Science Association, September, Boston, MA.

Rodney, Walter. 1980. *How Europe Underdeveloped Africa.* Washington, DC: Howard University Press.

Rousseau, David L., Christopher Gelpi, Dan Reiter, and Paul K. Huth. 1996. "Assessing the Dyadic Nature of the Democratic Peace, 1918–1988." *American Political Science Review* 90, 3 (September): 512–532.

Rummel, Rudolph. 1968. "The Relationship Between National Attributes and Foreign Conflict Behavior," in J. David Singer, ed., *Quantitative International Politics.* New York: Free Press, pp. 187–214.

————. 1979. *Understanding Conflict and War,* Vol. 4. Beverly Hills, CA: Sage.

————. 1983. "Libertarianism and International Violence," *Journal of Conflict Resolution* 27 (March): 27–71.

————. 1995. "Democracies ARE Less Warlike Than Other Regimes," *European Journal of International Relations* 1, 4 (December): 457–479.

————. 1997. "Is Collective Violence Correlated with Social Pluralism?" *Journal of Peace Research* 34, 2: 163–175.

Russett, Bruce. 1990. "Economic Decline, Electoral Pressure, and the Initiation of Interstate Conflict," in Charles Gochman and Alan Sabrosky, eds., *Prisoners of War? Nation-States in the Modern Era.* Lexington, MA: DC Heath, pp. 123–140.

————. 1993. *Grasping the Democratic Peace.* Princeton: Princeton University Press.

————. 1995. "Correspondence: And Yet It Moves," *International Security* 19 (Spring): 164–175.

Russett, Bruce, and R. J. Monsen. 1975. "Bureaucracy and Polyarchy as Predictors of Performance: A Cross-National Examination. *Comparative Political Studies* 8: 5–31.

Russett, Bruce, and John Oneal. 2001. *Triangulating Peace.* New York: W. W. Norton.

Russett, Bruce, John Oneal, and Michaelene Cox. 2000. "Clash of Civilizations, or Realism and Liberalism Déjà Vu? Some Evidence," *Journal of Peace Research* 37: 583–608.

Russett, Bruce, and Harvey Starr. 2000. "From Democratic Peace to Kantian Peace: Democracy and Conflict in the International System," in Manus Midlarsky, ed., *Handbook of War Studies II*. Ann Arbor, MI: University of Michigan Press, pp. 93–128.

Salmore, Stephan, and Charles Hermann. 1969. "The Effect of Size, Development and Accountability on Foreign Policy," *Peace Science Society Papers* 14: 16–30.

Schlichte, Klaus. 1994. "Is Ethnicity a Cause of War?" *Peace Review* 6, 1: 59–65.

Schultz, Kenneth. 1998. "Domestic Opposition and Signaling in International Crises," *American Political Science Review* 92 (December): 829–844.

———. 1999. "Do Democratic Institutions Constrain or Inform? Contrasting Two Institutional Perspectives on Democracy and War," *International Organization* 52 (Spring): 233–266.

Simon, Michael, and Erik Gartzke. 1996. "Do Democracies Flock Together, or Do Opposites Attract?" *Journal of Conflict Resolution* 40 (December): 617–635.

Singer, J. David. 1958. "Threat-Perception and the Armament-Tension Dilemma," *Journal of Conflict Resolution* 2: 90–105.

———. 1961. "The Level-of-Analysis Problem in International Relations," *World Politics* 14, 1 (October): 77–92.

———. 1995. *Cultural Composition of States Data, 1820–1990*. Correlates of War Project. Ann Arbor: University of Michigan, Department of Political Science.

———. 1996. "Armed Conflict in the Former Colonial Regions: From Classification to Explanation," in Luc Van de Goor, Kumar Rupesinghe, and Paul Sciarone, eds. *Between Development and Destruction: An Enquiry into the Causes of Conflict in Post-Colonial States*. New York: Macmillan, pp. 35–49.

Singer, J. David, and Melvin Small. 1994. *International and Civil War Data, 1816–1992*. Correlates of War Project. Ann Arbor: University of Michigan, Department of Political Science.

———. 1995. *National Material Capabilities Data, 1816–1992*. Correlates of War Project. Ann Arbor: University of Michigan, Department of Political Science.

Singer, Max, and Aaron Wildavsky. 1993. *The Real World Order: Zones of Peace, Zones of Turmoil*. Chatham, NJ: Chatham House.

Siverson, Randolph, and Juliann Emmons. 1991. "Birds of a Feather: Democratic Political Systems and Alliance Choices in the Twentieth Century," *Journal of Conflict Resolution* 35 (June): 285–306.

Siverson, Randolph, and Joel King. 1979. "Alliances and the Expansion of War," in J. David Singer and Michael Wallace, eds., *To Augur Well.* Beverly Hills, CA: Sage, pp. 37–49.

Small, Melvin, and J. David Singer. 1976. "The War-Proneness of Democratic Regimes, 1816–1965," *Jerusalem Journal of International Relations* 1 (Summer): 50–69.

———. 1979. "Conflict in the International System, 1816–1977: Historical Trends and Policy Futures," in J. David Singer, ed., *Explaining War.* Beverly Hills, CA: Sage, pp. 57–82.

———. 1982. *Resort to Arms: International and Civil Wars, 1816–1980.* Beverly Hills, CA: Sage.

Smith, Roger K. 1987. "Explaining the Non-Proliferation Regime: Anomalies for Contemporary International Relations Theory," *International Organization* 41 (Spring): 253–281.

Smith, Tony. 1994. *America's Mission: The U.S. and the Global Struggle for Democracy in the Twentieth Century.* Princeton, NJ: Princeton University Press.

Snidal, Duncan. 1991a. "International Cooperation Among Relative Gain Maximizers," *International Studies Quarterly* 35 (December): 387–402.

———. 1991b. "Relative Gains and the Pattern of International Cooperation," *American Political Science Review* 85 (September): 701–726.

Snyder, Jack. 2000. *From Voting to Violence: Democratization and Nationalist Conflict.* New York: W. W. Norton.

Spiro, David. 1994. "The Insignificance of the Liberal Peace," *International Security* 19 (Fall): 50–86.

Stam, Allan. 1996. *Win, Lose, or Draw: Domestic Politics and the Crucible of War.* Ann Arbor, MI: University of Michigan Press.

Stedman, Stephen. 1996. "Conflict and Conciliation in Sub-Saharan Africa," in Michael Brown, ed., *The International Dimensions of Internal Conflict.* Cambridge, MA: MIT Press, pp. 235–265.

Stein, Arthur. 1990. *Why Nations Cooperate.* Ithaca, NY: Cornell University Press.

Stoessinger, John. 1998. *Why Nations Go to War*, 7th ed. New York: St. Martin's.

Stuart, Douglas. 1989. "Continuity and Change in the Southern Region of the Atlantic Alliance," in James Golden, Daniel Kaufman, Asa Clark IV, and David Petraeus, eds., *NATO at Forty.* Boulder, CO: Westview.

Summers, Anthony. 2000. *The Arrogance of Power: The Secret World of Richard Nixon.* New York: Viking.

Tate, Trevor M. 1990. "Regime Building in the Non-Proliferation System," *Journal of Peace Research* 27 (November): 399–414.

Thompson, Leonard. 1975. *Survival in Two Worlds: Moshoeshoe of Lesotho, 1786–1870.* Oxford: Oxford University Press.

Thompson, William, and Richard Tucker. 1997a. "A Tale of Two Democratic Peace Critiques," *Journal of Conflict Resolution* 41, 3: 428–454.

————. 1997b. "Bewitched, Bothered, and Bewildered: A Reply to Farber and Gowa and to Mansfield and Snyder," *Journal of Conflict Resolution* 41, 3: 462–477.

Tilly, Charles. 1978. *From Mobilization to Revolution*. Reading, MA: Addison-Wesley.

Tilly, Charles, ed. 1975. *The Formation of National States in Western Europe*. Princeton: Princeton University Press.

Vasquez, John. 1991. "The Deterrence Myth: Nuclear Weapons and the Prevention of Nuclear War," in Charles W. Kegley, ed. *The Long Postwar Peace*. New York: HarperCollins, pp. 205–223.

————. 1993. *The War Puzzle*. Cambridge: Cambridge University Press.

Wallace, Michael. 1973. *War and Rank Among Nations*. Toronto: Lexington.

Waltz, Kenneth. 1979. *Theory of International Politics*. Reading, MA: Addison-Wesley.

Wamba-Dia-Wamba, Ernest. 1985. "Experiences of Democracy in Africa: Reflections on Practices of Communalist Palaver as a Social Method of Resolving Contradictions Among the People," *Philosophy and Social Action* 11, 3: 5–23.

Ward, Michael, and Kristian Gleditsch. 1998. "Democratizing for Peace." *American Political Science Review* 92 (March): 701–726.

Wayman, Frank. 1984. "Bipolarity and War: The Role of Capability Concentration and Alliance Patterns Among Major Powers, 1816–1965," *Journal of Peace Research* 21, 1: 61–78.

————. 1990. "Alliances and War: A Time-Series Analysis," in Charles Gochman and Alan Sabrosky, eds. *Prisoners of War? Nation-States in the Modern Era*. Lexington, MA: Lexington, pp. 93–113.

Wayman, Frank, J. David Singer, and Gary Goertz. 1983. "Capabilities, Allocations, and Success in Militarized Disputes and Wars, 1816–1976," *International Studies Quarterly* 27 (December): 497–515.

Weart, Spencer. 1994. "Peace Among Democratic and Oligarchic Republics," *Journal of Peace Research* 31 (August): 299–316.

————. 1998. *Never at War: Why Democracies Will Not Fight One Another*. New Haven, CT: Yale University Press.

Weede, Erich. 1970. "Conflict Behavior of Nation-States," *Journal of Peace Research* 7: 229–237.

————. 1981. "Income Inequality, Average Income, and Domestic Violence," *Journal of Conflict Resolution* 25, 4: 639–654.

————. 1983. "Extended Deterrence by Superpower Alliance," *Journal of Conflict Resolution* 27 (June): 231–254.

————. 1984. "Democracy and War Involvement," *Journal of Peace Research* 28: 649–664.

————. 1992. "Some Simple Calculations on Democracy and War Involvement," *Journal of Peace Research* 29 (November): 377–383.

Werner, Suzanne. 1997. "In Search of Security: Relative Gains and Losses in Dyadic Relations," *Journal of Peace Research* 34 (August): 289–302.

Wohlstetter, Albert. 1959. "The Delicate Balance of Terror," *Foreign Affairs* 37 (January): 211–234.

Wright, Quincy. 1942. *A Study of War.* Chicago: University of Chicago Press.

Young, Oran. 1989. *International Cooperation: Building Resources for Natural Resources and the Environment.* Ithaca, NY: Cornell University Press.

Zinnes, Dina, and Jonathan Wilkenfeld. 1971. "An Analysis of Foreign Conflict Behavior of Nations," in Wolfram Hanreider, ed., *Comparative Foreign Policy.* New York: Mckay, pp. 167–213.

Index

About the Book

Errol Henderson critically examines what is nearly a law in world politics, the concept of the democratic peace.

Henderson tests three versions of the democratic peace proposition (DPP)—that democracies rarely if ever fight one another, that democracies are more peaceful in general than nondemocracies, and that democracies rarely experience civil wars—using exactly the same data and statistical techniques as their proponents. In effect hoisting the thesis on its own petard, he finds that the ostensible "democratic peace" has in fact been the result of a confluence of several processes during the post–World War II era. It seems clear, Henderson maintains, that the presence of democracy is hardly a guarantor of peace—and under certain conditions, it *increases* the probability of war.

Errol A. Henderson is associate professor of political science at Wayne State University, where he teaches world politics, foreign policy, and the analysis of war, and he is research associate with the Correlates of War project. His recent articles include "Clear and Present Strangers: The Clash of Civilizations and International Conflict" and "Democracy, Threats, and Political Repression in Developing Countries," and he is author of *Afrocentrism and World Politics*.